TWELVE ORDINARY MEN

OTHER BOOKS BY JOHN MACARTHUR

Twelve Extraordinary Women

Hard to Believe

The Book on Leadership

The Battle for the Beginning

God in the Manger

The God Who Loves

The Gospel According to the Apostles

How to Survive in a World of Unbelievers

Introduction to Biblical Counseling

The Murder of Jesus

Rediscovering Expository Preaching

Rediscovering Pastoral Ministry

Terrorism, Jihad, and the Bible

The Vanishing Conscience

Whose Money Is It, Anyway?

Why Government Can't Save You

Why One Way?

BIBLE PRODUCTS BY JOHN MACARTHUR

Biblical Parenting for Life Study

MacArthur Bible Studies

MacArthur's Quick Reference Guide to the Bible

The MacArthur Student Bible

The MacArthur Study Bible (New King James Version)

TWELVE ORDINARY MEN

HOW *the* MASTER
SHAPED HIS DISCIPLES *for*
GREATNESS,
and WHAT HE WANTS TO DO *with*
YOU

JOHN MACARTHUR

NELSON BOOKS
A Division of Thomas Nelson Publishers
Since 1798

www.thomasnelson.com

TWELVE ORDINARY MEN

Copyright © 2002 by John MacArthur

Nelson Books,
a division of Thomas Nelson, Inc.,
P. O. Box 141000
Nashville, TN 37214

All Scripture quotations in this book, except those noted otherwise,
are from the New King James Version, © 1979, 1980, 1982, 1984
by Thomas Nelson, Inc.

Quotations marked NASB are from the New American Standard Bible,
© 1960, 1962, 1963, 1968, 1971, 1972, 1973, 1975, 1977, 1988, and 1995
by The Lockman Foundation, and are used by permission.

Quotations marked NIV are from
The Holy Bible: New International Version.
Copyright © 1973, 1978, 1984 by the International Bible Society.
All rights reserved.
Used by permission of Zondervan Bible Publishers.

Quotations marked KJV are from the King James Version of the Bible.

ISBN 0-8499-1773-5 (hc)
ISBN 0-7852-8824-4 (tp)
ISBN 0-7852-2677-x

Printed in the United States of America
06 07 08 09 10 QW 9 8 7 6 5 4 3 2 1

DEDICATION

To Irv Busenitz, for his loyal friendship and devoted service over three decades. Irv is a true teacher and selfless servant who has faithfully invested his own life in the lives of other men who come to study at The Master's Seminary. Irv is the ideal model of both disciple and disciple-maker, having dedicated himself to fulfilling 2 Timothy 2:2: "The things you have heard from me among many witnesses, commit these to faithful men who will be able to teach others also."

ACKNOWLEDGMENTS

THIS BOOK IS IN NO SMALL MEASURE thanks to the faithful support and encouragement of David Moberg, Mark Sweeney, and the rest of the staff of the W Publishing Group. We have enjoyed a close and fruitful partnership over the years, and I am grateful to the Lord for the ministry these dear friends have had in so many of my published works.

I am particularly grateful to Mary Hollingsworth and Kathryn Murray of the W Group, who worked hard under very short deadlines to keep this book on schedule throughout the editorial and typesetting process. Their kindness, patience, and diligence have been examplary, even under difficult circumstances.

Thanks also to Garry Knussman, who proofread this material at several different stages and offered many helpful editorial suggestions.

My special thanks goes to Phil Johnson, who has worked alongside me as my main editor for more than twenty years. He applied his skills in the process of translating this material from transcripts of my sermons on Matthew 10 and Luke 6, collating both series into one seamless whole and making sure the text was clear and readable.

CONTENTS

INTRODUCTION

MORE THAN TWENTY YEARS AGO, while preaching through the Gospel of Matthew, I gave a series of character studies on the twelve apostles. The messages were extremely well received, and we produced a tape album and study guide from that series, titled *The Master's Men*. Over the years we have broadcast the entire series several times on the *Grace to You* radio broadcast. Each time it airs, it generates a greater outpouring of affirmative response from listeners. After twenty years, that album continues to be one of the most popular series we have ever produced.

A few years ago, I started teaching a verse-by-verse exposition of Luke's Gospel in our church. When I reached Luke 6:13–16 (where Luke records Jesus' calling of the Twelve) I preached a new series of messages on the apostles. Once again, the response was overwhelming and enthusiastic. While preaching the series I realized that an entire generation had been born and reached adulthood in the years since we had last studied the lives of the disciples. They identified with these men in the same way their parents had done more than two decades before.

Even people who had practically memorized the tapes from the earlier series said they still found the lives of the disciples as fresh and relevant and practical as ever. The new series quickly became another favorite, and people began urging me to combine all the material on the apostles in a book. I didn't need much prodding for such a project. The book you are holding in your hands is the result.

I have always been fascinated with the lives of the twelve apostles. Who isn't? The personality types of these men are familiar to us. They are just like us, and they are like other people we know. They are approachable. They are real and living characters we can identify with. Their faults and foibles, as well as their triumphs and endearing features, are chronicled in some of the most fascinating accounts of the Bible. These are men we *want* to know.

That's because they were perfectly ordinary men in every way. Not one of them was renowned for scholarship or great erudition. They had no track record as orators or theologians. In fact, they were outsiders as far as the religious establishment of Jesus' day was concerned. They were not outstanding because of any natural talents or intellectual abilities. On the contrary, they were all too prone to mistakes, misstatements, wrong attitudes, lapses of faith, and bitter failure—no one more so than the leader of the group, Peter. Even Jesus remarked that they were slow learners and somewhat spiritually dense (Luke 24:25).

They spanned the political spectrum. One was a former Zealot—a radical, determined to overthrow Roman rule. But another had been a tax collector—virtually a traitor to the Jewish nation and in collusion with Rome. At least four, and possibly seven, were fishermen and close friends from Capernaum, probably having known one another from childhood. The others must have been tradesmen or craftsmen, but we are not told what they did before becoming followers of Christ. Most of them were from Galilee, an agricultural region at the intersection of trade routes. And Galilee remained their home base for most of Jesus' ministry—not (as some might think) Jerusalem in Judea, which was the political and religious capital of Israel.

Yet with all their faults and character flaws—as remarkably ordinary as they were—these men carried on a ministry after Jesus' ascension that left an indelible impact on the world. Their ministry continues to influence us even today. God graciously empowered and used these men to inaugurate the spread of the gospel message and to turn the world upside down (Acts 17:6). Ordinary men—people like you and me—became the instruments by which Christ's message was carried to the ends of the earth. No wonder they are such fascinating characters.

The Twelve were personally selected and called by Christ. He knew them as only their Creator could know them (cf. John 1:47). In other words, He knew all their faults long before He chose them. He even knew Judas would betray Him (John 6:70; 13:21–27), and yet He chose the traitor anyway and gave him all the same privileges and blessings He gave to the others.

Think about the ramifications of this: From our human perspective, the propagation of the gospel and the founding of the church hinged entirely on twelve men whose most outstanding characteristic was their ordinariness. They were chosen by Christ and trained for a time that is best measured in months, not years. He taught them the Scriptures and theology. He discipled them in the ways of godly living (teaching them and showing them how to pray, how to forgive, and how to serve one another with humility). He gave them moral instruction. He spoke to them of things to come. And He employed them as His instruments to heal the sick, cast out demons, and do other miraculous works. Three of them—Peter, James, and John—even got a brief glimpse of Him in His glory on the Mount of Transfiguration (Matthew 17:1–9).

It was a brief but intensive schedule of discipleship. And when it was over, on the night of Jesus' betrayal, "all the disciples forsook Him and fled" (Matthew 26:56). From an earthly point of view, the training program looked like a monumental failure. It seemed the disciples had forgotten or ignored everything Christ had ever taught them about taking up the cross and following Him. In fact, their own sense of failure was so profound that they went back to their old vocations for a time. And even at that, it appeared they would fail (John 21:3–4).

But encouraged by the risen Lord, they returned to their apostolic calling. Empowered by the Holy Spirit at Pentecost, they valiantly undertook the task to which Jesus had called them. The work they subsequently began continues today, two thousand years later. They are living proof that God's strength is made perfect in weakness. In and of themselves they were clearly not sufficient for the task (cf. 2 Corinthians 2:16). But God led them in triumph in Christ, and through them He diffused "the fragrance of His knowledge in every place" (v. 14).

To get an appreciation for the brevity of their earthly time with Christ, consider the fact that Jesus' entire ministry from baptism to resurrection lasted only about three years. And the intensive training time with the disciples was only about half that long. In A. B. Bruce's classic work, *The Training of the Twelve*, he points out that by the time Jesus identified and called the Twelve from the larger group of His followers (Matthew 10:1–4; Luke 6:12–16), half of his earthly ministry was already over:

The selection by Jesus of the twelve . . . is an important landmark in the Gospel history. It divides the ministry of our Lord into two portions, nearly equal, probably, as to duration, but unequal as to the extent and importance of the work done in each respectively. In the earlier period Jesus labored single-handed; His miraculous deeds were confined for the most part to a limited area, and His teaching was in the main of an elementary character. But by the time when the twelve were chosen, the work of the kingdom had assumed such dimensions as to require organization and division of labor; and the teaching of Jesus was beginning to be of a deeper and more elaborate nature, and His gracious activities were taking on ever-widening range.

It is probable that the selection of a limited number to be His close and constant companions had become a necessity to Christ, in consequence of His very success in gaining disciples. His followers, we imagine, had grown so numerous as to be an incumbrance and an impediment to his movements, especially in the long journeys which mark the later part of His ministry. It was impossible that all who believed could continue henceforth to follow Him, in the literal sense, whithersoever He might go: the greater number could now only be occasional followers. But it was His wish that certain selected men should be with Him at all times and in all places,—His traveling companions in all His wanderings, witnessing all His work, and ministering to His daily needs. And so, in the quaint words of Mark, "Jesus calleth unto Him whom He would, and they came unto Him, and He [ordained] twelve, that they should be with Him." (Mark 3:13–14)[1]

That means these few men, whose backgrounds were in mundane trades and earthly occupations, had little more than eighteen months' training for the monumental task to which they were called. There was no second string, no backup players, no plan B if the Twelve should fail.

The strategy sounds risky in the extreme. In earthly terms, the founding of the church and the spread of the gospel message depended entirely on those twelve ordinary men with their many obvious weaknesses—and one of them so devilish as to betray the Lord of the universe. And the entirety of their training for the task took less than half as long as it typically takes to get a degree from a seminary today.

But Christ knew what He was doing. From His divine perspective, the ultimate success of the strategy actually depended on the Holy Spirit working in those men to accomplish His sovereign will. It was a mission that could not be thwarted. That's why it was a work for which God alone deserves praise and glory. Those men were merely instruments in His hands—just as you and I can be God's instruments today. God delights to use such ordinary means—"the foolish things of the world to put to shame the things which are mighty; and the base things of the world and the things which are despised God has chosen, and the things which are not, to bring to nothing the things that are, that no flesh should glory in His presence" (1 Corinthians 1:27–29). The two-thousand-year triumph of the apostolic endeavor is a testimony to the wisdom and power of the divine strategy.

Sometimes in Scripture the Twelve are called "disciples"—*mathetes* in the Greek text (Matthew 10:1; 11:1; 20:17; Luke 9:1). The word means "learners, students." That is what they were during those months they spent under the direct and personal tutelage of the Lord. He had multi-

tudes of disciples, but these twelve were specifically called
and chosen to a unique apostolic office. Therefore they are
also designated "apostles"—*apostoloi* in the Greek. The
word simply means "messengers, sent ones." They were
given a unique ambassadorial office of authority and
spokesmanship for Christ. Luke especially uses this term in
his gospel and throughout the Book of Acts, and he
reserves the term almost exclusively for the Twelve.
Matthew speaks of "apostles" only once (Matthew 10:2);
elsewhere, he refers to "twelve disciples" (11:1; 20:17) or
"the twelve" (26:14, 20, 47). Likewise, Mark uses the term
"apostles" only once (Mark 6:30). Other than that, he
always refers to the apostles as "the twelve" (3:14; 4:10; 6:7;
9:35; 10:32; 11:11; 14:10, 17, 20, 43). John, too, uses the
word *apostolos* just once, in a nontechnical sense (John
13:16—where most English versions render the expression, "he who is sent"). Like Mark, John always refers to the
apostolic band as "the twelve" (John 6:67, 70–71; 20:24).

Luke 10 describes an incident where seventy of Jesus'
followers were chosen and sent out two by two. They were
obviously "sent ones" and some commentators therefore
refer to them as "apostles," but Luke does not employ that
term to describe them.

The Twelve were called to a specific office. And in the
Gospels and Acts, the term *apostoloi* almost always refers to
that office and the twelve men who were specifically called
and ordained to the office. Acts 14:14 and the Pauline epistles make it clear that the apostle Paul was likewise called
to fill a special apostolic office—that of "apostle to the
Gentiles" (Romans 11:13; 1 Timothy 2:7; 2 Timothy 1:11).
Paul's apostleship was a unique calling. He obviously had
the same authority and privileges as that of the Twelve (2
Corinthians 11:5). But Paul's apostleship is not subject

matter for this book, because our focus here is on the twelve men who shared Jesus' public ministry with Him as His closest friends and companions. Paul wasn't converted until after Christ's ascension (Acts 9). He was an apostle "born out of due time" (1 Corinthians 15:8). He spoke with the same authority and manifested the same miraculous ability as the Twelve—and the Twelve embraced him and recognized his authority (cf. 2 Peter 3:15–16)—but he was not one of them.

The number twelve was significant, because Luke describes how, after Jesus' ascension, the apostles chose Matthias to fill the office vacated by Judas (Acts 1:23–26).

The role of an apostle (including the special office to which the apostle Paul was called) involved a position of leadership and exclusive teaching authority in the early church. The New Testament Scriptures were all written by the apostles or their close associates. And before the New Testament was written, the apostles' teaching was the rule in the early church. Beginning with the very first converts at Pentecost, all true believers looked to the apostles' leadership (Acts 2:37). And as the church grew, its faithfulness to the truth was described in these terms: "They continued steadfastly in the apostles' doctrine" (Acts 2:42).

The apostles were given a supernatural power to work signs and wonders (Matthew 10:1; Mark 6:7, 13; Luke 9:1–2; Acts 2:3–4; 5:12). Those signs bore witness to the truth of the gospel, which the apostles had received from Christ, and which they introduced on His behalf to the world (2 Corinthians 12:12; Hebrews 2:3–4).

In other words, their role was a pivotal, foundational role. They *are* in a true sense, the very foundation of the Christian church, "Jesus Christ Himself being the chief cornerstone" (Ephesians 2:20).

These studies in the lives of the apostles have been a particular delight for me—and one of the most fruitful endeavors of my life. My greatest joy is preaching Christ. Eleven of these men shared that passion, devoted their lives to it, and triumphed in it against overwhelming opposition. They are fitting heroes and role models for us, despite their shortcomings. To study their lives is to get to know the men who were closest to Christ during His earthly life. To realize that they were ordinary people just like us is a great blessing. May the Spirit of Christ who taught them transform us the way He transformed them, into precious vessels fit for the Master's use. And may we learn from their example what it means to be disciples indeed.

1

COMMON MEN,
UNCOMMON CALLING

*For you see your calling, brethren, that not
many wise according to the flesh, not many
mighty, not many noble, are called. But God
has chosen the foolish things of the world to put
to shame the wise, and God has chosen the
weak things of the world to put to shame the
things which are mighty; and the base things of
the world and the things which are despised
God has chosen, and the things which are not,
to bring to nothing the things that are, that no
flesh should glory in His presence.*

—1 CORINTHIANS 1:26–29

FROM THE TIME JESUS BEGAN His public ministry in
His hometown of Nazareth, He was enormously
controversial. The people from His own community
literally tried to kill Him immediately after His first public
message in the local synagogue. "All those in the synagogue, when they heard these things, were filled with
wrath, and rose up and thrust Him out of the city; and they
led Him to the brow of the hill on which their city was

1

built, that they might throw Him down over the cliff. Then passing through the midst of them, He went His way" (Luke 4:28–30).

Ironically, Jesus became tremendously popular among the people of the larger Galilee region. As word of His miracles began to circulate throughout the district, massive hordes of people came out to see Him and hear Him speak. Luke 5:1 records how "the multitude pressed about Him to hear the word of God." One day, the crowds were so thick and so aggressive that He got into a boat, pushed it offshore far enough to get away from the press of people, and taught the multitudes from there. Not by mere happenstance, the boat Jesus chose belonged to Simon. Jesus would rename him Peter, and he would become the dominant person in Jesus' closest inner circle of disciples.

Some might imagine that if Christ had wanted His message to have maximum impact, He could have played off His popularity more effectively. Modern conventional wisdom would suggest that Jesus ought to have done every-thing possible to exploit His fame, tone down the controversies that arose out of His teaching, and employ whatever strategies He could use to maximize the crowds around Him. But He did not do that. In fact, He did precisely the opposite. Instead of taking the populist route and exploiting His fame, He began to emphasize the very things that made His message so controversial. At about the time the crowds reached their peak, He preached a message so boldly confrontive and so offensive in its content that the multitude melted away, leaving only the most devoted few (John 6:66–67).

Among those who stayed with Christ were the Twelve, whom He had personally selected and appointed to repre-sent Him. They were twelve perfectly ordinary, unexceptional men. But Christ's strategy for advancing His kingdom hinged on those twelve men rather than on the clamoring multitudes. He chose to work through the instrumentality of those few fallible individuals rather than advance His agenda through mob force, military might, personal popularity, or a public-relations campaign. From a human perspective, the future of the church and the long-term success of the gospel depended entirely on the faithfulness of that handful of disciples. There was no plan B if they failed.

The strategy Jesus chose typified the character of the kingdom itself. "The kingdom of God does not come with observation; nor will they say, 'See here!' or 'See there!' For indeed, the kingdom of God is within you" (Luke 17:20–21). The kingdom advances " 'Not by might nor by power, but by My Spirit,' says the LORD of hosts" (Zechariah 4:6). A dozen men under the power of the Holy Spirit are a more potent force than the teeming masses whose initial enthusiasm for Jesus was apparently provoked by little more than sheer curiosity.

Christ personally chose the Twelve and invested most of His energies in them. He chose them before they chose Him (John 15:16). The process of choosing and calling them happened in distinct stages. Careless readers of Scripture sometimes imagine that John 1:35–51, Luke 5:3-11, and the formal calling of the Twelve in Luke 6:12–16 are contradictory accounts of how Christ called His apostles. But there is no contradiction. The passages are simply describing different stages of the apostles' calling.

In John 1:35–51, for example, Andrew, John, Peter, Philip, and Nathaniel encounter Jesus for the first time. This event occurs near the beginning of Jesus' ministry, in the wilderness near the Jordan River, where John the

Baptist was ministering. Andrew, John, and the others were there because they were already disciples of John the Baptist. But when they heard their teacher single out Jesus and say, "Behold the Lamb of God!" they followed Jesus.

That was phase one of their calling. It was a calling to *conversion*. It illustrates how every disciple is called first to salvation. We must recognize Jesus as the true Lamb of God and Lord of all, and embrace Him by faith. That stage of the disciples' call did not involve full-time discipleship. The Gospel narratives suggest that although they followed Jesus in the sense that they gladly heard His teaching and submitted to Him as their Teacher, they remained at their full-time jobs, earning a living through regular employment. That is why from this point until Jesus called them to full-time ministry, we often see them fishing and mending their nets.

Phase two of their calling was a call to *ministry*. Luke 5 describes the event in detail. This was the occasion when Jesus pushed out from shore to escape the press of the multitudes and taught from Peter's boat. After He finished teaching, He instructed Peter to launch out to the deep water and put in his nets. Peter did so, even though the timing was wrong (fish were easier to catch at night when the water was cooler and the fish surfaced to feed), the place was wrong (fish normally fed in shallower waters and were easier to catch there), and Peter was exhausted (having fished all night without any success). He told Jesus, "Master, we have toiled all night and caught nothing; nevertheless at Your word I will let down the net" (Luke 5:5). The resulting catch of fish overwhelmed their nets and nearly sank two of their fishing boats! (vv. 6–7).

It was on the heels of that miracle that Jesus said, "Follow Me, and I will make you fishers of men"

(Matthew 4:19). Scripture says it was at this point that "they forsook all and followed Him" (Luke 5:11). According to Matthew, Andrew and Peter "immediately left their nets and followed Him" (Matthew 4:20). And James and John "immediately . . . left the boat and their father, and followed Him" (v. 22). From that point on, they were inseparable from the Lord.

Matthew 10:1–4 and Luke 6:12–16 describe a third phase of their calling. This was their calling to *apostleship*. It was at this point that Christ selected and appointed twelve men in particular and made them His apostles. Here is Luke's account of the incident:

> Now it came to pass in those days that He went out to the mountain to pray, and continued all night in prayer to God. And when it was day, He called His disciples to Himself; and from them He chose twelve whom He also named apostles: Simon, whom He also named Peter, and Andrew his brother; James and John; Philip and Bartholomew; Matthew and Thomas; James the son of Alphaeus, and Simon called the Zealot; Judas the son of James, and Judas Iscariot who also became a traitor.

Their apostleship began with a kind of internship. Christ sends them out. Mark 6:7 says they were sent out two by two. At this stage they were not quite ready to go out alone, so Christ teamed them in pairs, so that they would offer one another mutual support.

Throughout this phase of their training, the Lord Himself stuck closely with them. He was like a mother eagle, watching the eaglets as they began to fly. They were always checking back with Him, reporting on how things were going (cf. Luke 9:10; 10:17). And after a couple of seasons of evangelistic labor, they returned to the Lord and remained with Him for an extended time of teaching, ministry, fellowship, and rest (Mark 6:30–34).

There was a fourth phase of their calling, which occurred after Jesus' resurrection. Judas was now missing from the group, having hanged himself after his betrayal of Christ. Jesus appeared to the remaining eleven in His resurrection body and sent them into all the world, commanding them to disciple the nations. This was, in effect, a call to *martyrdom*. Each of them ultimately gave his life for the sake of the gospel. History records that all but one of them were killed for their testimony. Only John is said to have lived to old age, and he was severely persecuted for Christ's sake, then exiled to the tiny island of Patmos.

Despite the obstacles they faced, they triumphed. In the midst of great persecution and even martyrdom, they fulfilled their task. Against all odds, they entered victorious into glory. And the continu-ing witness of the gospel— spanning two thousand years' time and reaching into virtually every corner of the world—is a testimony to the wisdom of the divine strategy. No wonder we are fascinated by these men.

Let's begin our study of the Twelve by looking carefully at phase three of their calling—their selection and appointment to *apostleship*. Notice the details as Luke gives them to us.

THE TIMING

First, the timing of this event is significant. Luke notes this with his opening phrase in Luke 6:12: "Now it came to pass in those days." The New American Standard Bible renders the phrase this way: "And it was at this time." Luke is not talking about clock time, or the specific days of a specific month. "At this time" and "in those days" refers to a period of time, a season, a distinct phase in Jesus' ministry. It was an interval in His ministry when the opposition to Him peaked.

"In those days" refers back to the immediately preceding account. This section of Luke's Gospel records the vicious opposition Christ was beginning to receive from the scribes and Pharisees. Luke 5:17 is Luke's first mention of the Pharisees, and verse 21 is his first use of the word "scribes." (The scribes are mentioned alongside the Pharisees as "teachers of the law" in verse 17.)

So we are first introduced to Jesus' chief adversaries in Luke 5:17, and Luke's account of their opposition fills the text through the end of chapter 5 and well into chapter 6. Luke describes the escalating conflict between Jesus and the religious leaders of Judaism. They opposed Him when He healed a paralytic and forgave his sins (5:17–26). They opposed Him for eating and drinking with tax collectors and sinners (5:27–39). They opposed Him when He permitted His disciples to pluck heads of grain and eat them on the Sabbath (6:1–5). And they opposed him for healing a man with a withered hand on the Sabbath (6:6–11). One after another, Luke recounts those incidents and highlights the growing opposition of the religious leaders.

The conflict reaches a high point in Luke 6:11. The scribes and Pharisees "were filled with rage, and discussed with one another what they might do to Jesus." Both Mark and Matthew are even more graphic. They report that the religious leaders wanted to destroy Jesus (Matthew 12:14; Mark 3:6). Mark says the religious leaders even got the

Herodians involved in their plot. The Herodians were a political faction that supported the dynasty of the Herods. They were not normally allied with the Pharisees, but the two groups joined together in collusion against Jesus. They were already hatching plans to murder Him.

It is at this precise point that Luke interjects his account of how the Twelve were chosen and appointed to be apostles. "It came to pass in those days"—when the hostility against Christ had escalated to a murderous fever pitch. Hatred for Him among the religious elite had reached its apex. Jesus could already feel the heat of His coming death. The crucifixion was now less than two years away. He already knew that He would suffer death on the cross, that He would rise from the dead, and that after forty days He would ascend to His Father. He therefore also knew that His earthly work would have to be handed off to someone else.

It was now time to select and prepare His official representatives. Jesus—knowing the hatred of the religious leaders, fully aware of the hostility against Him, seeing the inevitability of His execution—therefore chose twelve key men to carry on the proclamation of His gospel for the salvation of Israel and the establishment of the church. Time was of the essence. There weren't many days left (about eighteen months, by most estimates) before His earthly ministry would end. Now was the time to choose His apostles. Their most intensive training would begin immediately and be complete within a matter of months.

The focus of Christ's ministry therefore turned at this point from the multitudes to the few. Clearly, it was the looming reality of His death at the hands of His adversaries that signaled the turning point.

There's another striking reality in this. When Jesus

chose the Twelve to be His official representatives—preachers of the gospel who would carry both His message and His authority—He didn't choose a single rabbi. He didn't choose a scribe. He didn't choose a Pharisee. He didn't choose a Sadducee. He didn't choose a priest. Not one of the men He chose came from the religious establishment. The choosing of the twelve apostles was a judgment against institutionalized Judaism. It was a renunciation of those men and their organizations, which had become totally corrupt. That is why the Lord didn't choose one recognized religious leader. He chose instead men who were not theologically trained—fishermen, a tax collector, and other common men.

Jesus had long been at war with those who saw themselves as the religious nobility of Israel. They resented Him. They rejected Him and His message. They hated Him. The Gospel of John puts it this way: "He came to His own, and His own did not receive Him" (John 1:11). The religious leaders of Judaism constituted the core of those who rejected Him.

Nearly a year and a half before this, in one of the first official acts of Jesus' ministry, He had challenged Israel's religious establishment on their own turf in Jerusalem during the Passover—the one time of year when the city was most populated with pilgrims coming to offer sacrifices. Jesus went to the temple mount, made a whip of small cords, drove the thieving money-changers out of the temple, poured out their money, overturned their tables, and chased their animals away (John 2:13–16). In doing that, He struck a devastating blow at institutionalized Judaism. He unmasked the religious nobility as thieves and hypocrites. He condemned their spiritual bankruptcy. He exposed their apostasy. He publicly rebuked their sin. He indicted them for gross corruption. He denounced their deception. That is how He *began* His ministry. It was an all-out assault on the religion of the Jewish establishment.

Now, many months later, at the height of His Galilean ministry, far removed from Jerusalem, the resentment that must have been inaugurated at that first event had reached a fever pitch. The religious leaders were now bloodthirsty. And they began to devise a scheme to execute Him.

Their rejection of Him was complete. They were hostile to the gospel He preached. They despised the doctrines of grace He stood for, spurned the repentance He demanded, looked with disdain upon the forgiveness He offered, and repudiated the faith He epitomized. In spite of the many miracles that proved His messianic credentials—despite actually seeing Him cast out demons, heal every conceivable sickness, and raise dead people to life—they would not accept the fact that He was God in human flesh. They hated Him. They hated His message. He was a threat to their power. And they desperately wanted to see Him dead.

So when it was time for Jesus to select twelve apostles, He naturally did not choose people from the establishment that was so determined to destroy Him. He turned instead to His own humble followers and selected twelve simple, ordinary, working-class men.

THE TWELVE

If you've ever visited the great cathedrals in Europe, you might assume that the apostles were larger-than-life stained-glass saints with shining halos who represented an exalted degree of spirituality. The fact of the matter is that they were very, very common men.

It's a shame they have so often been put on pedestals as magnificent marble figures or portrayed in paintings like some kind of Roman gods. That dehumanizes them. They were just twelve completely ordinary men—perfectly human in every way. We mustn't lose touch with who they really were.

I recently read a biography of William Tyndale, who pioneered the translation of Scripture into English. He thought it wrong that common people heard the Bible only in Latin and not in their own language. The church leaders of his day, incredibly, did not want the Bible in the language of the people because (like the Pharisees of Jesus' day) they feared losing their ecclesiastical power. But against their opposition, Tyndale translated the New Testament into English and had it published. For his efforts he was rewarded with exile, poverty, and persecution. Finally, in 1536, he was strangled and burned at the stake.

One of the main things that motivated Tyndale to translate Scripture into the common language was a survey of English clergy that revealed that most of them did not even know who the twelve apostles were. Only a few of them could name more than four or five of the apostles. Church leaders and Christians of today might fare just as poorly on the test. The way the institutional church has canonized these men has actually dehumanized them and made them seem remote and otherworldly. It is a strange irony, because when Jesus chose them, He selected them not for any extraordinary abilities or spiritual superiority. He seems to have deliberately chosen men who were notable only for their ordinariness.

What qualified these men to be apostles? Obviously it was not any intrinsic ability or outstanding talent of their own. They were Galileans. They were not the elite.

Galileans were deemed low-class, rural, uneducated people. They were commoners—nobodies. But again, they were not selected because they were any more distinguished or more talented than others in Israel at the time.

Certainly, there are some rather clear moral and spiritual qualifications that have to be met by men who would fill this or any other kind of leadership role in the church. In fact, the standard for spiritual leadership in the church is extremely high. Consider, for example, the qualifications for being an elder or a pastor, listed in 1 Timothy 3:2–7:

> [He] must be blameless, the husband of one wife, temperate, sober-minded, of good behavior, hospitable, able to teach; not given to wine, not violent, not greedy for money, but gentle, not quarrelsome, not covetous; one who rules his own house well, having his children in submission with all reverence (for if a man does not know how to rule his own house, how will he take care of the church of God?); not a novice, lest being puffed up with pride he fall into the same condemnation as the devil. Moreover he must have a good testimony among those who are outside, lest he fall into reproach and the snare of the devil.

Titus 1:6–9 gives a similar list. Hebrews 13:7 also suggests that church leaders must be exemplary moral and spiritual examples, because their faith must be the kind others can follow, and they will be required to give an account to God for how they conduct themselves. These are very, very high standards.

By the way, the standard is no lower for people in the congregation. Leaders are examples for everyone else. There's no acceptable "lower" standard for rank-and-file church members. In fact, in Matthew 5:48, Jesus said to *all* believers, "Be perfect, just as your Father in heaven is perfect."

Frankly, no one meets such a standard. Humanly speaking, no one "qualifies" when the standard is utter perfection. No one is fit to be in God's kingdom, and no one is inherently worthy to be in God's service. All have sinned and fall short of God's glory (Romans 3:23). There is none righteous, no not one (Romans 3:10). Remember, it was the mature apostle Paul who confessed, "I know that in me (that is, in my flesh) nothing good dwells" (Romans 7:18). In 1 Timothy 1:15 he called himself the chief of sinners.

So there are no intrinsically qualified people. God Himself must save sinners, sanctify them, and then transform them from unqualified into instruments He can use.

The Twelve were like the rest of us; they were selected from the unworthy and the unqualified. They were, like Elijah, men "with a nature like ours" (James 5:17). They did not rise to the highest usefulness because they were somehow *different* from us. Their transformation into vessels of honor was solely the work of the Potter.

Many Christians become discouraged and disheartened when their spiritual life and witness suffer because of sin or failure. We tend to think we're worthless nobodies— and left to ourselves, that would be true! But worthless nobodies are just the kind of people God uses, because that is all He has to work with.

Satan may even attempt to convince us that our shortcomings render us useless to God and to His church. But Christ's choice of the apostles testifies to the fact that God can use the unworthy and the unqualified. He can use nobodies. They turned the world upside down, these twelve (Acts 17:6). It was not because they had extraordinary talents, unusual intellectual abilities, powerful political influence, or some special social status. They turned the world upside down because God worked in them to do it.

God chooses the humble, the lowly, the meek, and the weak so that there's never any question about the source of power when their lives change the world. It's not the man; it's the truth of God and the power of God *in* the man. (We need to remind some preachers today of this. It's not their cleverness or their personality. The power is in the Word— the truth that we preach—not in us.) And apart from one Person—one extraordinary human being who was God incarnate, the Lord Jesus Christ—the history of God's work on earth is the story of His using the unworthy and molding them for His use the same careful way a potter fashions clay. The Twelve were no exception to that.

The apostles properly hold an exalted place in redemptive history, of course. They are certainly worthy of being regarded as heroes of the faith. The book of Revelation describes how their names will adorn the twelve gates of the heavenly city, the New Jerusalem. So heaven itself features an eternal tribute to them. But that doesn't diminish the truth that they were as ordinary as you and I. We need to remember them not from their stained-glass images, but from the down-to-earth way the Bible presents them to us. We need to lift them out of their otherworldly obscurity and get to know them as real people. We need to think of them as actual men, and not as some kind of exalted figures from the pantheon of religious ritualism.

Let's not, however, underestimate the importance of their office. Upon their selection, the twelve apostles in effect became the true spiritual leaders of Israel. The religious elite of *apostate* Israel were symbolically set aside when Jesus chose them. The apostles became the first preachers of the new covenant. They were the ones to whom the Christian gospel was first entrusted. They represented the true Israel of God—a genuinely repentant and believing Israel. They also became the foundation stones of the church, with Jesus Himself as the chief cornerstone (Ephesians 2:20). Those truths are heightened, not diminished, by the fact that these men were so ordinary.

Again, that is perfectly consistent with the way the Lord always works. In 1 Corinthians 1:20–21 we read, "Where is the wise? Where is the scribe? Where is the disputer of this age? Has not God made foolish the wisdom of this world? For since, in the wisdom of God, the world through wisdom did not know God, it pleased God through the foolishness of the message preached to save those who believe." That is the very reason there were no philosophers, no brilliant writers, no famous debaters, no eminent teachers, and no men who had ever distinguished themselves as great orators among the twelve men Christ chose. They *became* great spiritual leaders and great preachers under the power of the Holy Spirit, but it was not because of any innate oratorical skill, leadership abilities, or academic qualifications these men had. Their influence is owing to one thing and one thing only: the power of the message they preached.

On a human level, the gospel was thought a foolish message and the apostles were deemed unsophisticated preachers. Their teaching was beneath the elite. They were mere fishermen and working-class nobodies. Peons. Rabble. That was the assessment of their contemporaries. (The same thing has been true of the genuine church of Christ throughout history. It is true in the evangelical world today. Where are the impressive intellects, the great writers, and the great orators esteemed by the world? They're not found, for the most part, in the church.) "For you see your calling, brethren, that not many wise according to the flesh, not many mighty, not many noble, are called" (v. 26).

"But God has chosen the foolish things of the world to put to shame the wise, and God has chosen the weak things of the world to put to shame the things which are mighty; and the base things of the world and the things which are despised God has chosen, and the things which are not, to bring to nothing the things that are, that no flesh should glory in His presence" (vv. 27–29). God's favorite instruments are nobodies, so that no man can boast before God. In other words, God chooses whom He chooses in order that *He* might receive the glory. He chooses weak instruments so that no one will attribute the power to human instruments rather than to God, who wields those instruments. Such a strategy is unacceptable to those whose whole pursuit in life is aimed toward the goal of human glory.

With the notable exception of Judas Iscariot, these men were not like that. They certainly struggled with pride and arrogance like every fallen human being. But the driving passion of their lives became the glory of Christ. And it was that passion, subjected to the influence of the Holy Spirit— not any innate skill or human talent—that explains why they left such an indelible impact on the world.

THE TEACHER

Bear in mind, then, that the selection of the Twelve took place at a time when Jesus was faced with the reality of His impending death. He had experienced the rising hostility of the religious leaders. He knew His earthly mission would soon culminate in His death, resurrection, and ascension. And so from this point on, the whole character of His ministry changed. It became his top priority to train the men who would be the chief spokesmen for the gospel after He was gone.

How did He choose them? He first went off to commune with His Father. "He went out to the mountain to pray, and continued all night in prayer to God" (Luke 6:12).

Throughout the first five chapters of his Gospel, Luke has already made clear that prayer was a pattern in the life of Jesus. Luke 5:16 says, "He Himself often withdrew into the wilderness and prayed." It was His habit to slip away in solitude to talk to His Father. He was always under pressure from the massive multitudes when He was in the towns and villages of Galilee. The wilderness and the mountain regions afforded solitude where He could pray.

We don't know *which* mountain this was. If it mattered, Scripture would tell us. There are lots of hills and mountains around the northern Galilee area. This one was probably in close walking distance to Capernaum, which was a sort of home base for Jesus' ministry. He went there and spent the entire night in prayer.

We often see Him praying in anticipation of crucial events in His ministry. (Remember, that is what He was doing on the night of His betrayal—praying in a garden where he found some solitude from the hectic atmosphere in Jerusalem. Judas knew he would find Jesus there because according to Luke 22:39 it was His habit to go there and pray.)

Here is Jesus in His true humanity. He was standing in a very volatile situation. The brewing hostility against Him was already threatening to bring about His death. He had a very brief amount of time remaining to train the men who would carry the gospel to the world after His departure. And the chilling reality of those matters drove Him to the top of a mountain so He could pray to God in total solitude. He had made Himself of no reputation and had taken the form of a bondservant, coming to earth as a man. The time was now approaching when He would further humble Himself unto death—even the death of the cross. And thus He goes to God as a man would go, to seek God's face in prayer and to commune with the Father about the men whom He would choose for this vital office.

Notice that He spent the entire night in prayer. If He went to the mountain before dark, that was probably around seven or eight o'clock in the evening. If He came back down after dawn, that would have been around six in the morning. In other words, He prayed for at least ten hours straight.

To say He spent the whole night requires several words in English. It's only one word in the Greek: *dianuktereuo*. The word is significant. It speaks of enduring at a task through the night. The word could not be used of sleeping all night. It's not an expression you would use if you wanted to say it was dark all night. It has the sense of toiling through the night, staying at a task all night. It suggests that He remained awake through the darkness until morning and that He was persevering all that time in prayer with an immense weight of duty upon Him.

Another interesting note comes through in the Greek language although we don't see it in the English. Our English version says that He "continued all night in prayer to God." Actually, the Greek expression means that He spent the whole night in the prayer *of* God. Whenever He prayed, it was quite literally the prayer of God. He was engaged in inter-Trinitarian communion. The prayer being offered was the very prayer of God. The Members of the Trinity were communing with one another. His prayers were all perfectly consistent with the mind and the will of God—for He Himself is God. And therein do we see the incredible mystery of His humanity and His deity brought together. Jesus in His humanity needed to pray all night, and Jesus in His deity was praying the very prayer of God.

Don't miss the point: The choice Christ would soon make was of such monumental importance that it required ten to twelve hours of prayer in preparation. What was He praying for? Clarity in the matter of whom to choose? I don't think so. As omniscient God incarnate, the divine will was no mystery to Him. He was no doubt praying for the men He would soon appoint, communing with the Father about the absolute wisdom of His choice, and acting in His capacity as Mediator on their behalf.

When the night of prayer was over, He returned to where His disciples were and summoned them. ("And when it was day, He called His disciples to Himself"—Luke 6:13.) It was not only the Twelve whom He summoned. The word *disciple* in this context speaks of His followers in a broad sense. The word itself means "student, learner." There must have been numerous disciples, and from them, He would choose twelve to fill the office of an apostle.

It was common, both in the Greek culture and the Jewish culture of Jesus' day, for a prominent rabbi or philosopher to attract students. Their teaching venue was not necessarily a classroom or an auditorium. Most were peripatetic instructors whose disciples simply followed them through the normal course of everyday life. That is the kind of ministry Jesus maintained with His followers. He was an itinerant teacher. He simply went from place to place, and as He taught, He attracted people who followed

His movements and listened to His teaching. We get a picture of this back in verse 1: "Now it happened on the second Sabbath after the first that He went through the grainfields. And His disciples plucked the heads of grain and ate them, rubbing them in their hands." They were walking with Him, following Him from place to place as He taught, gleaning grain for food as they walked.

We don't know how many disciples Jesus had. At one point, he sent seventy out in pairs to evangelize in communities where He was preparing to visit (Luke 10:1). But the total number of His followers was undoubtedly far more than seventy. Scripture indicates that multitudes followed Him. And why not? His teaching was absolutely unlike anything anyone had ever heard in its clarity and obvious, inherent authority; He had the ability to heal diseases, cast out demons, and raise the dead; He was full of grace and truth. It's not amazing that He drew so many disciples. What is amazing is that anyone rejected Him. But reject Him they did, because His message was more than they could bear.

We see something of the dynamics of this in John 6. At the beginning of the chapter, He feeds more than five thousand people who had come out to see Him. (John 6:10 says the men alone numbered five thousand. Counting women and children, the crowd might have easily been double that number or more.) It was an amazing day. Many of those people were already following Him as disciples; many others were no doubt prepared to do so. John writes, "Then those men, when they had seen the sign that Jesus did, said, 'This is truly the Prophet who is to come into the world'" (v. 14). Who was this man who could produce food out of nothing? *They* spent most of their lives farming, harvesting, raising animals, and preparing meals. *Jesus* could just create food!

That would change their lives. They must have had visions of leisure and free food, already prepared. This was the kind of Messiah they had hoped for! According to John, "They were about to come and take Him by force to make Him king" (v. 15). He escaped by a series of supernatural events that culminated in His walking on the water.

The next day the people found Him in Capernaum, on the other side of the lake. Crowds of them had come looking for Him, obviously hoping He would give them more food. He chided them for following Him out of wrong motives: "You seek Me, not because you saw the signs, but because you ate of the loaves and were filled" (v. 26). When they continued to ask for more food, He told them, "I am the living bread which came down from heaven. If anyone eats of this bread, he will live forever; and the bread that I shall give is My flesh, which I shall give for the life of the world" (v. 51). The saying was so hard for them to understand that they pressed Him to explain. He continued:

> "Most assuredly, I say to you, unless you eat the flesh of the Son of Man and drink His blood, you have no life in you. Whoever eats My flesh and drinks My blood has eternal life, and I will raise him up at the last day. For My flesh is food indeed, and My blood is drink indeed. He who eats My flesh and drinks My blood abides in Me, and I in him. As the living Father sent Me, and I live because of the Father, so he who feeds on Me will live because of Me. This is the bread which came down from heaven; not as your fathers ate the manna, and are dead. He who eats this bread will live forever." These things He said in the synagogue as He taught in Capernaum. (vv. 53–59)

This was so offensive that even many of His disciples began to have second thoughts about following Him. John writes, "From that time many of His disciples went back and walked with Him no more" (v. 66).

So disciples were coming and going. People were attracted, then disillusioned. And on that particular occasion described in John 6, Jesus even said to the Twelve, "Do you also want to go away?" (v. 67). Peter spoke for the group when he answered, "Lord, to whom shall we go? You have the words of eternal life. Also we have come to believe and know that You are the Christ, the Son of the living God" (vv. 68–69).

Those who stayed were people whom God had sovereignly drawn to His own Son (v. 44). Jesus had also drawn them to Himself in particular. He told them, "You did not choose Me, but I chose you and appointed you that you should go and bear fruit, and that your fruit should remain" (John 15:16). He sovereignly selected them and (with the exception of Judas Iscariot, whom Christ knew would betray Him) He sovereignly worked in them and through them to guarantee that they would persevere with Him, that they would bear fruit, and that their fruit would remain. Here we see the principle of God's electing grace at work.

The sovereignty of His choice is seen in an extraordinary way by the selection of the Twelve. Out of the larger group of disciples, perhaps hundreds of them, He chose twelve men in particular and appointed them to the apostolic office. It was not a job for which applicants or volunteers were sought. Christ *chose* them sovereignly and appointed them, in the presence of the larger group.

This was a remarkable moment for those twelve. Up to this point, Peter, James, John, Andrew, Nathanael,

Matthew, and the others were just part of the crowd. They were learners like everyone else in the group. They had been following and listening and observing and absorbing His teaching. But they didn't yet have any official role of leadership. They had not yet been appointed to any role that set them apart from the others. They were faces in the crowd until Christ selected them and made twelve of them apostles.

Why twelve? Why not eight? Why not twenty-four? The number twelve was filled with symbolic importance. There were twelve tribes in Israel. But Israel was apostate. The Judaism of Jesus' time represented a corruption of the faith of the Old Testament. Israel had abandoned divine grace in favor of works-religion. Their religion was legalistic. It was shot through with hypocrisy, self-righteous works, man-made regulations, and meaningless ceremonies. It was heretical. It was based on physical descent from Abraham rather than the *faith* of Abraham. In choosing twelve apostles, Christ was in effect appointing new leadership for the new covenant. And the apostles represented the new leaders of the true Israel of God—consisting of people who believed the gospel and were following the faith of Abraham (cf. Romans 4:16). In other words, the twelve apostles symbolized judgment against the twelve tribes of Old Testament Israel.

Jesus Himself made the connection plainly. In Luke 22:29–30, He told the apostles, "I bestow upon you a kingdom, just as My Father bestowed one upon Me, that you may eat and drink at My table in My kingdom, and sit on thrones judging the twelve tribes of Israel."

The significance of the number twelve would have been immediately obvious to almost every Israelite. Jesus' messianic claims were clear to all who listened to His teaching. He constantly spoke of His coming kingdom. Meanwhile, throughout Israel, expectation was running high that the Messiah would very soon appear and establish His kingdom. Some had thought John the Baptist would be that Messiah, but John pointed them to Christ (cf. John 1:19–27). They knew very well that Christ had all the messianic credentials (John 10:41-42). He wasn't the kind of political leader they expected, so they were slow to believe (John 10:24–25). But they surely understood the claims He was making, and they were filled with anticipation.

So when He publicly appointed twelve men to be His apostles, the significance of that number was loud and clear. The apostles represented a whole new Israel, under the new covenant. And their appointment—bypassing the religious establishment of official Judaism—signified a message of judgment against national Israel. Clearly, these twelve ordinary men were not destined for an ordinary role. They stood in the place of the heads of twelve tribes. They were living proof that the kingdom Jesus was about to establish was al-together different from the kingdom most Israelites anticipated.

Luke 6:13 says, "He chose twelve whom He also named apostles." The title alone was significant. The Greek verb *apostello* means "to send out." The noun form, *apostolos,* means "one who is sent." The English word *apostle* is a transliteration, rather than a translation, of the Greek word. The apostles were "sent ones." But they were not mere messengers. The Greek word for "messenger" was *angelos,* from which we get our word "angel." An *apostolos* was something more significant than a courier or a herald; *apostolos* conveyed the idea of an ambassador, a delegate, an official representative.

The word has an exact parallel in Aramaic—*shaliah.*

(Remember that the common language in Israel in Jesus' time—the language Jesus Himself spoke—was not Hebrew, but Aramaic.) In that first-century Jewish culture, the *shaliah* was an official representative of the Sanhedrin, the ruling council of Israel. A *shaliah* exercised the full rights of the Sanhedrin. He spoke for them, and when he spoke, he spoke with their authority. He was owed the same respect and deference as the council itself. But he never delivered his own message; his task was to deliver the message of the group whom he represented. The office of a *shaliah* was well known. *Shaliah* were sent out to settle legal or religious disputes, and they acted with the full authority of the whole council. Some prominent rabbis also had their *shaliah,* "sent ones" who taught their message and represented them with their full authority. Even the Jewish Mishnah (a collection of oral traditions originally conceived as a commentary on the Law) recognized the role of the *shaliah*. It says, "The one sent by the man is as the man himself." So the nature of the office was well known to the Jewish people.

Thus when Jesus appointed apostles, He was saying something very familiar to people in that culture. These were His delegates. They were His trusted *shaliah*. They spoke with His authority, delivered His message, and exercised His authority.

THE TASK

The familiar role of the *shaliah* in that culture virtually defined the task of the apostles. Obviously, Christ would delegate His authority to these twelve and send them out with His message. They would represent Him as official delegates. Virtually everyone in that culture would have instantly understood the nature of the office. These twelve men, commissioned as Jesus' apostles, would speak and act with the same authority as the One who sent them. "Apostle" was therefore a title of great respect and privilege.

Mark 3:14 records this same event: "Then He appointed twelve, that they might be with Him and that He might send them out to preach." Notice the two-step process. Before they could be sent out to preach, they had to be pulled in. It was absolutely critical that they be with Jesus before they be sent out. In fact, it isn't until Luke 9:1 that Jesus calls the Twelve together and gives them authority over the demons and power to heal diseases. At that point, He literally delegates to them His miracle power. So in Luke 6, He identifies and appoints them and brings them under His direct and personal tutelage ("that they might be with Him"). In Luke 9, several months later, He gives them power to work miracles and cast out demons. Not until then did He "send them out to preach."

Up to this point, Jesus was speaking to huge crowds most of the time. With the calling of the Twelve in Luke 6, His teaching ministry becomes more intimate, focused primarily on them. He would still draw large crowds and teach them, but His focus was on the disciples and their training.

Notice the natural progression in their training program. At first, they simply followed Jesus, gleaning from His sermons to the multitudes and listening to His instructions along with a larger group of disciples. They apparently did not do this full-time, but as opportunity allowed in the course of their regular lives. Next (as recorded in Matthew 4), He called them to leave everything and follow Him exclusively. Now (in the incident recorded in Luke 6 and

Matthew 10), He selects twelve men out of that group of full-time disciples, identifies them as apostles, and begins to focus most of His energies on their personal instruction. Later, He will gift them with authority and miracle power. Finally, He will send them out. At first, they go on short-term mission assignments, but they keep coming back. But when He leaves to return to the Father, they will go out for good on their own. There's a clear progression in their training and entry into full-time ministry.

No longer just disciples, they are now apostles—*shaliah*. They occupy an important office. Luke uses the word "apostles" six times in his Gospel and about thirty times in the book of Acts. Their role in the Gospels pertains primarily to taking the kingdom message to Israel. In Acts, they are engaged in the founding of the church.

Although they were common men, theirs was an uncommon calling. In other words, the task they were called to, and not anything about the men per se, is what makes them so important. Consider how unique their role was to be.

Not only would they found the church and play a pivotal leadership role as the early church grew and branched out, but they also became the channels through which most of the New Testament would be given. They received truth from God by divine revelation. Ephesians 3:5 is very explicit. Paul says that the mystery of Christ, which in earlier ages was not made known, "has now been revealed by the Spirit to His holy apostles and prophets." They did not preach a human message. The truth was given to them by direct revelation.

They were therefore the source of all true church doctrine. Acts 2:42 describes the activities of the early church in these terms: "They continued steadfastly in the apostles' doctrine and fellowship, in the breaking of bread, and in prayers." Before the New Testament was complete, the apostles' teaching was the *only* source of truth about Christ and church doctrine. And their teaching was received with the same authority as the written Word. In fact, the written New Testament is nothing other than the Spirit-inspired, inscripturated record of the apostles' teaching.

In short, the apostles were given to edify the church. Ephesians 4:11–12 says Christ gave the apostles "for the equipping of the saints for the work of ministry, for the edifying of the body of Christ." They were the original Christian teachers and preachers. Their teaching, as recorded in the New Testament, is the only rule by which sound doctrine can be tested, even today.

They were also examples of virtue. Ephesians 3:5 calls them "holy apostles." They set a standard for godliness and true spirituality. They were the first examples for believers to emulate. They were men of character and integrity, and they set the standard for all who would subsequently become leaders in the church.

They had unique power to perform miracles that confirmed their message. Hebrews 2:3–4 says that the gospel "first began to be spoken by the Lord, and was confirmed to us by those who heard Him, God also bearing witness both with signs and wonders, with various miracles, and gifts of the Holy Spirit." In other words, God confirmed His Word through the apostles by the miracles that they were able to do. The New Testament indicates that *only* the apostles and those who were closely associated with them had the power to do miracles. That is why 2 Corinthians 12:12 speaks of such miracles as "the signs of an apostle."

As a result of all this, the disciples were greatly blessed and held in high esteem by the people of God. Jesus' expectations for them were met through their faithful perseverance. And His promise to them was fulfilled in the growth and expansion of the church. You may recall that in Luke 18:28, Peter said to Jesus, "See, we have left all and followed You." The disciples were apparently concerned about the way things were going and what might happen to them. Peter's words were actually a plea. It is as if he was saying, on behalf of the others, "What's going to happen to us?"

Jesus replied, "Assuredly, I say to you, there is no one who has left house or parents or brothers or wife or children, for the sake of the kingdom of God, who shall not receive many times more in this present time, and in the age to come eternal life." They had not left anything that He would not more than make up to them. And God did bless them in this life (even though, as we shall see when we examine each life, most of them were martyred). God blessed them in this life through the founding and growth of the church. They not only gained influence, respect, and honor among the people of God; but as for their homes and families, they gained multitudes of spiritual children and brethren as the church grew and believers multiplied. And they will be greatly honored in the age to come as well.

THE TRAINING

All of that might have seemed remote and uncertain on the morning Jesus summoned His disciples and appointed the Twelve. They still needed to be taught. All their shortcomings and human failings seemed to overshadow their potential. Time was short. They had already left whatever vocations they were expert in. They had abandoned their nets, forsaken their fields, and left the tax tables behind. They had relinquished everything they knew, in order to be trained for something for which they had no natural aptitude.

But when they forsook their jobs, they by no means became idle. They became full-time students, learners—*disciples.* Now the next eighteen months of their lives would be filled with even more intensive training—the best seminary education ever. They had the example of Christ perpetually before them. They could listen to His teaching, ask Him questions, watch how He dealt with people, and enjoy intimate fellowship with Him in every kind of setting. He gave them ministry opportunities, instructing them and sending them out on special assignments. He graciously encouraged them, lovingly corrected them, and patiently instructed them. That is how the best learning always occurs. It isn't just information passed on; it's one life invested in another.

But it was not an *easy* process. The Twelve could be amazingly thick headed. There was a reason they weren't the academic elite. Jesus Himself often said things like, "Are you also still without understanding? Do you not yet understand?" (Matthew 15:16–17; cf. 16:9). "O foolish ones, and slow of heart to believe" (Luke 24:25). It is significant that Scripture doesn't cover their defects. The point is not to portray them as superholy luminaries or to elevate them above mere mortals. If that were the aim, there would be no reason to record their character flaws. But instead of whitewashing the blemishes, Scripture seems to make a great deal of their human weaknesses. It's a brilliant reminder that "[our] faith should not be in the wisdom of men but in the power of God" (1 Corinthians 2:5).

Why was the learning process so difficult for the apostles? First of all, they lacked spiritual understanding. They were slow to hear and slow to understand. They were at various times thick, dull, stupid, and blind. All those terms or their equivalents are used to describe them in the New Testament. So how did Jesus remedy their lack of spiritual understanding? He just kept teaching. Even after His resurrection, He stayed forty days on earth. Acts 1:3 says that during that time He was "speaking of the things pertaining to the kingdom of God." He was still persistently teaching them until the moment He ascended into heaven.

A second problem that made the learning process difficult for the disciples is that they lacked humility. They were self-absorbed, self-centered, self-promoting, and proud. They spent an enormous amount of time arguing about who would be the greatest among them (Matthew 20:20–28; Mark 9:33–37; Luke 9:46). How did Jesus overcome their lack of humility? By being an example of humility to them. He washed their feet. He modeled servanthood. He humbled Himself, even unto the death of the cross.

Third, not only did they lack understanding and humility, but they also lacked faith. Four times in the Gospel of Matthew alone Jesus says to them, "O you of little faith" (6:30; 8:26; 14:31; 16:8). In Mark 4:40, He asked them, "How is it that you have no faith?" At the end of Mark's Gospel, after they had spent months in intensive training with Jesus—even after He had risen from the dead—Mark writes, "He rebuked their unbelief and hardness of heart" (Mark 16:14). What remedy did Jesus have for their lack of faith? He kept doing miracles and wonderful works. The miracles were not primarily for the benefit of unbelievers; most of His miracles were deliberately done "in the presence of His disciples" so that *their* faith could be strengthened (John 20:30).

Fourth, they lacked commitment. While the crowds were cheering and the miracles were being multiplied, they were thrilled. But as soon as the soldiers came into the garden to arrest Jesus, they all forsook Him and fled (Mark 14:50). Their leader ended up denying Jesus and swearing he didn't even know the man. How did Jesus remedy their proneness to defection? By interceding for them in prayer. John 17 records how Jesus prayed that they would remain ultimately faithful and that the Father would bring them to heaven (vv. 11–26).

Fifth, they lacked power. On their own, they were weak and helpless, especially when confronted with the enemy. There were times when they tried but could not cast out demons. Their faithlessness left them unable to harness the power that was available to them. What did Jesus do to remedy their weakness? On the day of Pentecost He sent the Holy Spirit to indwell and empower them. This was His promise to them: "You shall receive power when the Holy Spirit has come upon you; and you shall be witnesses to Me in Jerusalem, and in all Judea and Samaria, and to the end of the earth" (Acts 1:8). That promise was mightily fulfilled.

We're inclined to look at this group with all their weaknesses and wonder why Jesus did not simply pick a different group of men. Why would He single out men with no understanding, no humility, no faith, no commitment, and no power? Simply this: His strength is made perfect in weakness (2 Corinthians 12:9). Again we see how He chooses the weak things of this world to confound the mighty. No one could ever examine this group of men and conclude that they did what they did because of their own innate abilities. There is no human explanation for the influence of the apostles. The glory goes to God alone.

Acts 4:13 says this about how the people of Jerusalem perceived the apostles: "Now when they saw the boldness of Peter and John, and perceived that they were uneducated and untrained men, they marveled. And they realized that they had been with Jesus." The Greek text says people perceived that they were *"aggramatoi . . . idiotai"*—literally, "illiterate ignoramuses." And that was true from a worldly viewpoint. But it was obvious that they had been with Jesus. The same thing should be said of every true disciple. Luke 6:40 says, "A disciple is not above his teacher, but everyone who is perfectly trained will be like his teacher."

The apostles' relatively brief time of training with Jesus bore eternal fruit. At first, it might have seemed that everything would be for naught. The night Jesus was betrayed, they were scattered like sheep whose shepherd had been smitten (Matthew 26:31). Even after the resurrection, they seemed timid, full of remorse over their failure, and too aware of their own weaknesses to minister with confidence.

But after Jesus ascended to heaven, the Holy Spirit came, infused them with power, and enabled them to do what Christ had trained them to do. The book of Acts records how the church was launched, and the rest is history. Those men, through the legacy of New Testament Scripture and the testimony they left, are still changing the world even today.

2

PETER—THE APOSTLE WITH THE FOOT-SHAPED MOUTH

And the Lord said, "Simon, Simon! Indeed, Satan has asked for you, that he may sift you as wheat. But I have prayed for you, that your faith should not fail; and when you have returned to Me, strengthen your brethren."

—LUKE 22:31–32

WE HAVE FOUR LISTS of the twelve apostles in the New Testament: Matthew 10:2–4, Mark 3:16–19, Luke 6:13–16, and Acts 1:13. Here's how the list appears in Luke's Gospel: "He chose twelve whom He also named apostles: Simon, whom He also named Peter, and Andrew his brother; James and John; Philip and Bartholomew; Matthew and Thomas; James the son of Alphaeus, and Simon called the Zealot; Judas the son of James, and Judas Iscariot who also became a traitor."

In all four biblical lists, the same twelve men are named, and the order in which they are given is strikingly similar. The first name in all four lists is Peter. He thus stands out as the leader and spokesman for the whole company of twelve. The Twelve are then arranged in three groups of four. Group one always has Peter at the head of the list, and that group always includes Andrew, James, and John. Group two always features Philip first and includes Bartholomew, Matthew, and Thomas. Group three is always led by James the son of Alphaeus, and it includes Simon the Zealot; Judas son of James (called "Thaddeaus" in Mark and "Lebbaeus, whose surname was Thaddeaus" in Matthew); and finally, Judas Iscariot. (Judas Iscariot is omitted from the list in Acts 1 because he was already dead by then. In the three lists where Judas's name is included, it always appears last, along with a remark identifying him as the traitor.)

The three names at the head of each group seem to have been the group leaders. The three groups always appear in the same order: first Peter's group, then the group led by Philip, then the group headed by James.

Matthew 10:2–4	Mark 3:16–19	Luke 6:14–16	Acts 1:13
Peter	Peter	Peter	Peter
Andrew	James	Andrew	James
James	John	James	John
John	Andrew	John	Andrew
Philip	Philip	Philip	Philip
Bartholomew	Bartholomew	Bartholomew	Thomas
Thomas	Matthew	Matthew	Bartholomew
Matthew	Thomas	Thomas	Matthew
James (son of Alphaeus)	James (son of Alphaeus)	James (son of Alphaeus)	James (son of Alphaeus)

Lebbaeus (surn. Thaddeus)	Thaddeus	Simon	Simon
Simon	Simon	Judas (son of James)	Judas (son of James)
Judas Iscariot	Judas Iscariot	Judas Iscariot	

The groups appear to be listed in descending order based on their level of intimacy with Christ. The members of group one were in all likelihood the first disciples Jesus called to Himself (John 1:35–42). Therefore they had been with Him the longest and occupied the most trusted position in His inner circle. They are often seen together in the presence of Christ at key times. Of the four in the first group, three—Peter, James, and John—form an even closer inner circle. Those three are with Jesus at major events in His ministry when the other apostles are either not present or not as close. The three in the inner circle were together, for example, on the Mount of Transfiguration and in the heart of the Garden of Gethsemane (cf. Matthew 17:1; Mark 5:37; 13:3; 14:33).

Group two does not have such a high profile, but they are still significant figures in the Gospel accounts. Group three is more distant, and they are rarely mentioned in the narrative accounts of Jesus' ministry. The only member of group three we know much about is Judas Iscariot—and we know him only because of his treachery at the very end. So although there were twelve apostles, only three seem to have had the most intimate relationship with Christ. The others seemed to enjoy somewhat lesser degrees of personal familiarity with Him.

This suggests that even a relatively small group of twelve is too large for one person to maintain the closest intimacy with each group member. Jesus kept three men very close to Him—Peter, James, and John. Next came Andrew, and then the others, obviously in declining degrees of close friendship. If Christ in His perfect humanity could not pour equal amounts of time and energy into everyone He drew around Him, no leader should expect to be able to do that.

The Twelve were an amazingly varied group. Their personalities and interests swept the spectrum. The four in group one seem to be the only ones tied together by common denominators. They were all four fishermen, they were two sets of brothers, they came from the same community, and they had apparently all been friends for a long time. By contrast, Matthew was a tax collector and a loner. Simon was a Zealot—a political activist—and a different kind of loner. The others all came from unknown occupations.

They all had vastly differing personalities. Peter was eager, aggressive, bold, and outspoken—with a habit of revving his mouth while his brain was in neutral. I have often referred to him as the apostle with the foot-shaped mouth. John, on the other hand, spoke very little. In the first twelve chapters of Acts, he and Peter are constant companions, but no words of John are ever recorded. Bartholomew (also known sometimes as Nathanael), was a true believer, openly confessing his faith in Christ and quick to have faith (cf. John 1:47–50). Significantly, he is in the same group as (and sometimes paired with) Thomas, who was an outspoken skeptic and doubter and wanted to have proof for everything.

Their political backgrounds were different, too.

Matthew, the former tax collector (who was sometimes called Levi), was considered one of the most despicable people in Israel before Jesus called him. He had taken a job with the Roman government to extort taxes from his own people—and that tax money went to pay for the Roman occupation army. The lesser-known of the two Simons, on the other hand, is called "the Zealot" in Luke 6:15 and Acts 1:13. Zealots were an outlaw political party who took their hatred of Rome to an extreme and conspired to overthrow Roman rule. Many of them were violent outlaws. Since they did not have an army, they used sabotage and assassination to advance their political agenda. They were, in effect, terrorists. One faction of the Zealots was known as *sicarii* (literally, "dagger-men") because of the small, curved blades they carried. They concealed those weapons beneath their robes and used them to dispatch people they perceived as political enemies—people like tax collectors. Roman soldiers were also favorite targets for their assassinations. The *sicarii* usually staged these acts of execution at public functions in order to heighten fear. That Matthew, a former tax collector, and Simon, a former Zealot, could be part of the same company of twelve apostles is a testimony to the life-changing power and grace of Christ.

It is interesting that the key men in the first and second groups of apostles were originally called at the very outset of Christ's ministry. John 1:35–42 describes how Jesus called John and Andrew. They, in turn, on that very same day, brought Peter, who was Andrew's brother. James, the remaining member of that group, was John's brother, so it was undoubtedly Andrew and John who brought him to Christ, too. In other words, the first group's association with Jesus went back to the very start of His public ministry.

John 1:43–55 likewise describes the calling of Philip

and Nathanael (also known as Bartholomew). They were called "the following day" (v. 43). So that group also had a history that went back to the beginning of Jesus' ministry. These were men who had known Jesus well and followed Him closely for a long time.

The first person in the first group—the man who became the spokesman and the overall leader of the group—was "Simon, whom He also named Peter" (Luke 6:14).

"SIMON . . . ALSO NAMED PETER"

Simon was a very common name. There are at least seven Simons in the Gospel accounts alone. Among the Twelve were two named Simon (Simon Peter and Simon the Zealot). In Matthew 13:55, Jesus' half brothers are listed, and one of them was also named Simon. Judas Iscariot's father was called Simon as well (John 6:71). Matthew 26:6 mentions that Jesus had a meal at the home of a man in Bethany named Simon the leper. Another Simon—a Pharisee—hosted Jesus at a similar meal (Luke 7:36–40). And the man conscripted to carry Jesus' cross partway to Calvary was Simon the Cyrene (Matthew 27:32).

Our Simon's full name at birth was Simon Bar-Jonah (Matthew 16:17), meaning "Simon, son of Jonah" (John 21:15–17). Simon Peter's father's name, then, was John (sometimes rendered Jonas or Jonah). We know nothing more about his parents.

But notice that the Lord gave him another name. Luke introduces him this way: "Simon, whom He also named Peter" (Luke 6:14). Luke's choice of words here is impor-tant. Jesus didn't merely give him a new name to replace the old one. He "also" named him Peter. This disciple was known sometimes as Simon, sometimes as Peter, and sometimes as Simon Peter.

"Peter" was a sort of nickname. It means "Rock." (*Petros* is the Greek word for "a piece of rock, a stone.") The Aramaic equivalent was *Cephas* (cf. 1 Corinthians 1:12; 3:22; 9:5; 15:5; Galatians 2:9). John 1:42 describes Jesus' first face-to-face meeting with Simon Peter: "Now when Jesus looked at him, He said, 'You are Simon the son of Jonah. You shall be called Cephas' (which is translated, A Stone)." Those were apparently the first words Jesus ever said to Peter. And from then on, "Rock" was his nickname.

Sometimes, however, the Lord continued to refer to him as Simon anyway. When you see that in Scripture, it is often a signal that Peter has done something that needs rebuke or correction.

The nickname was significant, and the Lord had a specific reason for choosing it. By nature Simon was brash, vacillating, and un-dependable. He tended to make great promises he couldn't follow through with. He was one of those people who appears to lunge wholeheartedly into something but then bails out before finishing. He was usually the first one in; and too often, he was the first one out. When Jesus met him, he fit James's description of a double-minded man, unstable in all his ways (James 1:8). Jesus changed Simon's name, it appears, because He wanted the nickname to be a perpetual reminder to him about who he *should* be. And from that point on, whatever Jesus called him sent him a subtle message. If He called him Simon, He was signaling him that he was acting like his old self. If He called him Rock, He was commending him for acting the way he ought to be acting.

Tommy Lasorda, former manager of the Los Angeles Dodgers, tells the story of a young, skinny pitcher who was new in the Dodgers' minor league system. The youngster was somewhat timid but had an extraordinarily powerful and accurate arm. Lasorda was convinced that the young pitcher had the potential to be one of the greatest ever. But, Lasorda says, the young man needed to be more fierce and competitive. He needed to lose his timidity. So Lasorda gave him a nickname that was exactly the opposite of his personality: "Bulldog." Over the years, that is exactly what Orel Hershiser became—one of the most tenacious competitors who ever took the mound in the major leagues. The nickname became a perpetual reminder of what he *ought* to be, and before long, it shaped his whole attitude.

This young man named Simon, who would become Peter, was impetuous, impulsive, and overeager. He needed to become like a rock, so that is what Jesus named him. From then on, the Lord could gently chide or commend him just by using one name or the other.

After Christ's first encounter with Simon Peter, we find two distinct contexts in which the name Simon is regularly applied to him. One is a *secular* context. When Scripture refers to his house, for example, it's usually "Simon's house" (Mark 1:29; Luke 4:38; Acts 10:17). When it speaks of his mother-in-law, it does so in similar terms: "Simon's wife's mother" (Mark 1:30; Luke 4:38). Luke 5, describing the fishing business, mentions "one of the boats, which was Simon's" (v. 3)—and Luke says James and John were "partners with Simon" (v. 10). All of those expressions refer to Simon by his given name in purely secular contexts. When he is called Simon in such a context, the use of his old name usually has nothing to do with his spirituality or his character. That is just the normal way of signifying what pertained to him as a natural man—his work, his home, or his family life. These are called "Simon's" things.

The second category of references where he is called Simon is seen whenever Peter was displaying the characteristics of his un-regenerate self—when he was sinning in word, attitude, or action. Whenever he begins to act like his old self, Jesus and the Gospel writers revert to calling him Simon. In Luke 5:5, for example, Luke writes, "Simon answered and said to Him, 'Master, we have toiled all night and caught nothing; nevertheless at Your word I will let down the net.'" That is young Simon the fisherman speaking. He is skeptical and reluctant. But as he obeys and his eyes are opened to who Jesus really is, Luke begins to refer to him by his new name. Verse 8 says, "When Simon Peter saw it, he fell down at Jesus' knees, saying, 'Depart from me, for I am a sinful man, O Lord!'"

We see Jesus calling him Simon in reference to the key failures in his career. In Luke 22:31, foretelling Peter's betrayal, Jesus said, "Simon, Simon! Indeed, Satan has asked for you, that he may sift you as wheat." Later, in the Garden of Gethsemane, when Peter should have been watching and praying with Christ, he fell asleep. Mark writes, "[Jesus] came and found them sleeping, and said to Peter, 'Simon, are you sleeping? Could you not watch one hour? Watch and pray, lest you enter into temptation. The spirit indeed is willing, but the flesh is weak'" (Mark 14:37–38). Thus usually when Peter needed rebuke or admonishment, Jesus referred to him as Simon. It must have reached the point where whenever the Lord said "Simon," Peter cringed. He must have been thinking, *Please call me Rock!* And the Lord might have replied, "I'll call you Rock when you act like a rock."

It is obvious from the Gospel narratives that the apostle John knew Peter very, very well. They were lifelong friends, business associates, and neighbors. Interestingly, in the Gospel of John, John refers to his friend fifteen times as

"Simon Peter." Apparently John couldn't make up his mind which name to use, because he saw both sides of Peter constantly. So he simply put both names together. In fact, "Simon Peter" is what Peter calls himself in the address of his second epistle: "Simon Peter, a bondservant and apostle of Jesus Christ" (2 Peter 1:1). In effect, he took Jesus' nickname for him and made it his surname (cf. Acts 10:32).

After the resurrection, Jesus instructed His disciples to return to Galilee, where He planned to appear to them (Matthew 28:7). Impatient Simon apparently got tired of waiting, so he announced that he was going back to fishing (John 21:3). As usual, the other disciples dutifully followed their leader. They got into the boat, fished all night, and caught nothing.

But Jesus met them on the shore the following morning, where He had prepared breakfast for them. The main purpose of the breakfast meeting seemed to be the restoration of Peter (who, of course, had sinned egregiously by denying Christ with curses on the night the Lord was betrayed). Three times Jesus addressed him as Simon and asked, "Simon, son of Jonah, do you love Me?" (John 21:15–17). Three times, Peter affirmed his love.

That was the last time Jesus ever had to call him Simon. A few weeks later, on Pentecost, Peter and the rest of the apostles were filled with the Holy Spirit. It was Peter, the Rock, who stood up and preached that day.

Peter was exactly like most Christians—both carnal and spiritual. He succumbed to the habits of the flesh sometimes; he functioned in the Spirit other times. He was sinful sometimes, but other times he acted the way a righteous man ought to act. This vacillating man—sometimes Simon, sometimes Peter—was the leader of the Twelve.

"FOLLOW ME, AND I WILL MAKE YOU FISHERS OF MEN"

Simon Peter was a fisherman by trade. He and his brother Andrew were heirs to a family fishing business, centered in Capernaum. They caught fish on the Sea of Galilee. Commercial fishermen on that lake in Jesus' day caught three types of fish. The "small fish" mentioned in John 6:9 in connection with the feeding of the five thousand are *sardines*. Sardines and a kind of flat bread were the staples of the region. Another kind of fish, known as *barbels* (because of the fleshy filaments at the corners of their mouths) are a kind of carp and hence are somewhat bony, but they can grow to be very large—weighing as much as fifteen pounds. (A barbel was probably the kind of fish Peter caught with a coin in its mouth in Matthew 17:27, because it is the only fish in the Sea of Galilee large enough to swallow a coin and also be caught on a hook.) The third and most common type of commercial fish are *musht*—a type of fish that swims and feeds in shoals and has a comblike dorsal fin. Musht of edible size range from six inches to a foot and a half long. Fried musht are still served in restaurants near the Sea of Galilee and are popularly known today as "St. Peter's Fish."

Simon and Andrew spent their nights netting those fish. The brothers were originally from a small village called Bethsaida on the north shore of the lake (John 1:44), but they had moved to a larger town nearby called Capernaum (Mark 1:21, 29).

In Jesus' day, Capernaum was the major town on the north tip of the Sea of Galilee. Jesus made Capernaum His home and the base of His ministry for several months. But He pronounced woe on both Capernaum and Bethsaida in Matthew 11:21–24. And those cities are merely ruins today.

The ruins of the synagogue in Capernaum are still visible. Nearby (just a block to the south) archaeologists found the ruins of an ancient church. Early tradition, dating back at least to the third century, claims this church was built over the house of Peter. Indeed, archaeologists have found many signs that Christians in the second century venerated this site. It may very well be the house where Peter lived. It is a short walk from there to the edge of the lake.

Simon Peter had a wife. We know this because in Luke 4:38 Jesus healed his mother-in-law. The apostle Paul said in 1 Corinthians 9:5 that Peter took his wife on his apostolic mission. That may indicate either that they had no children or that their children were already grown by the time he took his wife. However, Scripture doesn't expressly say that they had any children. Peter was married. That's really all we know for certain about his domestic life.

We know Simon Peter was the leader of the apostles—and not only from the fact that his name heads every list of the Twelve. We also have the explicit statement of Matthew 10:2: "Now the names of the twelve apostles are these: first, Simon, who is called Peter." The word translated "first" in that verse is the Greek term *protos*. It doesn't refer to the first in a list; it speaks of the chief, the leader of the group. Peter's leadership is further evident in the way he normally acts as spokesman for the whole group. He is always in the foreground, taking the lead. He seems to have had a naturally dominant personality, and the Lord put it to good use among the Twelve.

It was, after all, the Lord who chose him to be the leader. Peter was formed and equipped by God's sovereign design to be the leader. Moreover, Christ Himself shaped and trained Peter to be the leader. Therefore when we look at Peter, we see how God builds a leader.

Peter's name is mentioned in the Gospels more than any other name except Jesus. No one speaks as often as Peter, and no one is spoken to by the Lord as often as Peter. No disciple is so frequently rebuked by the Lord as Peter; and no disciple ever rebukes the Lord except Peter (Matthew 16:22). No one else confessed Christ more boldly or acknowledged His lordship more explicitly; yet no other disciple ever verbally denied Christ as forcefully or as publicly as Peter did. No one is praised and blessed by Christ the way Peter was; yet Peter was also the only one Christ ever addressed as Satan. The Lord had harsher things to say to Peter than He ever said to any of the others.

All of that contributed to making him the leader Christ wanted him to be. God took a common man with an ambivalent, vacillating, impulsive, unsubmissive personality and shaped him into a rocklike leader—the greatest preacher among the apostles and in every sense the dominant figure in the first twelve chapters of Acts, where the church was born.

We see in Peter's life three key elements that go into the making of a true leader: the right raw material, the right life experiences, and the right character qualities. Let me show you exactly what I mean.

THE RAW MATERIAL THAT
MAKES A TRUE LEADER

There is an age-old debate about whether true leaders are born or made. Peter is a strong argument for the belief that leaders are born with certain innate gifts, but must also be properly shaped and made into a true leader.

Peter had the God-given fabric of leadership woven into

his personality from the beginning. He was made of the right raw material. Of course, it was the Lord who fashioned him this way in his mother's womb (cf. Psalm 139:13–16).

There are certain rather obvious features in Simon Peter's natural disposition that were critical to his leadership ability. These are not generally characteristics that can be developed merely by training; they were innate features of Peter's temperament.

The first one is *inquisitiveness*. When you're looking for a leader, you want someone who asks lots of questions. People who are not inquisitive simply don't make good leaders. Curiosity is crucial to leadership. People who are content with what they don't know, happy to remain ignorant about what they don't understand, complacent about what they haven't analyzed, and comfortable living with problems they haven't solved—such people cannot lead. Leaders need to have an insatiable curiosity. They need to be people who are hungry to find answers. Knowledge is power. Whoever has the information has the lead. If you want to find a leader, look for someone who is asking the right questions and genuinely looking for answers.

This sort of inquisitiveness normally manifests itself in early childhood. Most of us have encountered children who ask question after question—wearying their parents and other adults with a nonstop barrage of petty puzzlers. (Some of us can even remember being like that as children!) That is part of the fabric of leadership. The best problem-solvers are people who are driven by an unquenchable enthusiasm for knowing and understanding things.

In the Gospel accounts, Peter asks more questions than all the other apostles combined. It was usually Peter who asked the Lord to explain His difficult sayings (Matthew 15:15; Luke 12:41). It was Peter who asked how often he needed to forgive (Matthew 18:21). It was Peter who asked what reward the disciples would get for having left everything to follow Jesus (Matthew 19:27). It was Peter who asked about the withered fig tree (Mark 11:21). It was Peter who asked questions of the risen Christ (John 21:20–22). He always wanted to know more, to understand better. And that sort of inquisitiveness is a foundational element of a true leader.

Another necessary ingredient is *initiative*. If a man is wired for leadership, he will have drive, ambition, and energy. A true leader must be the kind of person who makes things happen. He is a starter. Notice that Peter not only *asked* questions; he was also usually the first one to *answer* any question posed by Christ. He often charged right in where angels fear to tread.

There was that famous occasion when Jesus asked, "Who do men say that I, the Son of Man, am?" (Matthew 16:13). Several opinions were circulating among the people about that. "So they said, 'Some say John the Baptist, some Elijah, and others Jeremiah or one of the prophets'" (v. 14). Jesus then asked the disciples in particular, "But who do *you* say that I am?" (v. 15, emphasis added). It was at that point that Peter boldly spoke out above the rest: "You are the Christ, the Son of the living God" (v. 16). The other disciples were still processing the question, like schoolboys afraid to speak up lest they give the wrong answer. Peter was bold and decisive. That's a vital characteristic of all great leaders. Sometimes he had to take a step back, undo, retract, or be rebuked. But the fact that he was always willing to grab opportunity by the throat marked him as a natural leader.

In the Garden of Gethsemane, when Roman soldiers from Fort Antonia came to arrest Jesus, all three synoptic Gospel writers say there was a "great multitude" armed with "with swords and staves" (Matthew 26:47; cf. Mark 14:43;

Luke 22:47). A typical Roman cohort consisted of six hundred soldiers, so in all likelihood there were hundreds of battle-ready Roman troops in and around the garden that night. Without hesitating, Peter pulled out his sword and took a swing at the head of Malchus, the servant of the high priest. (The high priest and his personal staff would have been in the front of the mob, because he was the dignitary ordering the arrest.) Peter was undoubtedly trying to cut the man's head off. But Peter was a fisherman, not a swordsman. Malchus ducked, and his ear was severed. So Jesus "touched his ear and healed him" (Luke 22:51). Then He told Peter, "Put your sword in its place, for all who take the sword will perish by the sword" (Matthew 26:52). (Thus He affirmed the equity of capital punishment as a divine law.)

Think about that incident. There was an entire detachment of Roman soldiers there—perhaps numbering in the hundreds. What did Peter think he was going to do? Behead them all, one by one? Sometimes in Peter's passion for taking the initiative, he overlooked the obvious big-picture realities.

But with all his brashness, Peter had the raw material from which a leader could be made. Better to work with a man like that than to try to motivate someone who is always passive and hesitant. As the familiar saying goes, it is much easier to tone down a fanatic than to resurrect a corpse. Some people have to be dragged tediously in any forward direction. Not Peter. He always wanted to move ahead. He wanted to know what he didn't know. He wanted to understand what he didn't understand. He was the first to ask questions and the first to try to answer questions. He was a man who always took the initiative, seized the moment, and charged ahead. That's the stuff of leadership.

Remember, these characteristics are only the raw

material from which a leader is made. Peter needed to be trained and shaped and matured. But to do the task Christ had for him, he needed moxie, chutzpa—courage to stand up in Jerusalem on Pentecost and preach the gospel in the face of the same population who had lately executed their own Messiah. But Peter was just the sort of fellow who could be trained to take that kind of courageous initiative.

There's a third element of the raw material that makes a true leader: *involvement*. True leaders are always in the middle of the action. They do not sit in the background telling everyone else what to do while they live a life of comfort away from the fray. A true leader goes through life with a cloud of dust around him. That is precisely why people follow him. People cannot *follow* someone who remains distant. The true leader must show the way. He goes before his followers into the battle.

Jesus came to the disciples one night out in the middle of the Sea of Galilee, walking on the water in the midst of a violent storm. Who out of all the disciples jumped out of the boat? Peter. *There's the Lord,* he must have thought. *I'm here; I've got to go where the action is.* The other disciples wondered if they were seeing a ghost (Matthew 14:26). But Peter said, "Lord, if it is You, command me to come to You on the water." Jesus answered, "Come" (vv. 27–28)—and before anyone knew it, Peter was out of the boat, walking on the water. The rest of the disciples were still clinging to their seats, trying to make sure they didn't fall overboard in the storm. But Peter was out of the boat without giving it a second thought. That is involvement—*serious* involvement. Only after he left the boat and walked some distance did Peter think about the danger and start to sink.

People often look at that incident and criticize Peter's lack of faith. But let's give him credit for having faith to leave that boat in the first place. Before we disparage Peter for the weakness that almost brought him down, we ought to remember where he was when he began to sink.

Similarly, although Peter denied Christ, keep in mind one significant fact: He and one other disciple (probably his lifelong friend, John) were the only ones who followed Jesus to the high priest's house to see what would become of Jesus (John 18:15). And in the courtyard of the high priest's house, Peter was the only one close enough for Jesus to turn and look him in the eyes when the rooster crowed (Luke 22:61). Long after the other disciples had forsaken Christ and fled in fear for their lives, Peter was virtually alone in a position where such a temptation could snare him, because despite his fear and weakness, he couldn't abandon Christ completely. That's the sign of a true leader. When almost everyone else bailed out, he tried to stay as close to his Lord as he could get. He wasn't the kind of leader who is content to send messages to the troops from afar. He had a passion to be personally involved, so he is always found close to the heart of the action.

That was the raw fabric of which Peter was made: an insatiable inquisitiveness, a willingness to take the initiative, and a passion to be personally involved. Now it was up to the Lord to train and shape him, because frankly, that kind of raw material, if not submitted to the Lord's control, can be downright dangerous.

THE LIFE EXPERIENCES
THAT SHAPE A TRUE LEADER

How did the Lord take a man cut from such rough fabric and refine him into a leader? For one thing, he made sure

Peter had the kind of life experiences that formed him into the kind of leader Christ wanted him to be. It is in this sense that true leaders are made, not just born.

Experience can be a hard teacher. In Peter's case the ups and downs of his experience were dramatic and often painful. His life was filled with tortuous zigs and zags. The Lord dragged him through three years of tests and difficulties that gave him a lifetime of the kind of experiences every true leader must endure.

Why did Jesus do this? Did He take some glee in tormenting Peter? Not at all; the experiences—even the difficult ones—were all necessary to shape Peter into the man he needed to become.

Recently I read the results of a study involving all the young people in America who have been involved in the epidemic of school shooting rampages. It turns out that the common denominator among the shooters is that virtually all of them are young people who were prescribed Ritalin or other antidepressant drugs to control behavior problems. Instead of being disciplined for wrong attitudes and bad behavior, they were drugged into a stupor. Instead of training them to behave and teaching them self-control, child psychologists prescribed mind-numbing drugs that only temporarily curbed their rebellious behavior. The defiant, rebellious attitudes that were the root of the problem were never confronted or dealt with. Those kids had been artificially sheltered from the consequences of their rebellion in their younger childhood. They missed the life experiences that might have shaped their character differently.

The apostle Peter learned a lot through hard experience. He learned, for example, that crushing defeat and deep humiliation often follow hard on the heels of our greatest victories. Just after Christ commended him for his great confession in Matthew 16:16 ("You are the Christ, the Son of the living God"), Peter suffered the harshest rebuke ever recorded of a disciple in the New Testament. One moment Christ called Peter blessed, promising him the keys of the kingdom (vv. 17–19). In the next paragraph, Christ addressed Peter as Satan and said, "Get behind me!" (v. 23)—meaning, "Don't stand in My way!"

That incident occurred shortly after Peter's triumphant confession. Jesus announced to the disciples that He was going to Jerusalem, where He would be turned over to the chief priests and scribes and be killed. Upon hearing that, "Peter took Him aside and began to rebuke Him, saying, 'Far be it from You, Lord; this shall not happen to You!'" (Matthew 16:22). Peter's sentiment is perfectly understandable. But he was thinking only from a human standpoint. He did not know the plan of God. Without realizing it, he was trying to dissuade Christ from the very thing He came to earth to do. As usual, he was speaking when he ought to have been listening. Jesus' words to Peter were as stern as anything He ever spoke to any individual: "He turned and said to Peter, 'Get behind Me, Satan! You are an offense to Me, for you are not mindful of the things of God, but the things of men'" (v. 23).

Peter had just learned that God would reveal truth to him and guide his speech as he submitted his mind to the truth. He wasn't dependent upon a human message. The message he was to proclaim was given to him by God (v. 17). He would also be given the keys to the kingdom— meaning that his life and message would be the unlocking of the kingdom of God for the salvation of many (v. 19).

But now, through the painful experience of being rebuked by the Lord, Peter also learned that he was vulnerable to Satan. Satan could fill his mouth just as surely as the Lord could fill it. If Peter minded the things of men rather than the things of God, or if he did not do the will of God, he could be an instrument of the enemy.

Later, Peter fell victim to Satan again on the night of Jesus' arrest. This time he learned the hard way that he was humanly weak and could not trust his own resolve. All his boasting promises and earnest resolutions did not keep him from falling. After declaring in front of everyone that he would *never* deny Christ, he denied Him anyway, and he punctuated his denials with passionate curses. Satan was sifting him as wheat. Thus Peter learned how much chaff and how little substance there was in him and how watchful and careful he must be to rely only on the Lord's strength.

At the same time, he learned that in spite of his own sinful tendencies and spiritual weaknesses, the Lord wanted to use him and would sustain him and preserve him no matter what.

All those things Peter learned by experience. Sometimes the experiences were bitter, distressing, humiliating, and painful. Other times they were encouraging, uplifting, and perfectly glorious—such as when Peter saw Christ's divine brilliance on the Mount of Trans-figuration. Either way, Peter made the most of his experiences, gleaning from them lessons that helped make him the great leader he became.

THE CHARACTER QUALITIES THAT DEFINE A TRUE LEADER

A third element in the making of a leader—besides the right raw material and the right life experiences—is the right character. Character, of course, is absolutely critical in leadership. America's current moral decline is directly linked to the fact that we have elected, appointed, and hired too many leaders who have no character. In recent years, some have tried to argue that character doesn't really matter in leadership; what a man does in his private life supposedly should not be a factor in whether he is deemed fit for a public leadership role. That perspective is diametrically opposed to what the Bible teaches. Character does matter in leadership. It matters a lot.

In fact, character is what makes leadership possible. People simply cannot respect or trust those who lack character. And if they do not respect a man, they will not follow him. Time and truth go hand in hand. Leaders without character eventually disappoint their followers and lose their confidence. The only reason such people are often popular is that they make other people who have no character feel better about themselves. But they aren't *real* leaders.

Lasting leadership is grounded in character. Character produces respect. Respect produces trust. And trust motivates followers.

Even in the purely human realm, most people do recognize that true leadership is properly associated with character qualities like integrity, trustworthiness, respectability, unselfishness, humility, self-discipline, self-control, and courage. Such virtues reflect the image of God in man. Although the divine image is severely tarnished in fallen humanity, it has not been entirely erased. That's why even pagans recognize those qualities as desirable virtues, important requirements for true leadership.

Christ Himself is the epitome of what a true leader ought to be like. He is perfect in all the attributes that make up the character of a leader. He is the embodiment of all the truest, purest, highest, and noblest qualities of leadership.

Obviously, in *spiritual* leadership, the great goal and objective is to bring people to Christlikeness. That is why the leader himself must manifest Christlike character. That is why the standard for leadership in the church is set so high. The apostle Paul summarized the spirit of the true leader when he wrote, "Imitate me, just as I also imitate Christ" (1 Corinthians 11:1).

Peter might just as well have written the same thing. His character was molded and shaped after the example he had witnessed in Christ. He had the raw material for becoming a leader, and that was important. His life experiences helped hone and sharpen his natural leadership abilities, and that was also vital. But the real key to everything—the essential foundation upon which true leadership always rises or falls—is character. It was the character qualities Peter developed through his intimate association with Christ that ultimately made him the great leader he became.

J. R. Miller wrote, "The only thing that walks back from the tomb with the mourners and refuses to be buried is the character of a man. What a man is survives him. It can never be buried."[1] That is a true sentiment, but there is something more important than what people think of us after we are dead. What is far more important is the impact we have while we are here.

What are some of the character qualities of a spiritual leader that were developed in the life of Peter? One is *submission*. At first glance that may seem an unusual quality to cultivate in a leader. After all, the leader is the person in charge, and he expects other people to submit to him, right? But a true leader doesn't just demand submission; he is an example of submission by the way he submits to the Lord and to those in authority over him. Everything the true spiritual leader does ought to be marked by submission to every legitimate authority—especially submission to God and to His Word.

Leaders tend to be confident and aggressive. They naturally dominate. Peter had that tendency in him. He was quick to speak and quick to act. As we have seen, he was a man of initiative. That means he was always inclined to try to take control of every situation. In order to balance that side of him, the Lord taught him submission.

He did it in some rather remarkable ways. One classic example of this is found in Matthew 17. This account comes at a time when Jesus was returning with the Twelve to Capernaum, their home base, after a period of itinerant ministry. A tax collector was in town making the rounds to collect the annual two-drachma (half-shekel) tax from each person twenty years old or older. This was not a tax paid to Rome, but a tax paid for the upkeep of the temple. It was prescribed in Exodus 30:11–16 (cf. 2 Chronicles 24:9). The tax was equal to two days' wages, so it was no small amount.

Matthew writes, "Those who received the temple tax came to Peter and said, 'Does your Teacher not pay the temple tax?'" (Matthew 17:24). Peter assured him that Jesus did pay His taxes.

But this particular tax apparently posed a bit of a problem in Peter's mind. Was Jesus morally obliged, as the incarnate Son of God, to pay for the upkeep of the temple like any mere man? The sons of earthly kings don't pay taxes in their fathers' kingdoms; why should Jesus? Jesus knew what Peter was thinking, so "when he had come into the house, Jesus anticipated him, saying, 'What do you think, Simon? From whom do the kings of the earth take customs or taxes, from their sons or from strangers?'" (v. 25).

Peter answered, "From strangers." Kings don't tax their own children.

Jesus drew the logical conclusion for Peter: "Then the sons are free" (v. 26). In other words, Jesus had absolute heavenly authority, if He desired, to opt out of the temple tax.

But if He did that, it would send the wrong message as far as *earthly* authority is concerned. Better to submit, pay the tax, and avoid a situation most people would not understand. So although Jesus was not technically *obligated* to pay the temple tax, he said, "Nevertheless, lest we offend them, go to the sea, cast in a hook, and take the fish that comes up first. And when you have opened its mouth, you will find a piece of money; take that and give it to them for Me and you" (v. 27).

The coin in the mouth of the fish was a stater—a single coin worth a shekel, or four drachma. It was exactly enough to pay the temple tax for two. In other words, Jesus arranged for Peter's tax to be paid in full, too.

It's intriguing that the miracle Jesus worked demonstrated His absolute *sovereignty,* and yet at the same time, He was being an example of human *submission.* Christ supernaturally directed a fish that had swallowed a coin to take the bait on Peter's hook. If Jesus was Lord over nature to such a degree, He certainly had authority to opt out of the temple tax. And yet he taught Peter by example how to submit willingly.

Submission is an indispensible character quality for leaders to cultivate. If they would teach people to submit, they must be examples of submission themselves. And sometimes a leader must submit even when there might seem to be very good arguments *against* submitting.

Peter learned the lesson well. Years later, in 1 Peter 2:13–18, he would write,

> Therefore submit yourselves to every ordinance of man for the Lord's sake, whether to the king as supreme, or to governors, as to those who are sent by him for the punishment of evildoers and for the praise of those who do good. For this is the will of God, that by doing good you may put to silence the ignorance of foolish men; as free, yet not using liberty as a cloak for vice, but as bondservants of God. Honor all people. Love the brotherhood. Fear God. Honor the king. Servants, be submissive to your masters with all fear, not only to the good and gentle, but also to the harsh.

This was the same lesson Peter learned from Christ: You are free in one sense, but don't use your freedom as a covering for evil. Rather, regard yourself as the Lord's bond-slave. You are a citizen of heaven and merely a sojourner on earth, but submit to every ordinance of man *for the Lord's sake.* You are first and foremost a subject of Christ's kingdom and a mere stranger and pilgrim on this earth. Nonetheless, to avoid offense, honor the earthly king. Honor all people. This is the will of God, and by submitting, you will put to silence the ignorance of ungodly men.

Remember, the man who wrote that epistle was the same man who when he was young and brash slashed off the ear of the high priest's servant. He is the same man who once struggled over the idea of Jesus' paying taxes. But he *learned* to submit—not an easy lesson for a natural leader. Peter especially was inclined to be dominant, forceful, aggressive, and resistant to the idea of submission. But Jesus taught him to submit willingly, even when he thought he had a good argument for refusing to submit.

A second character quality Peter learned was *restraint*. Most people with natural leadership abilities do not naturally excel when it comes to exercising restraint. Self-control, discipline, moderation, and reserve don't necessarily come naturally to someone who lives life at the head of the pack. That is why so many leaders have problems with anger and out-of-control passions. Perhaps you have noticed recently that anger-management seminars have become the latest fad for CEOs and people in high positions of leadership in American business. It is clear that anger is a common and serious problem among people who rise to such a high level of leadership.

Peter had similar tendencies. Hotheadedness goes naturally with the sort of active, decisive, initiative-taking personality that made him a leader in the first place. Such a man easily grows impatient with people who lack vision or underperform. He can be quickly irritated by those who throw up obstacles to success. Therefore he must learn restraint in order to be a good leader.

The Lord more or less put a bit in Peter's mouth and taught him restraint. That is one of the main reasons Peter bore the brunt of so many rebukes when he spoke too soon or acted too hastily. The Lord was *constantly* teaching him restraint.

That scene in the garden where Peter tried to decapitate Malchus is a classic example of his natural lack of restraint. Even surrounded by hundreds of Roman soldiers, all armed to the teeth, Peter unthinkingly pulled out his sword and was ready to wade into the crowd, swinging. It was fortunate for him that Malchus lost nothing more than an ear and that Jesus immediately healed the damage. As we have already seen, Jesus rebuked Peter sternly.

That rebuke must have been especially difficult for

Peter, coming as it did in front of a horde of enemies. But he learned much from what he witnessed that night. Later in life, he would write, "Christ also suffered for us, leaving us an example, that you should follow His steps: 'Who committed no sin, nor was deceit found in His mouth'; who, when He was reviled, did not revile in return; when He suffered, He did not threaten, but committed Himself to Him who judges righteously" (1 Peter 2:21–23).

How different that is from the young man who tried to grab a sword and whack his way through his opposers! Peter had learned the lesson of restraint.

He also had to learn *humility*. Leaders are often tempted by the sin of pride. In fact, the besetting sin of leadership may be the tendency to think more of oneself than one ought to think. When people are following your lead, constantly praising you, looking up to you, and admiring you, it is too easy to be overcome with pride.

We can observe in Peter a tremendous amount of self-confidence. It is obvious by the way he jumps in with answers to all the questions. It is obvious in most of his actions, such as when he stepped out of the boat and began to walk on water. It became obvious in the worst and most disastrous way on that fateful occasion when Jesus foretold that His disciples would forsake Him.

Jesus said, "All of you will be made to stumble because of Me this night, for it is written: 'I will strike the Shepherd, and the sheep of the flock will be scattered'" (Matthew 26:31).

But Peter was cocksure: "Even if all are made to stumble because of You, I will *never* be made to stumble" (v. 33, emphasis added). Then he added, "Lord, I am ready to go with You, both to prison and to death" (Luke 22:33).

Of course, as usual, Peter was wrong and Jesus was

right. Peter *did* deny Christ not once, but multiple times, just as Jesus had warned. Peter's shame and disgrace at having dishonored Christ so flagrantly were only magnified by the fact he had boasted so stubbornly about being impervious to such sins!

But the Lord used all of this to make Peter humble. And when Peter wrote his first epistle, he said, "be clothed with humility, for 'God resists the proud, but gives grace to the humble.' Therefore humble yourselves under the mighty hand of God, that He may exalt you in due time" (1 Peter 5:5–6). He specifically told church leaders, "[Don't act like] lords over those entrusted to you, but [be] examples to the flock" (v. 3). Humility became one of the virtues that characterized Peter's life, his message, and his leadership style.

Peter also learned *love*. All the disciples struggled with learning that true spiritual leadership means loving service to one another. The real leader is someone who serves, not someone who demands to be waited upon.

This is a hard lesson for many natural leaders to learn. They tend to see people as a means to their end. Leaders are usually task-oriented rather than people-oriented. And so they often use people, or plow over people, in order to achieve their goals. Peter and the rest of the disciples needed to learn that leadership is rooted and grounded in loving service to others. The true leader loves and serves those whom he leads.

Jesus said, "If anyone desires to be first, he shall be last of all and servant of all" (Mark 9:35). The Lord Himself constantly modeled that kind of loving servant-leadership for the disciples. But nowhere is it more plainly on display than in the Upper Room on the night of His betrayal.

Jesus and the disciples had come to celebrate the Passover in a rented room in Jerusalem. The Passover seder was an extended, ceremonious meal lasting as long as four or five hours. Celebrants in that culture usually reclined at a low table rather than sitting upright in chairs. That meant one person's head would be next to another person's feet. Of course, all the roads were either muddy or dusty, so feet were constantly dirty. Therefore the common custom was that when you went into a house for a meal, there was usually a servant whose job it was to wash guests' feet. This was practically the lowliest and least desirable of all jobs. But for any host to neglect to arrange for his guests' feet to be washed was a significant affront (cf. Luke 7:44).

Apparently on this busy Passover night, in that rented room, no provision had been made for any servant to wash the guests' feet. The disciples were evidently prepared to overlook the breach of etiquette rather than volunteering to do such a menial task themselves. So they gathered around the table as if they were prepared to start the meal without any foot-washing. Therefore, Scripture says, Jesus Himself "rose from supper and laid aside His garments, took a towel and girded Himself. After that, He poured water into a basin and began to wash the disciples' feet, and to wipe them with the towel with which He was girded" (John 13:4–5).[2]

Jesus Himself—the One they rightly called Lord— took on the role of the lowest slave and washed the dirty feet of His disciples. According to Luke, at about the same time this occurred, the disciples were in the midst of an argument about which one of them was the greatest (Luke 22:24). They were interested in being elevated, not humiliated. So Jesus did what none of them would do. He gave them a lesson about the humility of genuine love.

Most of them probably sat there in stunned silence. But when the Lord came to Simon Peter, "Peter said to Him,

'Lord, are You washing my feet?'" (John 13:6). The sense of the statement is, *What do You think You're doing?* Here is the brash and bold Simon, speaking without carefully thinking things through. He even went on to say, "You shall never wash my feet!" (v. 8).

Peter was the master of the absolute statement: "I will *never* deny You" (cf. Matthew 26:33). "You shall *never* wash my feet!" There are no shades of gray in Peter's life; everything is in absolute black and white.

Jesus answered him, "If I do not wash you, you have no part with Me" (John 13:8). Jesus, of course, was speaking of the necessity of *spiritual* cleansing. Obviously, it wasn't the literal foot-washing that made the disciples fit for fellowship with Christ; Jesus was speaking about cleansing from sin. That was the spiritual reality this humble act of foot-washing was meant to symbolize. (Proof that He was speaking of *spiritual* cleansing is found in verse 10, when He said, "You are clean, but not all of you." He had just washed their feet, so they were all clean in the external, physical sense. But the apostle John says in verse 11, "He knew who would betray Him; therefore He said, 'You are not all clean' "—signifying that Judas was not clean in the spiritual sense of which He spoke.)

Peter's answer is typical of his usual unbridled wholeheartedness: "Lord, not my feet only, but also my hands and my head!" (v. 9). Again, there was never any middle ground with Peter. It was always all or nothing. So Jesus assured him that he was already "completely clean." (The Lord was still speaking in spiritual terms about forgiveness and cleansing from sin.) Peter now needed nothing more than a foot-washing.

In other words, Peter, as a believer, was already fully justified. The forgiveness and cleansing he needed was not the kind of summary pardon one would seek from the Judge of the universe—as if Peter were seeking to have his eternal destiny settled. He had already received that kind of cleansing and forgiveness. But now Peter was coming to God as any child would approach a parent, seeking fatherly grace and forgiveness for his wrongdoings. That was the kind of cleansing Peter needed. It is the same kind of forgiveness Jesus taught all believers to pray for daily (Luke 11:4). Here, Jesus likens such daily forgiveness to a foot-washing.

Those truths were all wrapped up in the symbolism when Jesus washed the disciples' feet. But the central lesson was about the way love ought to be shown. Jesus' example was a consummate act of loving, lowly service.

Later that evening, after Judas had left, Jesus told the other eleven, "A new commandment I give to you, that you love one another; as I have loved you, that you also love one another. By this all will know that you are My disciples, if you have love for one another" (vv. 34–35). How had He loved them? He washed their feet. While they were arguing about who was the greatest, He showed them what loving, humble service for one another looks like.

It's hard for most leaders to stoop and wash the feet of those whom they perceive as subordinates. But that was the example of leadership Jesus gave, and He urged His disciples to follow it. In fact, He told them that showing love to one another in such a way was the mark of a true disciple.

Did Peter learn to love? He certainly did. Love became one of the hallmarks of his teaching. In 1 Peter 4:8 he wrote, "Above all things have fervent love for one another, for 'love will cover a multitude of sins.'" The Greek word translated "fervent" in that verse is *ektenes,* literally meaning "stretched to the limit." Peter was urging us to love to the maximum of our capacity. The love he spoke of is not about a feeling. It's not about how we respond to people who are naturally lovable. It's about a love that covers and compensates for others' failures and weaknesses: "Love will cover a multitude of sins." This is the sort of love that washes a brother's dirty feet. Peter himself had learned that lesson from Christ's example.

Another important character quality Peter needed to learn was *compassion*. When the Lord warned Peter that he would deny Him, He said, "Satan has asked for you, that he may sift you as wheat" (Luke 22:31). Wheat was typically separated from the chaff by being shaken and tossed up into the air in a stiff wind. The chaff was blown away and the wheat would fall into a pile, thus purified.

We might have expected Jesus to reassure Peter by saying, "I'm not going to allow Satan to sift you." But He didn't. He essentially let Peter know that He had given Satan the permission he sought. He would allow the devil to put Peter to the test (as God did in the case of Job). He said, in essence, "I'm going to let him do it. I'm going to let Satan shake the very foundations of your life. Then I'm going to let him toss you to the wind—until there's nothing left but the reality of your faith." Jesus did reassure Peter that the apostle's faith would survive the ordeal. "I have prayed for you," Jesus told him, "that your faith should not fail; and when you have returned to Me, strengthen your brethren" (v. 32).

It was then that Peter arrogantly insisted that he would never stumble. Yet despite his protestations, before the night was over, he *did* deny Jesus, and his whole world was severely shaken. His ego was deflated. His self-confidence was annihilated. His pride suffered greatly. But his faith never failed.

What was this all about? Jesus was equipping Peter to

strengthen the brethren. People with natural leadership abilities often tend to be short on compassion, lousy comforters, and impatient with others. They don't stop very long to care for the wounded as they pursue their goals. Peter needed to learn compassion through his own ordeal, so that when it was over, he could strengthen others in theirs.

For the rest of his life, Peter would need to show compassion to people who were struggling. After being sifted by Satan, Peter was well equipped to empathize with others' weaknesses. He could hardly help having great compassion for those who succumbed to temptation or fell into sin. He had been there. And by that experience he learned to be compassionate, tender-hearted, gracious, kind, and comforting to others who were lacerated by sin and personal failure.

In 1 Peter 5:8–10, he wrote, "Be sober, be vigilant; because your adversary the devil walks about like a roaring lion, seeking whom he may devour. Resist him, steadfast in the faith, knowing that the same sufferings are experienced by your brotherhood in the world. But may the God of all grace, who called us to His eternal glory by Christ Jesus, after you have suffered a while, perfect, establish, strengthen, and settle you."

Peter understood human weakness, and he understood it well. He had been to the bottom. His own weaknesses had been thrown in his face. But he had been perfected, established, strengthened, and settled by the Lord. As usual, he was writing out of his own experience. These were not theoretical precepts he taught.

Finally, he had to learn *courage*. Not the impetuous, headlong, false kind of "courage" that caused him to swing his sword so wildly at Malchus, but a mature, settled, intrepid willingness to suffer for Christ's sake.

The kingdom of darkness is set against the kingdom of light. Lies are set against the truth. Satan is set against God. And demons are set against the holy purposes of Christ. Therefore Peter would face difficulty wherever he went. Christ told him, "Most assuredly, I say to you, when you were younger, you girded yourself and walked where you wished; but when you are old, you will stretch out your hands, and another will gird you and carry you where you do not wish" (John 21:18).

What did that mean? The apostle John gives a clear answer: "This He spoke, signifying by what death [Peter] would glorify God" (v. 19).

The price of preaching would be death for Peter. Persecution. Oppression. Trouble. Torture. Ultimately, martyrdom. Peter would need rock-solid courage to persevere.

You can practically see the birth of real courage in Peter's heart at Pentecost, when he was filled and empowered by the Holy Spirit. Prior to that, he had shown flashes of a fickle kind of courage. That is why he impetuously drew his sword in front of a multitude of armed soldiers one minute but denied Jesus when challenged by a servant girl a few hours later. His courage, like everything in his life, was marred by instability.

After Pentecost, however, we see a different Peter. Acts 4 describes how Peter and John were brought before the Sanhedrin, the Jewish ruling counsel. They were solemnly instructed "not to speak at all nor teach in the name of Jesus" (v. 18).

Peter and John boldly replied, "Whether it is right in the sight of God to listen to you more than to God, you judge. For we cannot but speak the things which we have seen and heard" (vv. 19–20). Soon they were brought back before the Sanhedrin for continuing to preach. Again they told them the same thing: "We ought to obey God rather than men" (Acts 5:29). Peter, filled with the Holy Spirit and driven by the knowledge that Christ had risen from the dead, had acquired an unshakable, rock-solid courage.

In Peter's first epistle we get a hint of why he was filled with such courage. Writing to Christians dispersed all over the Roman Empire because of persecution, he tells them:

> Blessed be the God and Father of our Lord Jesus Christ, who according to His abundant mercy has begotten us again to a living hope through the resurrection of Jesus Christ from the dead, to an inheritance incorruptible and undefiled and that does not fade away, reserved in heaven for you, who are kept by the power of God through faith for salvation ready to be revealed in the last time. In this you greatly rejoice, though now for a little while, if need be, you have been grieved by various trials, that the genuineness of your faith, being much more precious than gold that perishes, though it is tested by fire, may be found to praise, honor, and glory at the revelation of Jesus Christ. (1 Peter 1:3–7)

He was secure in Christ, and he knew it. He had seen the risen Christ, so he knew Christ had conquered death. He knew that whatever earthly trials came his way, they were merely temporary. The trials, though often painful and always distasteful, were nothing compared to the hope of eternal glory (cf. Romans 8:18). The genuineness of true faith, he knew, was infinitely more precious than any perishing earthly riches, because his faith would redound to the praise and glory of Christ at His appearing. That hope is what gave Peter such courage.

As Peter learned all these lessons and his character was transformed—as he became the man Christ wanted him to be—he gradually changed from Simon into Rock. He learned submission, restraint, humility, love, compassion, and courage from the Lord's example. And because of the Holy Spirit's work in his heart, he did become a great leader.

He preached at Pentecost and three thousand people were saved (Acts 2:14–41). He and John healed a lame man (Acts 3:1–10). He was so powerful that people were healed in his shadow (Acts 5:15–16). He raised Dorcas from the dead (Acts 9:36–42). He introduced the gospel to the Gentiles (Acts 10). And he wrote two epistles, 1 and 2 Peter, in which he featured the very same lessons he had learned from the Lord about true character.

What a man Peter was! Was he perfect? No. In Galatians 2 the apostle Paul relates an incident in which Peter compromised. He acted like a hypocrite. We see a brief flash of the old Simon. Peter was eating with Gentiles, fellowshiping with them as true brethren in Christ—until some false teachers showed up. These heretics insisted that unless the Gentiles were circumcised and following Old Testament ceremonial law, they could not be saved and should not be treated as brethren. Peter, apparently intimidated by the false teachers, stopped eating with the Gentile brethren (Galatians 2:12). Verse 13 says that when Peter did it, everybody else did it, too, because Peter was their leader. So the apostle Paul writes, "I withstood him to his face, because he was to be blamed" (v. 11). Paul rebuked Peter in the presence of everyone (v. 14).

To Peter's credit, he responded to Paul's correction. And when the error of the Judaizers was finally confronted at a full council of church leaders and apostles in Jerusalem, it was Peter who spoke up first in defense of the gospel of divine grace. He introduced the argument that won the day (Acts 15:7–14). He was in effect defending the apostle Paul's ministry. The whole episode shows how Simon Peter remained teachable, humble, and sensitive to the Holy Spirit's conviction and correction.

How did Peter's life end? We know that Jesus told Peter he would die as a martyr (John 21:18–19). But Scripture doesn't record the death of Peter. All the records of early church history indicate that Peter was crucified. Eusebius cites the testimony of Clement, who says that before Peter was crucified he was forced to watch the crucifixion of his own wife. As he watched her being led to her death, Clement says, Peter called to her by name, saying, "Remember the Lord." When it was Peter's turn to die, he pleaded to be crucified upside down because he wasn't worthy to die as his Lord had died. And thus he was nailed to a cross head-downward.[3]

Peter's life could be summed up in the final words of his second epistle: "Grow in grace and in the knowledge of our Lord and Savior, Jesus Christ" (2 Peter 3:18). That is exactly what Simon Peter did, and that is why he became Rock—the great leader of the early church.

3

ANDREW—THE APOSTLE OF SMALL THINGS

One of the two who heard John speak, and followed Him, was Andrew, Simon Peter's brother. He first found his own brother Simon, and said to him, "We have found the Messiah" (which is translated, the Christ). And he brought him to Jesus.

—JOHN 1:40–42

PETER'S BROTHER, ANDREW, is the least-known of the four disciples in the lead group. Although he was a member of that dominant foursome, Andrew ordinarily is left very much in the background. He was not included in several of the important events where we see Peter, James, and John together with Christ (Matthew 17:1; Mark 5:37; 14:33). At other key times, however, he was featured as part of the inner circle (cf. Mark 1:29; 13:3). There is no question that he had a particularly close relationship with Christ, because he was so often the means by which other people were personally introduced to the Master.

Andrew was the first of all the disciples to be called

(John 1:35–40). As we shall shortly see, he was responsible for introducing his more dominant brother, Peter, to Christ (vv. 41–42). His eagerness to follow Christ, combined with his zeal for introducing others to Him, fairly typifies Andrew's character.

Peter and Andrew were originally from the village of Bethsaida (John 1:44). Archaeologists have not yet determined the exact location of Bethsaida, but from its description in the New Testament, it is clear that it lay in the northern Galilee region. At some point, the brothers relocated to the larger city of Capernaum, close by their hometown. In fact, Peter and Andrew shared a house in Capernaum (Mark 1:29) and operated a fishing business together from there. Capernaum afforded an especially advantageous location, situated as it was on the north shore of the Sea of Galilee (where fishing was good)—and located at the junction of key trade routes.

Peter and Andrew had probably been lifelong companions with the other set of fishermen—brothers from Capernaum—James and John, sons of Zebedee. The four of them apparently shared common spiritual interests even before they met Christ. They evidently took a sabbatical from the fishing business, visited the wilderness where John the Baptist was preaching, and became disciples of John. That is where they were when they first met Christ. And when they returned to fishing (before Jesus called them to be full-time disciples), they remained together as partners. So it was quite natural that this little group formed a cohesive unit within the Twelve. In many ways these four seemed inseparable.

All four of them obviously *wanted* to be leaders. As a group, they exercised a sort of collective leadership over the other disciples. We have already seen that Peter was without question the dominant one of the group and the usual spokesman for all twelve—sometimes whether they liked it or not. But it is clear that the four disciples in the inner circle all aspired to be leaders. That is why they sometimes had those shameful arguments over who was the greatest.

Their eagerness to lead, which caused so many clashes when they were together as a group, ultimately became immensely valuable when these men went their separate ways as apostles in the early church. Jesus was training them for leadership, and in the end, they all filled important leadership roles in the early church. That is why Scripture likens them to the very foundation of the church: "Jesus Christ Himself being the chief cornerstone" (Ephesians 2:20).

Of the four in the inner circle, however, Andrew was the least conspicuous. Scripture doesn't tell us a lot about him. You can practically count on your fingers the number of times he is mentioned specifically in the Gospels. (In fact, apart from the places where all twelve disciples are listed, Andrew's name appears in the New Testament only nine times, and most of those references simply mention him in passing.)

Andrew lived his life in the shadow of his better-known brother. Many of the verses that name him add that he was Peter's brother, as if that were the fact that made him significant.

In such situations, where one brother overshadows another to such a degree, it is common to find resentment, strong sibling rivalry, or even estrangement. But in Andrew's case, there is no evidence that he begrudged Peter's dominance. Again, it was Andrew who brought Peter to Christ in the first place. He did this immediately and without hesitation. Of course, Andrew would have been fully aware of

Peter's tendency to domineer. He must have known full well that as soon as Peter entered the company of disciples, he would take charge and Andrew would be relegated to a secondary status. Yet Andrew brought his older brother anyway. That fact alone says much about his character.

Almost everything Scripture tells us about Andrew shows that he had the right heart for effective ministry in the background. He did not seek to be the center of attention. He did not seem to resent those who labored in the limelight. He was evidently pleased to do what he could with the gifts and calling God had bestowed on him, and he allowed the others to do likewise.

Of all the disciples in the inner circle, Andrew appears the least contentious and the most thoughtful. As we know already, Peter tended to be impetuous, to rush ahead foolishly, and to say the wrong thing at the wrong time. He was often brash, clumsy, hasty, and impulsive. James and John were nicknamed "Sons of Thunder" because of their reckless tendencies. They were also evidently the ones who provoked many of the arguments about who was the greatest. But there's never a hint of that with Andrew. Whenever he speaks—which is rare in Scripture—he always says the right thing, not the wrong thing. Whenever he acts apart from the other disciples, he does what is right. Scripture never attaches any dishonor to Andrew's actions when it mentions him by name.

There were certainly times when, following Peter's lead, or acting in concert with all the disciples, Andrew made the same mistakes they made. But whenever his name is expressly mentioned—whenever he rises above the others and acts or speaks as an individual—Scripture commends him for what he does. He was an effective leader even though he never took the spotlight.

Andrew and Peter, though brothers, had totally different leadership styles. But just as Peter was perfectly suited for his calling, Andrew was perfectly suited for his. In fact, Andrew may be a *better* model for most church leaders than Peter, because most who enter the ministry will labor in relative obscurity, like Andrew, as opposed to being renowned and prominent, like Peter.

Andrew's name means "manly," and it seems a fitting description. Of course, the kind of net-fishing he and the others did required no small degree of physical strength and machismo. But Andrew also had other characteristics of manliness. He was bold, decisive, and deliberate. Nothing about him is feeble or wimpish. He was driven by a hearty passion for the truth, and he was willing to subject himself to the most extreme kinds of hardship and austerity in pursuit of that objective.

Remember that when Jesus met him for the first time, Andrew was already a devout man who had joined the ranks of John the Baptist's disciples. The Baptist was well known for his rugged appearance and his spartan lifestyle. He "was clothed in camel's hair, with a leather belt around his waist; and his food was locusts and wild honey" (Matthew 3:4). He lived and ministered in the wilderness, cut off from all the comforts and conveniences of city life. To follow John the Baptist as a disciple, one could hardly be soft.

John's Gospel describes Andrew's first meeting with Jesus. It took place in the wilderness, where John the Baptist was preaching repentance and baptizing converts. The apostle John records the incident as an eyewitness, because he and Andrew were there together as disciples of John the Baptist. (The apostle John doesn't identify himself by name. He keeps himself anonymous in his Gospel right up to the very end. But the way he relates the details of this encounter, right down to giving us the time of day, suggests that he had firsthand knowledge of this incident. He was obviously the other disciple mentioned in the account.)

Andrew's personal encounter with Jesus took place the day after Jesus' baptism (vv. 29–34). Andrew and John were standing next to the Baptist when Jesus walked by and John the Baptist said, "Behold the Lamb of God!" (John 1:35–36). They immediately left John's side and began to follow Jesus (v. 37). Don't imagine that they were being fickle or untrue to their mentor. Quite the opposite. John the Baptist had already expressly denied that he was the Messiah: "When the Jews sent priests and Levites from Jerusalem to ask him, 'Who are you?' He confessed, and did not deny, but confessed, 'I am not the Christ'" (vv. 19–20). When people pressed John for an explanation of who he was, he said, "I am 'The voice of one crying in the wilderness: "Make straight the way of the LORD,"' as the prophet Isaiah said" (v. 23).

So John had already said in the most plain and forthright terms that he was only the forerunner of the Messiah. He had come to prepare the way and to point people in the right direction. In fact, the very heart of John the Baptist's message was preparation for the Messiah, who was coming speedily. Andrew and John would therefore have been caught up in the thrill of messianic expectation, waiting only for the right Person to be identified. That is why as soon as they heard John the Baptist identify Christ as the Lamb of God, the two disciples instantly, eagerly left John to follow Christ. They did the right thing. The Baptist himself surely would have approved of their choice.

The biblical account continues: "Then Jesus turned, and seeing them following, said to them, 'What do you seek?' They said to Him, 'Rabbi' (which is to say, when translated, Teacher), 'where are You staying?' He said to them, 'Come and see.' They came and saw where He was staying, and remained with Him that day" (vv. 38–39).

It was about four o' clock in the afternoon ("the tenth hour," acc-ording to verse 39) when they met Christ. They followed Him to the place where He was staying and spent the remainder of that day with Him. Since this was near John the Baptist in the wilderness, it was prob- ably a rented house or possibly just a room in a rustic inn. But these two disciples were privileged to spend the after- noon and evening in private fellowship with Jesus, and they left convinced that they had found the true Messiah. They met, became acquainted, and began to be taught by Jesus that very day. Thus Andrew and John became Jesus' first disciples.

Notice the first thing Andrew did: "He first found his own brother Simon, and said to him, 'We have found the Messiah' (which is translated, the Christ). And he brought him to Jesus" (vv. 41–42). The news was too good to keep to himself, so Andrew went and found the one person in the world whom he most loved—whom he most wanted to know Jesus—and he led him to Christ.

As we saw in the previous chapter, Peter and Andrew went back to Capernaum and continued their fishing career after that initial meeting with Christ. It was at a later time— perhaps several months later—that Jesus came to Galilee to minister. He had begun His ministry in and around Jerusalem, where He cleansed the temple and stirred the hostility of the religious leaders. But then He returned to Galilee to preach and heal, and He eventually came to Capernaum. There He encountered the four brothers again, while they were fishing.

Matthew 4 records that encounter:

> And Jesus, walking by the Sea of Galilee, saw two brothers, Simon called Peter, and Andrew his brother, casting a net into the sea; for they were fishermen. Then He said to them, "Follow Me, and I will make you fishers of men." They immediately left their nets and followed Him. Going on from there, He saw two other brothers, James the son of Zebedee, and John his brother, in the boat with Zebedee their father, mending their nets. He called them, and immediately they left the boat and their father, and followed Him. (vv. 18–22)

This was where they left fishing for a more permanent, full-time discipleship.

A parallel account of this event is recorded in Luke 5:1–11. But in Luke's account, Andrew's name is not mentioned. We know he was there and was included, because Matthew's record makes that clear. But Andrew was so much in the background that Luke doesn't even mention his name. Again, he was the kind of person who seldom came to the forefront. He remained somewhat hidden. He was certainly part of the group, and he must have followed Christ as eagerly and as quickly as the others, but he played a quiet, unsung role in obscurity.

He had lived his whole life in the shadow of Peter, and he apparently accepted that role. This was the very thing that made him so useful. His willingness to be a supporting actor often gave him insights into things the other disciples had trouble grasping. Thus whenever he does come to the forefront, the thing that shines is his uncanny ability to see immense value in small and modest things.

HE SAW THE VALUE
OF INDIVIDUAL PEOPLE

When it came to dealing with people, for example, Andrew fully appreciated the value of a single soul. He was known for bringing individuals, not crowds, to Jesus. Almost every time we see him in the Gospel accounts, he is bringing someone to Jesus.

Remember that his first act after discovering Christ was to go and get Peter. That incident set the tone for Andrew's style of ministry. At the feeding of the five thousand, for example, it was Andrew who brought the boy with the loaves and fishes to Christ. All the other disciples were at a loss to know how to obtain food for the multitude. It was Andrew who took the young boy to Jesus and said, "There is a lad here who has five barley loaves and two small fish" (John 6:9).

John 12:20–22 tells of some Greeks who sought out Philip and asked to see Jesus. These were probably Gentiles who knew of Jesus' reputation and wanted to meet Him. John 12:21 says these men "came to Philip, who was from Bethsaida of Galilee, and asked him, saying, 'Sir, we wish to see Jesus.' Philip came and told Andrew, and in turn Andrew and Philip told Jesus."

It is significant that these men approached Philip, but Philip took the men to Andrew and let Andrew introduce them to the Master. Why didn't Philip just take them to Jesus himself? Perhaps he was naturally timid, or maybe he wasn't confident enough in his own relationship with Christ. Maybe Philip just became flustered and confused about the proper protocol. Or it's possible that Philip wasn't sure Jesus would want to see *them*. In any case, Philip knew Andrew could introduce individuals to Christ.

Andrew was not confused when someone wanted to see Jesus. He simply brought them to Him. He understood that Jesus would want to meet anyone who wanted to meet Him (cf. John 6:37).

Andrew was obviously poised and comfortable introducing people to Christ, because he did it so often. He apparently knew Jesus well and had no insecurities about bringing others to Him. In John 1 he brought Peter to Christ, which made him the first home missionary. Now he brings some Greeks to Christ, making him the first foreign missionary.

One thing I have observed in all my years of ministry is that the most effective and important aspects of evangelism usually take place on an individual, personal level. Most people do not come to Christ as an immediate response to a sermon they hear in a crowded setting. They come to Christ because of the influence of an individual.

The church I pastor seeks to foster an evangelistic environment. And people are coming to Christ on a regular basis. Almost every Sunday in our evening services we baptize several new believers. Each one gives a testimony before being baptized. And in the overwhelming majority of instances, they tell us they came to Christ primarily because of the testimony of a coworker, a neighbor, a relative, or a friend. Occasionally we hear people say they were converted in direct response to a message they heard in church or a sermon that was broadcast on the radio. But even in those cases, it is usually owing to the influence of an individual who encouraged the person to listen or brought him to church in the first place. There's no question that the most effective means for bringing people to Christ is one at a time, on an individual basis.

Both Andrew and his brother Peter had evangelistic

hearts, but their methods were dramatically different. Peter preached at Pentecost, and three thousand people were added to the church. Nothing in Scripture indicates that Andrew ever preached to a crowd or stirred masses of people. But remember that it was he who brought Peter to Christ. In the sovereign providence of God, Andrew's act of faithfulness in bringing his own brother to Christ was the individual act that led to the conversion of the man who would preach that great sermon at Pentecost. All the fruit of Peter's ministry is ultimately also the fruit of Andrew's faithful, individual witness.

God often works that way. Few have ever heard of Edward Kimball. His name is a footnote in the annals of church history. But he was the Sunday school teacher who led D. L. Moody to Christ. He went one afternoon to the Boston shoe store where the nineteen-year-old Moody was working, cornered him in the stockroom, and introduced him to Christ.

Kimball was the antithesis of the bold evangelist. He was a timid, soft-spoken man. He went to that shoe shop frightened, trembling, and unsure of whether he had enough courage to confront this young man with the gospel. At the time, Moody was crude and obviously illiterate, but the thought of speaking to him about Christ had Kimball trembling in his boots. Kimball recalled the incident years later. Moody had begun to attend his Sunday school class. It was obvious that Moody was totally untaught and ignorant about the Bible. Kimball said,

I decided to speak to Moody about Christ and about his soul. I started down town to Holton's shoe store. When I was nearly there I began to wonder whether I ought to go just then during business hours. And I thought maybe my mission might embarrass the boy, that when I went away the other clerks might ask who I was, and when they learned might taunt Moody and ask if I was trying to make a good boy out of him. While I was pondering over it all I passed the store without noticing it. Then, when I found I had gone by the door I determined to make a dash for it and have it over at once.[1]

Kimball found Moody working in the stockroom, wrapping and shelving shoes. Kimball said he spoke with "limping words." He later said, "I never could remember just what I *did* say: something about Christ and His love; that was all." He admitted it was "a weak appeal."[2] But Moody then and there gave his heart to Christ.

Of course, D. L. Moody was used mightily by the Lord as an evangelist both in America and in England. His ministry made a massive impact on both sides of the Atlantic, spanning most of the second half of the nineteenth century. Tens of thousands testified that they came to Christ because of his ministry. Among Moody's converts were people like C. T. Studd, the great pioneer missionary, and Wilbur Chapman, who himself became a well-known evangelist. Moody subsequently founded Moody Bible Institute, where thousands of missionaries, evangelists, and other Christian workers have been trained during the past century and sent out into all the world. All of that began when one man was faithful to introduce another individual to Christ.

That's the way Andrew usually seemed to minister: one-on-one. Most pastors would love to have their churches populated by people with Andrew's mentality. Too many Christians think that because they can't speak in front of groups or because they don't have leadership gifts, they aren't responsible to evangelize. There are few who, like Andrew, understand the value of befriending just one person and bringing him or her to Christ.

HE SAW THE VALUE OF
INSIGNIFICANT GIFTS

Some people see the big picture more clearly just because they appreciate the value of small things. Andrew fits that category. This comes through clearly in John's account of the feeding of the five thousand.

Jesus had gone to a mountain to try to be alone with His disciples. As often happened when He took a break from public ministry, the clamoring multitudes tracked Him down. It was just before Passover, the most important holiday on the Jewish calendar. That means it was precisely one year before Christ would be crucified.

Suddenly a huge throng of people approached. Somehow they had discovered where Jesus was. It was nearing time to eat, and bread would be the object lesson in the message Jesus would preach to the multitude. So He made it clear that He wanted to feed the multitude. He asked Philip where they might buy bread. John adds an editorial comment to stress the fact that Christ was sovereignly in control of these circumstances: "This He said to test him, for He Himself knew what He would do" (John 6:6).

Philip did a quick accounting and determined that they had only two hundred denarii in their treasury. A denarius was a day's pay for a common laborer, so two hundred denarii would be approximately eight months' wages. It was a significant sum, but the crowd was so large that even two hundred denarii was inadequate to buy enough food for them. Philip's vision was overwhelmed by the size of the need. He and the other disciples were at a loss to know what to do. Matthew, recounting this same incident, reports that the disciples said, "This is a deserted place, and the hour is already late. Send the multitudes away, that they may go into the villages and buy themselves food" (Matthew 14:15).

But Jesus answered, "They do not need to go away. You give them something to eat" (v. 16). The disciples must have been stymied by this. Jesus' demand seemed unreasonable.

At that point, Andrew spoke up. "There is a lad here who has five barley loaves and two small fish" (John 6:9). Of course, even Andrew knew that five barley loaves and two small fish would not be enough to feed five thousand people, but (in his typical fashion) he brought the boy to Jesus anyway. Jesus had commanded the disciples to feed the people, and Andrew knew He would not issue such a command without making it possible for them to obey. So Andrew did the best he could. He identified the one food source available, and he made sure Jesus knew about it. Something in him seemed to understand that no gift is insignificant in the hands of Jesus.

John continues the narrative:

Then Jesus said, "Make the people sit down." Now there was much grass in the place. So the men sat down, in number about five thousand. And Jesus took the loaves, and when He had given thanks He distributed them to the disciples, and the disciples to those sitting down; and likewise of the fish, as much as they wanted. So when they were filled, He said to His disciples, "Gather up the fragments that remain, so that nothing is lost." Therefore they gathered them up, and filled twelve baskets with the frag-

ments of the five barley loaves which were left over by
those who had eaten. (vv. 10–13)

What an amazing lesson! That so little could be used to
accomplish so much was a testimony to the power of
Christ. No gift is really insignificant in His hands.

Our Lord Himself taught the disciples that same lesson
in Luke 21:1–4: "He looked up and saw the rich putting
their gifts into the treasury, and He saw also a certain poor
widow putting in two mites. So He said, 'Truly I say to you
that this poor widow has put in more than all; for all these
out of their abundance have put in offerings for God, but she
out of her poverty put in all the livelihood that she had.'"

In other words, the poor person who gives everything
he or she has is giving a greater gift than rich people who
gave much more out of their abundance. God's ability to
use a gift is in no way hindered or enhanced by the size of
that gift. And it is the sacrificial faithfulness of the giver, not
the size of the gift, that is the true measure of the gift's
significance.

That's a difficult concept for the human mind to
comprehend. But somehow, Andrew seemed instinctively
to know that he was not wasting Jesus' time by bringing
such a paltry gift. It is not the greatness of the gift that
counts, but rather the greatness of the God to whom it is
given. Andrew set the stage for the miracle.

Of course, Jesus didn't even need to have that boy's
lunch in order to serve the crowd. He could have created
food from nothing just as easily. But the way He fed the
five thousand illustrates the way God always works. He
takes the sacrificial and often insignificant gifts of people
who give faithfully, and He multiplies them to accomplish
monumental things.

HE SAW THE VALUE
OF INCONSPICUOUS SERVICE

Some people won't play in the band unless they can hit the big drum. James and John had that tendency. So did Peter. But not Andrew. He is never named as a participant in the big debates. He was more concerned about bringing people to Jesus than about who got the credit or who was in charge. He had little craving for honor. We never hear him say anything unless it related to bringing someone to Jesus.

Andrew is the very picture of all those who labor quietly in humble places, "not with eyeservice, as men-pleasers, but as bond-servants of Christ, doing the will of God from the heart" (Ephesians 6:6). He was not an impressive pillar like Peter, James, and John. He was a humbler stone. He was one of those rare people who is willing to take second place and to be in the place of support. He did not mind being hidden as long as the work was being done.

This is a lesson many Christians today would do well to learn. Scripture cautions against seeking roles of prominence, and it warns those who would be teachers that they face a higher standard of judgment: "My brethren, let not many of you become teachers, knowing that we shall receive a stricter judgment" (James 3:11).

Jesus taught the disciples, "If any man desire to be first, the same shall be last of all, and servant of all" (Mark 9:35). It takes a special kind of person to be a leader with a servant's heart. Andrew was like that.

As far as we know, Andrew never preached to multitudes or founded any churches. He never wrote an epistle. He isn't mentioned in the book of Acts or any of the epistles. Andrew is more a silhouette than a portrait on the pages of Scripture.

In fact, the Bible does not record what happened to Andrew after Pentecost. Whatever role he played in early church history, he remained behind the scenes. Tradition says he took the gospel north. Eusebius, the ancient church historian, says Andrew went as far as Scythia. (That's why Andrew is the patron saint of Russia. He is also the patron saint of Scotland.) He was ultimately crucified in Achaia, which is in southern Greece, near Athens. One account says he led the wife of a provincial Roman governor to Christ, and that infuriated her husband. He demanded that his wife recant her devotion to Jesus Christ and she refused. So the governor had Andrew crucified.

By the governor's orders, those who crucified him lashed him to his cross instead of nailing him, in order to prolong his sufferings. (Tradition says it was a saltire, or an X-shaped cross.) By most accounts, he hung on the cross for two days, exhorting passersby to turn to Christ for salvation. After a lifetime of ministry in the shadow of his more famous brother and in the service of His Lord, he met a similar fate as theirs, remaining faithful and still endeavoring to bring people to Christ, right to the end.

Was he slighted? No. He was privileged. He was the first to hear that Jesus was the Lamb of God. He was the first to follow Christ. He was part of the inner circle, given intimate access to Christ. His name will be inscribed, along with the names of the other apostles, on the foundations of the eternal city—the New Jerusalem. Best of all, he had a whole lifetime of privilege, doing what he loved best: introducing individuals to the Lord.

Thank God for people like Andrew. They're the quiet individuals, laboring faithfully but inconspicuously, giving insignificant, sacrificial gifts, who accomplish the most for the Lord. They don't receive much recognition, but they don't seek it. They only want to hear the Lord say, "Well done."

And Andrew's legacy is the example he left to show us that in effective ministry it's often the little things that count—the individual people, the insignificant gifts, and the inconspicuous service. God delights to use such things, because He has "chosen the foolish things of the world to put to shame the wise, and God has chosen the weak things of the world to put to shame the things which are mighty; and the base things of the world and the things which are despised God has chosen, and the things which are not, to bring to nothing the things that are, that no flesh should glory in His presence" (1 Corinthians 1:27–29).

4

JAMES—THE APOSTLE OF PASSION

Herod the king stretched out his hand to harass some from the church. Then he killed James the brother of John with the sword.

—ACTS 12:1–2

OF THE THREE DISCIPLES IN JESUS' CLOSEST INNER CIRCLE, James is the least familiar to us. The biblical account is practically devoid of any explicit details about his life and character. He never appears as a stand-alone character in the Gospel accounts, but he is always paired with his younger and better-known brother, John. The only time he is mentioned by himself is in the book of Acts, where his martyrdom is recorded.

This relative silence about James is ironic, because from a human perspective, he might have seemed the logical one to dominate the group. Between James and John, James was the eldest. (That is doubtless why his name always appears first when those two names appear together.) And between the two sets of brothers, the family of James and John seems to have been much more prominent than the family of Peter and Andrew. This is hinted at by the fact that James and John are often referred to simply as "the sons of

Zebedee" (Matthew 20:20; 26:37; 27:56; Mark 10:35; Luke 5:10; John 21:2)—signifying that Zebedee was a man of some importance.

Zebedee's prestige might have stemmed from his financial success, his family lineage, or both. He was apparently quite well-to-do. His fishing business was large enough to employ multiple hired servants (Mark 1:20). Moreover, Zebedee's entire family had enough status that the apostle John "was known to the high priest," and that is how John was able to get Peter admitted to the high priest's courtyard on the night of Jesus' arrest (John 18:15–16). There is some evidence from the early church record that Zebedee was a Levite and closely related to the high priest's family. Whatever the reason for Zebedee's prominence, it is clear from Scripture that he was a man of importance, and his family's reputation reached from Galilee all the way to the high priest's household in Jerusalem.

James, as the elder brother from such a prominent family, might have felt that by all rights he ought to have been the chief apostle. Indeed, that may be one of the main reasons there were so many disputes about "which of them should be considered the greatest" (Luke 22:24). But James never did actually take first place among the apostles except in one regard: He was the first to be martyred.

James is a much more significant figure than we might consider, based on the little we know about him. In two of the lists of apostles his name comes immediately after Peter's (Mark 3:16–19; Acts 1:13). So there is good reason to assume he was a strong leader—and probably second in influence after Peter.

Of course, James also figures prominently in the close inner circle of three. He, Peter, and John were the only ones Jesus permitted to go with Him when He raised

Jairus's daughter from the dead (Mark 5:37). The same group of three witnessed Jesus' glory on the Mount of Transfiguration (Matthew 17:1). James was among four disciples who questioned Jesus privately on the Mount of Olives (Mark 13:3). And he was included again with John and Peter when the Lord urged those three to pray with Him privately in Gethsemane (Mark 14:33). So as a member of the small inner circle, he was privileged to witness Jesus' *power* in the raising of the dead, he saw His *glory* when Jesus was transfigured, he saw Christ's *sovereignty* in the way the Lord unfolded the future to them on the Mount of Olives, and he saw the Savior's *agony* in the garden. All of these events must have strengthened his faith immensely and equipped him for the suffering and martyrdom he himself would eventually face.

If there's a key word that applies to the life of the apostle James, that word is *passion*. From the little we know about him, it is obvious that he was a man of intense fervor and intensity. In fact, Jesus gave James and John a nickname: *Boanerges*—"Sons of Thunder." That defines James's personality in very vivid terms. He was zealous, thunderous, passionate, and fervent. He reminds us of Jehu in the Old Testament, who was known for driving his chariot at breakneck speed (2 Kings 9:20), and who said, "Come with me, and see my zeal for the LORD"—then annihilated the house of Ahab and swept away Baal-worship from the land. But Jehu's passion was a passion out of control, and his "zeal for the Lord" turned out to be tainted with selfish, worldly ambition and the most bloodthirsty kinds of cruelty. Scripture says, "Jehu took no heed to walk in the law of the LORD God of Israel with all his heart; for he did not depart from the sins of Jeroboam, who had made Israel sin" (2 Kings 10:31). The apostle James's zeal was mixed with similar ambitious and bloodthirsty tendencies (though in much milder doses), and he may have even been headed down a similar road to ruin when Jesus met him. But by God's grace, he was transformed into a man of God and became one of the leading apostles.

Mark, who records that Jesus called James and John "Sons of Thunder," includes that fact in his list of the Twelve, mentioning it in the same way he notes that Simon was named Peter (Mark 3:17). We don't know how often Jesus employed His nickname for James and John; Mark's mention of it is the only time it appears in all of Scripture. Unlike Peter's name, which was obviously intended to help encourage and shape Peter's character toward a rocklike steadfastness, "Boanerges" seems to have been bestowed on the sons of Zebedee to chide them when they allowed their naturally feverish temperaments to get out of hand. Perhaps the Lord even used it for humorous effect while employing it as a gentle admonishment.

What little we know about James underscores the fact that he had a fiery, vehement disposition. While Andrew was quietly bringing individuals to Jesus, James was wishing he could call down fire from heaven and destroy whole villages of people. Even the fact that James was the first to be martyred—and that his martyrdom was accomplished by no less a figure than Herod—suggests that James was not a passive or subtle man, but rather he had a style that stirred things up, so that he made deadly enemies very rapidly.

There is a legitimate place in spiritual leadership for people who have thunderous personalities. Elijah was that kind of character. (Indeed, Elijah was the role model James thought he was following when he pleaded for fire from heaven.) Nehemiah was similarly passionate (cf. Nehemiah 13:25). John the Baptist had a fiery temperament, too.

James apparently was cut from similar fabric. He was outspoken, intense, and impatient with evildoers.

There is nothing inherently wrong with such zeal. Remember that Jesus Himself made a whip and cleansed the temple. And when he did, "His disciples remembered that it was written, 'Zeal for Your house has eaten Me up'" (John 2:17; cf. Psalm 69:9). James of all people knew what it was to be eaten up with zeal for the Lord. Much of what James saw Jesus do probably helped stoke his zeal—such as when the Lord rebuked the Jewish leaders, when He cursed the cities of Chorazin and Bethsaida, and when He confronted and destroyed demonic powers. Zeal is a virtue when it is truly zeal for righteousness' sake.

But sometimes zeal is less than righteous. Zeal apart from knowledge can be damning (cf. Romans 10:2). Zeal without wisdom is dangerous. Zeal mixed with insensitivity is often cruel. Whenever zeal disintegrates into uncontrolled passion, it can be deadly. And James sometimes had a tendency to let such misguided zeal get the better of him. Two incidents in particular illustrate this. One is the episode where James wanted to call down fire. The other is the time James and John enlisted their mother's help to lobby for the highest seats in the kingdom. Let's look at these individually.

FIRE FROM HEAVEN

We get our best glimpse of why James and John were known as the Sons of Thunder in Luke 9:51–56. Jesus was preparing to pass through Samaria. He was headed to Jerusalem for the final Passover, which He knew would culminate in His death, burial, and resurrection. Luke writes, "Now it came to pass, when the time had come for Him to be received up, that He steadfastly set His face to go to Jerusalem, and sent messengers before His face. And as they went, they entered a village of the Samaritans, to prepare for Him. But they did not receive Him, because His face was set for the journey to Jerusalem" (vv. 51–53).

It was significant that Jesus chose to travel through Samaria. Even though the shortest route from Galilee to Jerusalem went right through Samaria, most Jews traveling between those two places deliberately took a route that required them to travel many miles out of the way through the barren desert of Perea—requiring them to cross the Jordan twice—just so that they could avoid Samaria.

The Samaritans were the mixed-race offspring of Israelites from the Northern Kingdom. When Israel was conquered by the Assyrians, the most prominent and influential people in their tribes were taken into captivity, and the land was resettled with pagans and foreigners who were loyal to the Assyrian king (2 Kings 17:24–34). Poor Israelites who remained in the land intermarried with those pagans.

From the very beginning, the interloping pagans did not prosper in the land because they did not fear the Lord. So the king of Assyria sent back one of the priests whom he had taken captive, in order to teach people how to fear the Lord (2 Kings 17:28). The result was a religion that blended elements of truth and paganism. "They feared the LORD, yet served their own gods; according to the rituals of the nations from among whom they were carried away" (v. 33). In other words, they still *claimed* to worship Jehovah as God (and ostensibly they accepted the Pentateuch as Scripture), but they founded their own priesthood, built their own temple, and devised a sacrificial system of their own making. In short, they made a new religion based in large part on pagan traditions. The Samaritans' religion is a classic example of what happens when the authority of Scripture is subjugated to human tradition.

The original site of the Samaritans' temple was on Mount Gerizim, in Samaria. That temple was built during the time of Alexander the Great, but it had been destroyed about one hundred twenty-five years before the birth of Christ. Gerizim was still deemed holy by the Samaritans, however, and they were convinced the mountain was the only place where God could properly be worshiped. That is why the Samaritan woman in John 4:20 said to Jesus, "Our fathers worshiped on this mountain, and you Jews say that in Jerusalem is the place where one ought to worship." Obviously, this was one of the chief points under dispute between the Jews and the Samaritans. (To this day a small group of the Samaritans' descendants still worship on Mount Gerizim.)

Many of the original Israelites' descendants who later returned to Samaria from captivity were also the product of intermarriage with pagans, so the culture of Samaria suited them perfectly. Of course, the Jews regarded the Samaritans as a mongrel race and their religion as a mongrel religion. That is why, during the time of Christ, such pains were taken to avoid all travel through Samaria. The entire region was deemed unclean.

But in this instance, Jesus' face was set for Jerusalem, and as He had done before (John 4:4), He chose the more direct route through Samaria. Along the way, He and His followers would need places to eat and spend the night. Since the party traveling with Jesus was fairly large, He sent messengers ahead to arrange accommodations.

Because it was obvious that Jesus was headed for

Jerusalem to celebrate the Passover, and the Samaritans were of the opinion that all such feasts and ceremonies ought to be observed on Mount Gerizim, Jesus' messengers were refused all accommodations. The Samaritans not only hated the Jews, but they also hated the worship that took place in Jerusalem. They therefore had no interest in Christ's agenda at all. He represented everything Jewish that they despised. So they summarily rejected the request. The problem was not that there was no room for them in the inn; the problem was that the Samaritans were being deliberately inhospitable. If Jesus intended to pass through their city on His way to Jerusalem to worship, they were going to make it as hard as possible for Him. They hated the Jews and their worship as much as the Jews hated them and their worship. As far as the Samaritans were concerned, turnabout was fair play.

Of course, Jesus had never shown anything but good-will toward the Samaritans. He had healed a Samaritan's leprosy and commended that man for his gratefulness (Luke 17:16). He had accepted water from a Samaritan woman and given her the water of life (John 4:7–29). He had stayed in that woman's village for two days, evangelizing her neighbors (John 4:39–43). He had made a Samaritan the hero of one of His best-known parables (Luke 10:30–37). Later He would command His disciples to preach the gospel in Samaria (Acts 1:8). He had always been full of kindness and goodwill toward the Samaritans.

But now they were treating Him with deliberate contempt.

James and John, the Sons of Thunder, were instantly filled with passionate outrage. They already had in mind a remedy for this situa-tion. They said, "Lord, do You want us to command fire to come down from heaven and consume them, just as Elijah did?" (Luke 9:54).

The reference to Elijah was full of significance. The incident to which James and John were referring had taken place in this very region. They were familiar with the Old Testament account, and they knew its historical relevance to Samaria. We see here how deeply the Jews felt their resentment toward Samaria.

It was a matter of historical fact that the name of Samaria had been associated with idolatry and apostasy long before the Assyrian conquest. *Samaria* was originally the name of one of the most important cities in the Northern Kingdom. During Ahab's reign, in the days of Elijah, Samaria was turned into a center for Baal-worship (1 Kings 16:32). This was also where Ahab had built his famous ivory palace (1 Kings 22:39; cf. Amos 3:12–15).

Ahab's palace became the permanent residence for subsequent kings of the Northern Kingdom. In fact, it was the very place where King Ahaziah fell through the lattice in his upper chamber and was seriously injured (2 Kings 1:2).

A *lattice* is a screen or a grate made of crisscrossed wooden strips. This could have been a decorative window covering. More likely it was a flimsy substitute for a parapet around the perimeter of the roof. Apparently, Ahaziah carelessly backed into some latticework or stupidly leaned on it, and when it gave way, he fell to the ground from the upper level of the palace.

Ahaziah was the son and successor of Ahab. His mother, Jezebel, was still living during his reign and still exercising her evil influence through her son's throne. When Ahaziah's accident occurred, the injuries were apparently life-threatening, and he wanted to know his fate. So he dispatched messengers, telling them, "Go, inquire of Baal-Zebub, the god of Ekron, whether I shall recover from this injury" (v. 2).

Inquiring of soothsayers was strictly forbidden by

Moses' law, of course (Deuteronomy 18:10–12). Seeking prophecies from fortune-tellers who were associated with Baal-Zebub was even worse. Baal–Zebub was a Philistine deity. His name meant "lord of the flies." The land of the Philistines was thick with flies, and the Philistines believed the lord of the flies lived in their land, so they made this fly-god one of their main deities. They had some famous oracles who claimed to be able to tell the future. They usually gave flattering prophecies with predictions so ambiguous they could hardly miss, but those oracles nonetheless had gained fame throughout Israel. They were the "Psychic Friends Network" of Elijah's time.

But Baal-Zebub was as vile a deity as anyone ever invented. He supposedly ruled the flies—those abhorrent insects that swarm around every kind of decay and filth and spread disease and spawn maggots. It was a fitting image for this kind of god. Who would ever think of worshiping a deity whose realm was everything foul and unclean? Such a god was so revolting to the Jews that they altered the name *Baal-Zebub* slightly to make it "Beelzebul," which means "god of dung." This vile being epitomized everything impure and unholy—everything that opposes the true God. (That is why, by the time of Jesus, the name *Beelzebub* had become a way to refer to Satan—Luke 11:15.) This was the god from whom Ahaziah sought knowledge of the future.

So the Lord sent Elijah to intercept the messengers. Scripture says, "The angel of the LORD said to Elijah the Tishbite, 'Arise, go up to meet the messengers of the king of Samaria, and say to them, "Is it because there is no God in Israel that you are going to inquire of Baal-Zebub, the god of Ekron?"'" (2 Kings 1:3). The angel also gave Ahab a solemn message for the injured king: "Now therefore, thus says the LORD: 'You shall not come down from the bed to which you have gone up, but you shall surely die' " (v. 4).

Elijah did as he was told and sent the prophecy back to Ahaziah via the king's messengers. The messengers did not even know who Elijah was. When they reported back to the king, they simply told him the prophecy had been given them by "a man [who] came up to meet us" (v. 6).

Ahaziah asked, "What kind of man was it who came up to meet you and told you these words?" (v. 7).

They answered, "A hairy man wearing a leather belt around his waist" (v. 8).

Ahaziah instantly knew who it was: "It is Elijah the Tishbite" (v. 8).

Elijah had been Ahab and Jezebel's nemesis for years, so he was well known to Ahaziah. Naturally, Ahaziah hated him and probably decided then and there to kill him. So he sent "a captain of fifty with his fifty men" to confront Elijah (v. 9). The fact that Ahaziah sent so many soldiers is proof his intentions were not peaceful. Their orders were probably to arrest him and bring him back to Ahaziah so that the king could actually witness Elijah's execution and gloat over it.

"So [the captain of the fifty] went up to him; and there he was, sitting on the top of a hill" (v. 9). Elijah was totally unfazed by the size of the regiment that came to get him. He wasn't hiding or running from them; he was sitting placidly atop the hill, where they would be sure to find him.

The captain spoke: "Man of God, the king has said, 'Come down!' " (v. 9).

Elijah's reply was to the point: " 'If I am a man of God, then let fire come down from heaven and consume you and your fifty men.' And fire came down from heaven and consumed him and his fifty" (v. 10). The Hebrew expression suggests that the entire company was utterly consumed, reduced to ashes in an instant. This apparently occurred in the presence of witnesses, who reported the matter back to the king.

But Ahaziah was a foolishly stubborn man. "Then he sent to him another captain of fifty with his fifty men. And he answered and said to him: 'Man of God, thus has the king said, "Come down quickly!"' So Elijah answered and said to them, 'If I am a man of God, let fire come down from heaven and consume you and your fifty men.' And the fire of God came down from heaven and consumed him and his fifty" (vv. 11–12).

Incredibly, Ahaziah was not through. He sent *another* company of fifty men. But the captain of this third group was wise. He approached Elijah humbly and pleaded for the lives of his men. So this time the angel of the Lord instructed Elijah to go with the soldiers and confront Ahaziah personally. Elijah went with them and delivered the message of doom to Ahaziah personally.

And Ahaziah died "according to the word of the LORD which Elijah had spoken" (vv. 13–17).

All of that had taken place in the very region through which Jesus proposed to travel to Jerusalem. The story of Elijah's fiery triumph was well known to the disciples. It was one of the classic Old Testament episodes they would have been reminded of merely by traveling through that district.

So when James and John suggested fire from heaven as a fitting response to the Samaritans' inhospitality, they probably thought they were standing on solid precedent. After all, Elijah was not condemned for his actions. On the contrary, at that time and under those circumstances, it was the appropriate response from Elijah.

But it was not a proper response for James and John. In

the first place, their motives were wrong. A tone of arrogance is evident in the way they asked the question: "Lord,
do You want *us* to command fire to come down from
heaven and consume them, just as Elijah did?" Of course,
they did not have the power to call down fire from heaven.
Christ was the only one in their company who had such
power. If that were an appropriate response, He could well
have done it Himself. James and John were brazenly
suggesting that He should give *them* power to call down
fire. Christ Himself had been challenged many times by His
adversaries to produce such cosmic miracles, and He had
always declined (cf. Matthew 12:39). James and John were
in effect asking Jesus to enable them to do what they knew
He would not do.

Furthermore, Jesus' mission was very different from
Elijah's. Christ had come to save, not to destroy. Therefore
He responded to the Boanerges Brothers with a firm
reproof: "But He turned and rebuked them, and said, 'You
do not know what manner of spirit you are of. For the Son
of Man did not come to destroy men's lives but to save
them'" (Luke 9:55–56).

After all this time with Jesus, how could they have
missed the spirit of so much He had taught? "The Son of
Man has come to seek and to save that which was lost"
(Luke 19:10). He was on a mission of rescue, not judgment.
Although He had every right to demand absolute worship,
"The Son of Man did not come to be served, but to serve,
and to give His life a ransom for many" (Matthew 20:28).
"For God did not send His Son into the world to condemn
the world, but that the world through Him might be saved"
(John 3:17). Jesus Himself had said, "I have come as a light
into the world, that whoever believes in Me should not
abide in darkness. And if anyone hears My words and does

not believe, I do not judge him; for I did not come to judge the world but to save the world" (John 12:46–47).

Of course, a time is coming when Christ *will* judge the world. Scripture says He will be "revealed from heaven with His mighty angels, in flaming fire taking vengeance on those who do not know God, and on those who do not obey the gospel of our Lord Jesus Christ. These shall be punished with everlasting destruction from the presence of the Lord and from the glory of His power" (2 Thessalonians 1:7–9). But this was not the time or the place for that.

As Solomon wrote, "To everything there is a season, a time for every purpose under heaven. . . . A time to kill, and a time to heal; a time to break down, and a time to build up . . . a time to cast away stones, and a time to gather stones . . . a time to keep silence, and a time to speak; a time to love, and a time to hate; a time of war, and a time of peace" (Ecclesiastes 3:1–8). James and John momentarily forgot that "now is the day of salvation" (2 Corinthians 6:2).

Perhaps, however, there is a touch of nobility in their indignation against the Samaritans. Their zeal to defend Christ's honor is surely a great virtue. It is far better to get fired up with righteous wrath than to sit passively and endure insults against Christ. So their resentment over seeing Christ deliberately slighted is admirable in some measure, even though their reaction was tainted with arrogance and their proposed remedy to the problem was completely out of line.

Note also that Jesus was not by any means condemning what Elijah had done in his day. Nor was our Lord advocating a purely pacifist approach to every conflict. What Elijah did he did for the sake of God's glory and with God's express approval. That fire from heaven was a public display of *God's* wrath (not Elijah's), and it was a deservedly severe judgment against an unthinkably evil regime that had sat on Israel's throne for generations. Such extreme wickedness called for extreme measures of judgment.

Of course, such instant destruction would be fitting every time anyone sinned, if that were how God chose to deal with us. But, thankfully, it ordinarily is not. "His tender mercies are over all His works" (Psalm 145:9). He is "merciful and gracious, longsuffering, and abounding in goodness and truth" (Exodus 34:6). He has "no pleasure in the death of the wicked, but that the wicked turn from his way and live" (Ezekiel 33:11).

Jesus' example taught James that loving-kindness and mercy are virtues to be cultivated as much as (and sometimes more than) righteous indignation and fiery zeal. Notice what happened. Instead of calling down fire from heaven, "They went to another village" (Luke 9:56). They simply found accommodations elsewhere. It was a little inconvenient, perhaps, but far better and far more appropriate in those circumstances than James and John's proposed remedy for the Samaritans' inhospitality.

A few years after this, as the early church began to grow and the gospel message spread beyond Judea, Philip the deacon "went down to the city of Samaria and preached Christ to them" (Acts 8:5). A marvelous thing happened. "The multitudes with one accord heeded the things spoken by Philip, hearing and seeing the miracles which he did. For unclean spirits, crying with a loud voice, came out of many who were possessed; and many who were paralyzed and lame were healed. And there was great joy in that city" (vv. 6–8).

Undoubtedly, many who were saved under Philip's preaching were some of the same people whom Jesus spared when James had wanted to incinerate them. And we can be certain that even James himself rejoiced greatly in the salvation of so many who once had dishonored Christ so flagrantly.

THRONES IN THE KINGDOM

We get another insight into James's character in Matthew 20:20–24. Here we discover that James was not only fervent, passionate, zealous, and insensitive; he was also ambitious and overconfident. And in this case, he and his brother John engaged in a furtive attempt to gain status over the other apostles:

> Then the mother of Zebedee's sons came to Him with her sons, kneeling down and asking something from Him. And He said to her, "What do you wish?" She said to Him, "Grant that these two sons of mine may sit, one on Your right hand and the other on the left, in Your kingdom." But Jesus answered and said, "You do not know what you ask. Are you able to drink the cup that I am about to drink, and be baptized with the baptism that I am baptized with?" They said to Him, "We are able." So He said to them, "You will indeed drink My cup, and be baptized with the baptism that I am baptized with; but to sit on My right hand and on My left is not Mine to give, but it is for those for whom it is prepared by My Father." And when the ten heard it, they were greatly displeased with the two brothers.

Mark also records this incident, but he doesn't mention that James and John enlisted their mother's intercession. Although Matthew records that she is the one who made this request of Jesus, a comparison with Mark's account makes it clear that she was put up to it by her sons.

By comparing Matthew 27:56 with Mark 16:1, we further discover that the mother of James and John was named Salome. She was one of "many women who followed Jesus from Galilee, ministering to Him" (Matthew 27:55)—meaning that they supplied financial support and probably helped prepare meals (cf. Luke 8:1–3). Because of the family's affluence, Salome would have been able to join her sons for extended periods of time, traveling with the company that followed Jesus everywhere and helping meet logistical, practical, and financial needs.

The idea for Salome's bold request was undoubtedly hatched in the minds of James and John because of Jesus' promise in Matthew 19:28: "Assuredly I say to you, that in the regeneration, when the Son of Man sits on the throne of His glory, you who have followed Me will also sit on twelve thrones, judging the twelve tribes of Israel." Jesus immediately followed up that promise with a reminder that "Many who are first will be last, and the last first" (v. 30). But it was the promise of thrones that caught the attention of James and John. So they decided to have their mother request that they be given the most prominent thrones.

They were already in the intimate circle of three. They had been disciples as long as anyone. They probably thought of numerous reasons why they deserved this honor, so why not simply ask for it?

For her part, Salome was clearly a willing participant. Obviously she had encouraged her sons' ambitions, which may help explain where some of their attitudes came from.

Jesus' reply subtly reminded them that suffering is the prelude to glory: "Are you able to drink the cup that I drink, and be baptized with the baptism that I am baptized with?" Although He had explained to them numerous times that He was about to be crucified, they clearly did not understand what kind of baptism He meant. They had no real concept of what was stirring in the cup He was asking them to drink.

So, of course, in their foolish, ambitious self-confidence, they assured Him, "We are able." They were clamoring for honor and position, so they were *still* eager to hear Him promise them those highest thrones.

But He did not make that promise. Instead, He assured them that they would indeed drink His cup and be baptized with the same baptism he was about to undergo. (At that moment they could not have appreciated what they had just volunteered for.) But the chief thrones, Jesus said, were not necessarily part of the bargain. "To sit on My right hand and on My left is not Mine to give, but it is for those for whom it is prepared by My Father" (Matthew 20:23).

Their ambition ultimately created conflicts among the apostles, because the other ten heard about it and were displeased. The question of who deserved the most prominent thrones became the big debate among them, and they carried it right to the table at the Last Supper (Luke 22:24).

James wanted a crown of glory; Jesus gave him a cup of suffering. He wanted power; Jesus gave him servanthood. He wanted a place of prominence; Jesus gave him a martyr's grave. He wanted to rule; Jesus gave him a sword—not to wield, but to be the instrument of his own execution. Fourteen years after this, James would become the first of the Twelve to be killed for his faith.

A CUP OF SUFFERING

The end of James's story from an earthly perspective is recorded in Acts 12:1–3: "Now about that time Herod the king stretched out his hand to harass some from the church. Then he killed James the brother of John with the sword. And because he saw that it pleased the Jews, he proceeded further to seize Peter also."

Remember, this is the one place in Scripture where James appears alone, apart from even his brother. Few details of James's martyrdom are given. Scripture records that Herod was the one who had him killed and that the instrument of execution was a sword (meaning, of course, that he was beheaded). This was not Herod Antipas, the one who killed John the Baptist and put Jesus on trial; this was his nephew and successor, Herod Agrippa I. We don't know why this Herod would be so hostile to the church. Of course, it was well known that his uncle had participated in the conspiracy to kill Christ, so the preaching of the cross would surely have been an embarrassment to the Herodian Dynasty per se (cf. Acts 4:27). In addition to that, it is clear that Herod wanted to use the tensions between the church and the Jewish religious leaders to his political advantage. He began with a campaign of harassment against Christians and soon moved to murder. When he saw how this pleased the Jewish leaders, he decided to target Peter as well.

Peter miraculously escaped, and Herod himself died under God's judgment shortly afterward. Scripture says that after Peter's escape, Herod had the prison guards killed and went to Caesarea (Acts 12:19). While there, he accepted the kind of worship that is appropriate only for God. "The people kept shouting, 'The voice of a god and not of a man!' Then immediately an angel of the Lord struck him, because he did not give glory to God. And he was eaten by worms and died" (vv. 22–23). And thus the immediate threat against the church posed by Herod's campaign of harassment and murder was ended.

But it is significant that James was the first of the apostles to be killed. (James is the only apostle whose death is actually recorded in Scripture.) Clearly, James was still a man of passion. His passion, now under the Holy Spirit's control, had been so instrumental in the spread of the truth that it had aroused the wrath of Herod. Obviously, James was right where he had always hoped to be and where Christ had trained him to be—on the front line as the gospel advanced and the church grew.

That Son of Thunder had been mentored by Christ, empowered by the Holy Spirit, and shaped by those means into a man whose zeal and ambition were useful instruments in the hands of God for spreading of the kingdom. Still courageous, zealous, and committed to the truth, he had apparently learned to use those qualities for the Lord's service, rather than for his own self-aggrandizement. And now his strength was so great that when Herod decided it was time to stop the church, James was the first man who had to die. He thus drank the cup Christ gave him to drink. His life was short, but his influence continues to this day.

History records that James's testimony bore fruit right up until the moment of his execution. Eusebius, the early church historian, passes on an account of James's death that came from Clement of Alexandria: "[Clement] says that the one who led James to the judgment-seat, when he saw him bearing his testimony, was moved, and confessed that he was himself also a Christian. They were both therefore, he says, led away together; and on the way he begged James to forgive him. And [James], after considering a little, said, 'Peace be with thee,' and kissed him. And thus they were both beheaded at the same time."[1] Thus in the end, James had learned to be more like Andrew, bringing people to Christ instead of itching to execute judgment.

James is the prototype of the passionate, zealous, front runner who is dynamic, strong, and ambitious. Ultimately, his passions were tempered by sensitivity and grace. Somewhere along the line he had learned to control his anger, bridle his tongue, redirect his zeal, eliminate his thirst for revenge, and completely lose his selfish ambition. And the Lord used him to do a wonderful work in the early church.

Such lessons are sometimes hard for a man of James's passions to learn. But if I have to choose between a man of burning, flaming, passionate, enthusiasm with a potential for failure on the one hand, and a cold compromiser on the other hand, I'll take the man with passion every time. Such zeal must always be harnessed and tempered with love. But if it is surrendered to the control of the Holy Spirit and blended with patience and longsuffering, such zeal is a marvelous instrument in the hands of God. The life of James offers clear proof of that.

5

JOHN—THE APOSTLE OF LOVE

*Now there was leaning on Jesus' bosom one of
His disciples, whom Jesus loved.*

—JOHN 13:23

THE APOSTLE JOHN IS FAMILIAR TO US because he
wrote so much of the New Testament. He was the
human author of a Gospel and three epistles that
bear his name, as well as the book of Revelation. Aside
from Luke and the apostle Paul, John wrote more of the
New Testament than any other human author. Scripture is
therefore full of insights into his personality and character.
In fact, most of what we know about John we extract from
his own writings. We see through his Gospel how he views
Christ. We observe in his epistles how he dealt with the
church. And in the book of Revelation we even see the
future through the visions God gave him.

Both Scripture and history record that John played a
major role in the early church. Of course, he was a member
of the Lord's most intimate inner circle, but he was by no
means the dominant member of that group. He was the
younger brother of James, and although he was a frequent
companion to Peter in the first twelve chapters of Acts,

Peter remained in the foreground and John remained in the background.

But John also had his turn at leadership. Ultimately, because he outlived all the others, he filled a unique and patriarchal role in the early church that lasted nearly to the end of the first century and reached deep into Asia Minor. His personal influence was therefore indelibly stamped on the primitive church, well into the post-apostolic era.

Almost everything we observed about the personality and character of James is also true of John, the younger half of the Boanerges Brothers' duo. The two men had similar temperaments, and as we noted in the previous chapter, they were inseparable in the Gospel accounts. John was right there with James, eager to call down fire from heaven against the Samaritans. He was also in the thick of the debates about who was the greatest. His zeal and ambition mirrored that of his elder brother.

Therefore it is all the more remarkable that John has often been nicknamed "the apostle of love." Indeed, he wrote more than any other New Testament author about the importance of love—laying particular stress on the Christian's love for Christ, Christ's love for His church, and the love for one another that is supposed to be the hallmark of true believers. The theme of love flows through his writings.

But love was a quality he *learned* from Christ, not something that came naturally to him. In his younger years, he was as much a Son of Thunder as James. If you imagine that John was the way he was often portrayed in medieval art—a meek, mild, pale-skinned, effeminate person, lying around on Jesus' shoulder looking up at Him with a dove-eyed stare—forget that caricature. He was rugged and hard-edged, just like the rest of the fishermen-disciples. And again, he was every bit as intolerant, ambitious, zealous, and explosive as his elder brother. In fact, the one and only time the synoptic Gospel writers recorded John speaking for himself, he displayed his trademark aggressive, self-assertive, impertinent intolerance.

If you study Matthew, Mark, and Luke you'll notice that John is nearly always named along with someone else—with Jesus, with Peter, or with James. Only one time does John appear and speak alone. And that was when he confessed to the Lord that he had rebuked a man for casting out demons in Jesus' name, because the man was not part of the disciples' group (Mark 9:38). We'll examine that episode shortly.

So it is clear from the Gospel accounts that John was capable of behaving in the most sectarian, narrow-minded, unbending, reckless, and impetuous fashion. He was volatile. He was brash. He was aggressive. He was passionate, zealous, and personally ambitious—just like his brother James. They were cut from the same bolt of cloth.

But John aged well. Under the control of the Holy Spirit, all his liabilities were exchanged for assets. Compare the young disciple with the aged patriarch, and you'll see that as he matured, his areas of greatest weakness all developed into his greatest strengths. He's an amazing example of what should happen to us as we grow in Christ—allowing the Lord's strength to be made perfect in our weakness.

When we think of the apostle John today, we usually think of a tender-hearted, elderly apostle. As the elder statesman of the church near the end of the first century, he was universally beloved and respected for his devotion to Christ and his great love for the saints worldwide. That is precisely why he earned the epithet, "apostle of love."

As we shall see, however, love did not nullify the apostle

John's passion for truth. Rather, it gave him the balance he needed. He retained to the end of his life a deep and abiding love for God's truth, and he remained bold in proclaiming it to the very end.

John's zeal for the truth shaped the way he wrote. Of all the writers of the New Testament, he is the most black and white in his thinking. He thinks and writes in absolutes. He deals with certainties. Everything is cut-and-dried with him. There aren't many gray areas in his teaching, because he tends to state things in unqualified, antithetical language.

For example, in his Gospel, he sets light against darkness, life against death, the kingdom of God against the kingdom of the devil, the children of God against the children of Satan, the judgment of the righteous against the judgment of the wicked, the resurrection of life against the resurrection of damnation, receiving Christ against rejecting Christ, fruit against fruitlessness, obedience against disobedience, and love against hatred. He loves dealing with truth in absolutes and opposites. He understands the necessity of drawing a clear line.

The same approach carries through in his epistles. He tells us we are either walking in the light or dwelling in darkness. If we are born of God, we do not sin—indeed, we *cannot* sin (1 John 3:9). We are either "of God" or "of the world" (1 John 4:4–5). If we love, we are born of God; and if we don't love, we are not born of God (vv. 7–8). John writes, "Whoever abides in Him does not sin. Whoever sins has neither seen Him nor known Him" (1 John 3:6). He says all these things without qualification and without any softening of the hard lines.

In his second epistle, he calls for complete, total separation from all that is false: "Whoever transgresses and does not abide in the doctrine of Christ does not have God. He who abides in the doctrine of Christ has both the Father and the Son. If anyone comes to you and does not bring this doctrine, do not receive him into your house nor greet him; for he who greets him shares in his evil deeds" (vv. 9–11). He ends his third epistle with these words in verse 11: "He who does good is of God, but he who does evil has not seen God."

John is just that black and white.

Of course, even as John is writing such things, he knows and understands very well that believers *do* sin (cf. 1 John 2:1; 1:8, 10), but he doesn't belabor or even develop the point. He is concerned primarily with the overall pattern of a person's life. He wants to underscore the fact that righteousness, not sin, is the dominant principle in a true believer's life. Those who read John carelessly or superficially might almost think he is saying there are no exceptions.

Paul is the apostle of the exceptions. Paul took time to explain the struggle all believers experience with sin in their lives (Romans 7). While Paul also states that those who are born of God do not continue in habitual sin as a pattern of life (Romans 6:6–7), he nonetheless acknowledges that we must still wage war against the remnants of sin in our members, resist the tendencies of our flesh, put off the old man, put on the new, and so on. From reading John, one might think that righteousness comes so easily and naturally to the Christian that every failure would be enough to shatter our assurance completely. That is why when I read heavy doses of John, I sometimes have to turn to Paul's epistles just to find some breathing space.

Of course, both Paul's and John's epistles are inspired Scripture, and both emphases are necessary. The exceptions

dealt with by Paul don't nullify the truths stated so defin-
itively by John. And the relentlessly unequivocal
statements of John don't rule out the careful qualifications given by Paul. Both are necessary aspects of God's
revealed truth.

But the way John wrote was a reflection of his personality. Truth was his passion, and he seemed to bend over
backwards not to make it fuzzy. He spoke in black-and-
white, absolute, certain terms, and he did not waste ink
coloring in all the gray areas. He gave rules of thumb
without listing all the exceptions. Jesus Himself often spoke
in absolutes just like that, and John no doubt learned his
teaching style from the Lord. Although John always wrote
with a warm, personal, pastoral tone, what he wrote does
not always make for soothing reading. It does, however,
always reflect his deep convictions and his absolute devotion to the truth.

It is probably fair to say that one of the dangerous
tendencies for a man with John's personality is that he
would have a natural inclination to push things to
extremes. And indeed, it does seem that John in his
younger years was a bit of an extremist. He seemed to lack
a sense of spiritual equilibrium. His zeal, his sectarianism,
his intolerance, and his selfish ambition were all sins of
imbalance. They were all potential virtues, pushed to sinful
extremes. That is why the greatest strengths of his character
sometimes ironically *caused* his most prominent failures.
Peter and James had a similar tendency to turn their
greatest strengths into weaknesses. Their *best* characteristics
frequently became pitfalls for them.

We all fall prey to this principle from time to time. It is
one of the effects of human depravity. Even our best characteristics, corrupted by sin, become an occasion of

stumbling. It is wonderful to have a high regard for the truth, but zeal for the truth must be balanced by a love for people, or it can give way to judgmentalism, harshness, and a lack of compassion. It is fine to be hardworking and ambitious, but if ambition is not balanced with humility, it becomes sinful pride—self-promotion at the expense of others. Confidence is a wonderful virtue, too, but when confidence becomes a sinful *self*-confidence, we become smug and spiritually careless.

Clearly, there is nothing inherently wrong with zeal for the truth, a desire to succeed, or a sense of confidence. Those are all legitimate virtues. But even a virtue out of balance can become an impediment to spiritual health— just as truth out of balance can lead to serious error. A person out of balance is unsteady. Imbalance in one's personal character is a form of intemperance—a lack of self-control—and that is a sin in and of itself. So it is a very dangerous thing to push any point of truth or any character quality to an undue extreme.

That is what we see in the life of the younger disciple John. At various times he behaved like an extremist, a bigot, and a harsh, reckless man who was selfishly committed to his own narrow perception of truth. In his early years he was the most *unlikely* candidate to be remembered as the apostle of love.

But three years with Jesus began to transform a self-centered fanatic into a mature man of balance. Three years with Jesus moved this Son of Thunder toward becoming an apostle of love. At the very points where he was most imbalanced, Christ gave him equilibrium, and in the process John was transformed from a bigoted hothead into a loving, godly elder statesman for the early church.

HE LEARNED THE BALANCE
OF LOVE AND TRUTH

John seems to have been committed to truth very early in
life. From the beginning we see him as a spiritually aware
man who sought to know and follow the truth. When we
first encounter John (John 1:35–37), both he and Andrew
are disciples of John the Baptist. But like Andrew, John
without hesitation began following Jesus as soon as John
the Baptist singled Him out as the true Messiah. It was not
that they were fickle or disloyal to the Baptist. But John the
Baptist himself said of Jesus, "He must increase, but I must
decrease" (John 3:30). John the disciple was interested in
the truth; he hadn't followed the Baptist in order to join a
personality cult. Therefore he left John to follow Jesus as
soon as John clearly identified Him as the Lamb of God.

John's love of truth is evident in all his writings. He
uses the Greek word for *truth* twenty-five times in his
Gospel and twenty more times in his epistles. He wrote, "I
have no greater joy than to hear that my children walk in
truth" (3 John 4). His strongest epithet for someone who
claimed to be a believer while walking in darkness was to
describe the person as "a liar, and the truth is not in him"
(1 John 2:4; cf. 1:6, 8). No one in all of Scripture, except
the Lord Himself, had more to say extolling the very
concept of truth.

But sometimes in his younger years, John's zeal for
truth was lacking in love and compassion for people. He
needed to learn the balance. The incident in Mark 9 where
John forbade a man to cast out demons in Jesus' name is a
good illustration of this.

Again, this is the one place in the synoptic Gospels
where John acts and speaks alone, so it is an important

insight into his character. Here we see a rare glimpse of John without James and without Peter, speaking for himself. This is pure John. This same incident is also recorded in Luke 9, just before Luke's account of the episode at the Samaritan village, when James and John wanted to call down fire. The similarity of the two occasions is striking. In both cases, John is displaying an appalling intolerance, elitism, and a lack of genuine love for people. In the incident with the Samaritans, James and John showed a lack of love for unbelievers. Here John is guilty of a similar kind of unloving spirit toward a fellow believer. He forbade the man to minister in Jesus' name "because he does not follow us" (Mark 9:38)—because he was not officially a member of the group.

This incident occurred shortly after Jesus' transfiguration. That glorious mountaintop experience, which was witnessed only by the inner circle of three (Peter, James, and John), actually sets the context for what happens later in the chapter. As always, it is vital that we understand the context.

In Mark 9:1, Jesus tells the disciples, "Assuredly, I say to you that there are some standing here who will not taste death till they see the kingdom of God present with power." Of course, that sounded to the disciples like a promise that the millennial kingdom would come in their lifetimes. Yet even today, more than nineteen hundred years after the death of the last disciple, we're still waiting for the establishment of the millennial kingdom on earth. So what was this promise about?

What happened immediately afterward clearly answers that question. Jesus was promising them a preview of coming attractions. Three of them would have the privilege of witnessing a brilliant foretaste of glory divine. They would see a glimpse of the glory and power of the coming kingdom. It happened less than a week after Jesus' promised that some of them would see the kingdom, present with power: "Now after six days Jesus took Peter, James, and John, and led them up on a high mountain apart by themselves; and He was transfigured before them" (v. 2).

Christ took His three most trusted, intimate friends and disciples to a mountain, where He pulled back the veil of His human flesh so that the shekinah glory—the very essence of the nature of the eternal God—was shining out in blazing brilliance. "His clothes became shining, exceedingly white, like snow, such as no launderer on earth can whiten them" (v. 3). Matthew says the sight was so shocking that the disciples fell on their faces (Matthew 17:6). No one on earth had experienced anything remotely like this since Moses caught a glimpse of God's back after being shielded in the cleft of a rock from the full display of His glory (Exodus 33:20–23). It was a transcendental experience, the likes of which the disciples had never even imagined.

To top that off, "Elijah appeared to them with Moses, and they were talking with Jesus" (Mark 9:4). According to verse 6, the disciples were so frightened, they didn't know what to say.

Peter, in typical fashion, spoke anyway: "Rabbi, it is good for us to be here; and let us make three tabernacles: one for You, one for Moses, and one for Elijah" (v. 5). Peter probably thought this appearance of Elijah and Moses signified the inauguration of the kingdom, and he was eager to make it permanent. He also seems to have been erroneously thinking of the three of them as a kind of triumvirate of equals, rather than realizing Christ was the one to whom Moses and Elijah had pointed, making Him superior to them. And so at that very moment ("While he was still

speaking"—Matthew 17:5), "A cloud came and overshad-
owed them; and a voice came out of the cloud, saying, 'This
is My beloved Son. Hear Him!'" (Mark 9:7). Those were
virtually the same words that had come from heaven at Jesus'
baptism (Mark 1:11).

This was an amazing experience for Peter, James, and
John to behold. They were being given a unique privilege,
unparalleled in the annals of redemptive history. But Mark
9:9 says, "As they came down from the mountain, [Jesus]
commanded them that they should tell no one the things
they had seen, till the Son of Man had risen from the dead."

Can you imagine how difficult that would have been?
They had just witnessed the most incredible thing anyone
had ever seen, but they weren't allowed to tell anyone else
about it. It was a formidable restraint to put upon them.

After all, the disciples—and these three in particular—
were constantly arguing about who was the greatest among
them. The subject seemed never very far from their thoughts
(and they are about to give evidence of that just a few verses
further into Mark's narrative). So it must have been exceedingly difficult for them not to use this experience as
ammunition for their own case. They might have come
down the mountain and said to the rest of the disciples,
"Guys, guess where we have been? We were up there on the
mountain and guess who showed up? Elijah and Moses!"
They had been given a glimpse of the kingdom. They had
seen things that never could be seen or known by anyone.
They had a vivid preview of the glory to come. How difficult it must have been to keep this experience to themselves!

It does seem to have fueled the debate about who was
the greatest. Later in the chapter, Mark says they came to
Capernaum. "And when He was in the house He asked
them, 'What was it you disputed among yourselves on the

road?'" (Mark 9:33). Jesus did not ask because He needed the *information;* He was looking for a *confession.* He knew exactly what they were talking about.

But they were embarrassed. So "they kept silent, for on the road they had disputed among themselves who would be the greatest" (v. 34). It's not hard to understand how the argument began. Peter, James, and John, brimming with confidence after their mountaintop experience, surely felt that now they had the inside track. They had seen things so wonderful that they were not permitted even to speak of them. And each one now was probably looking for some sign that he was the greatest of the three—possibly arguing among themselves about things like which one was standing closer to Jesus when He was trans-figured, reminding Peter that he was rebuked by a voice from heaven, and so on.

But when Jesus asked them what they were arguing about, they instantly grew silent. They realized they were wrong to debate these things. Their own consciences obviously were smiting them. That is why they couldn't bear to admit what all the fuss was about.

Of course, Jesus knew. And He seized the opportunity to teach them once again. "He sat down, called the twelve, and said to them, 'If anyone desires to be first, he shall be last of all and servant of all.' Then He took a little child and set him in the midst of them. And when He had taken him in His arms, He said to them, 'Whoever receives one of these little children in My name receives Me; and whoever receives Me, receives not Me but Him who sent Me'" (vv. 35–37).

They had it backward. If they wanted to be first in the kingdom, they needed to be servants. If they wanted to be truly great, they needed to be more childlike. Instead of arguing and fighting with each other, instead of putting each other down, instead of rejecting each other and exalting themselves, they needed to take the role of a servant.

It was a lesson about love. "Love does not parade itself, is not puffed up; does not behave rudely, does not seek its own" (1 Corinthians 13:4–5). Love is manifested in service to one another, not by lording it over each other.

This apparently cut John to the heart. It was a serious rebuke, and John obviously got the message. This is where we find the only time John speaks in the synoptic Gospels: "Now John answered Him, saying, 'Teacher, we saw someone who does not follow us casting out demons in Your name, and we forbade him because he does not follow us'" (v. 38). This was sectarianism—rebuking a man for ministering in Jesus' name just because he didn't belong to the group. This shows the intolerance of John, a Son of Thunder. This was the narrowness, the ambition, the desire to have the status all for himself and not share it with anybody else—all of which too often characterized John in his younger years.

Here we see clearly that John was not a passive personality. He was aggressive. He was competitive. He condemned a man who was ministering in the name of Jesus, just because the man wasn't part of the group. John had actually stepped in and tried to shut down this man's ministry for no other reason than that.

I am inclined to think John confessed this to Jesus because he was convicted. I believe he was feeling the sting of Jesus' rebuke, and he spoke these words as a penitent. Something in John was beginning to change, and he was beginning to see his own lack of love as undesirable. The fact that John made this confession was indicative of the transformation that was taking place in him. His conscience was bothering him. He was being tenderized. He had always been zealous and passionate for the truth, but now the Lord was teaching him to love. This is a major turning point in his life and thinking. He was beginning to understand the necessary equilibrium between love and truth.

The kingdom needs men who have courage, ambition, drive, passion, boldness, and a zeal for the truth. John certainly had all of those things. But to reach his full potential, he needed to balance those things with love. I think this episode was a critical rebuke that started to move him toward becoming the apostle of love he ultimately became.

John was always committed to truth, and there's certainly nothing wrong with that, but it is not enough. Zeal for the truth must be balanced by love for people. Truth without love has no decency; it's just *brutality*. On the other hand, love without truth has no character; it's just *hypocrisy*.

Many people are just as imbalanced as John was, only in the other direction. They place too much emphasis on the love side of the fulcrum. Some are merely ignorant; others are deceived; still others simply do not care about what is true. In each case, truth is missing, and all they are left with is error, clothed in a shallow, tolerant sentimentality. It is a poor substitute for genuine love. They talk a lot about love and tolerance, but they utterly lack any concern for the truth. Therefore even the "love" they speak of is a tainted love. Real love "does not rejoice in iniquity, but rejoices in the truth" (1 Corinthians 13:6).

On the other hand, there are many who have all their theological ducks in a row and know their doctrine but are unloving and self-exalting. They are left with truth as cold facts, stifling and unattractive. Their lack of love cripples the power of the truth they profess to revere.

The truly godly person must cultivate both virtues in

equal proportions. If you could wish for anything in your sanctification, wish for that. If you pursue anything in the spiritual realm, pursue a perfect balance of truth and love. Know the truth, and uphold it in love.

In Ephesians 4, the apostle Paul describes this balance of truth and love as the very pinnacle of spiritual maturity. He writes of "the measure of the stature of the fullness of Christ" (v. 13). He is speaking about full maturity, perfect Christlikeness. This is how he epitomizes the goal for which we ought to strive: "[That] speaking the truth in love, [we] may grow up in all things into Him who is the head; Christ" (v. 15). This is what it means to share Christ's likeness. He is the perfect expression of truth and the perfect expression of love. He is our model.

Manifesting both truth and love is possible only for the mature believer who has grown into the measure of the stature that belongs to the fullness of Christ. That is how true spiritual maturity is defined. The authentically Christlike person knows the truth and speaks it in love. He knows the truth as Christ has revealed it, and he loves as Christ loves.

As a mature apostle, John learned the lesson well. His brief second epistle offers vivid proof of how well he balanced the twin virtues of truth and love. Throughout that epistle, John repeatedly couples the concepts of love and truth. He writes, "To the elect lady and her children, whom I love in truth" (v. 1). He says, "I rejoiced greatly that I have found some of your children walking in truth" (v. 4), and then he spends the first half of the epistle urging them to walk in love as well. He reminds them of the New Commandment, which of course is not really new, but simply restates the commandment we have heard from the beginning: "that we love one another" (v. 5).

So the first half of this short epistle is all about love. He urges this woman and her children not only to continue walking in truth, but also to remember that the sum and substance of God's law is *love*. There is therefore no greater truth than love. The two are inseparable. After all, the First and Great Commandment is this: "You shall love the LORD your God with all your heart, with all your soul, and with all your mind" (Matthew 22:37). And the second is like unto it: "You shall love your neighbor as yourself" (v. 39). In other words, love is what real truth is ultimately all about.

But John balances that emphasis on love in the second half of the epistle by urging this woman not to compromise her love by receiving and blessing false teachers who undermine the truth. Genuine love is not some saccharine sentiment that disregards the truth and tolerates everything:

> For many deceivers have gone out into the world who do not confess Jesus Christ as coming in the flesh. This is a deceiver and an antichrist. Look to yourselves, that we do not lose those things we worked for, but that we may receive a full reward. Whoever transgresses and does not abide in the doctrine of Christ does not have God. He who abides in the doctrine of Christ has both the Father and the Son. If anyone comes to you and does not bring this doctrine, do not receive him into your house nor greet him; for he who greets him shares in his evil deeds. (vv. 7–11)

John is no longer calling down fire from heaven against the enemies of truth, but he cautions this lady not to go to the other extreme, either. She is not to open her home or even bestow a verbal blessing on people who make a living twisting and opposing the truth.

Of course, the apostle is not urging this woman to be

unkind or abusive to anyone. We are commanded to do good to those who persecute us, be kind to those who hate us, bless those who oppose us, and pray for those who despitefully use us (Luke 6:27–28). But our blessing on our enemies must stop short of encouraging or assisting a false teacher who is corrupting the gospel.

Love and truth must be maintained in perfect balance. Truth is never to be abandoned in the name of love. But love is not to be deposed in the name of truth. That is what John learned from Christ, and it gave him the balance he so desperately needed.

HE LEARNED THE BALANCE OF AMBITION AND HUMILITY

In his youth, John had some ambitious plans for himself. It's not inherently wrong to aspire to have influence or to desire success. But it is wrong to have selfish motives, as John apparently did. And it is especially wrong to be ambitious without also being humble.

Here is another important balance that must be struck, or else a virtue turns into a vice. Ambition without humility becomes egotism, or even megalomania.

In Mark 10, one chapter after the incident where John rebuked a man who was ministering in Jesus' name, we find Mark's description of how James and John approached Jesus with their request to be seated on His right and left in the kingdom. Ironically, Jesus had just reiterated the importance of humility. In Mark 10:31, He told them, "Many who are first will be last, and the last first." (Remember, this was virtually the same statement that provoked John's earlier confession in Mark 9. There, Jesus had set a child in their midst as an object lesson about humility and told them, "If anyone desires to be first, he shall be last of all and servant of all"—Mark 9:35.) Jesus was simply reiterating the same lesson He had taught them over and over about humility.

Nonetheless, just a few verses later (10:35–37), Mark records that James and John came to Jesus with their infamous request for the chief thrones. In our study of the apostle James, we looked at Matthew's account of this incident, and we learned that James and John actually enlisted their mother to intercede for them. Here we discover that they were seeking this favor secretly, because the other disciples learned of it afterward (v. 41).

Coming as it did on the heels of so many admonitions from Jesus about humility, the brothers' request shows amazing audacity. It reveals how utterly devoid of true humility they were.

Again, there is nothing wrong with ambition. In fact, there was nothing intrinsically wrong with James and John's desire to sit next to Jesus in the kingdom. Who would not desire that? The other disciples certainly desired it, and that is why they were displeased with James and John. Jesus did not rebuke them for that desire per se.

Their error was in desiring *to obtain* the position more than they desired *to be worthy* of such a position. Their ambition was untempered by humility. And Jesus had repeatedly made clear that the highest positions in the kingdom are reserved for the most humble saints on earth. Notice His response in verses 42–45:

> Jesus called them to Himself and said to them, "You know that those who are considered rulers over the Gentiles lord it over them, and their great ones exercise authority over them. Yet it shall not be so among you; but whoever desires

to become great among you shall be your servant. And whoever of you desires to be first shall be slave of all. For even the Son of Man did not come to be served, but to serve, and to give His life a ransom for many."

Those who want to be great must first learn to be humble. Christ Himself was the perfection of true humility. Furthermore, His kingdom is advanced by humble service, not by politics, status, power, or dominion. This was Jesus' whole point when He set the child in the midst of the disciples and talked to them about the childlikeness of the true believer. Elsewhere, He had also told them, "Everyone who exalts himself will be humbled, and he who humbles himself will be exalted" (Luke 18:14). Even before that, He had said,

When you are invited by anyone to a wedding feast, do not sit down in the best place, lest one more honorable than you be invited by him; and he who invited you and him come and say to you, "Give place to this man," and then you begin with shame to take the lowest place. But when you are invited, go and sit down in the lowest place, so that when he who invited you comes he may say to you, "Friend, go up higher." Then you will have glory in the presence of those who sit at the table with you. For whoever exalts himself will be humbled, and he who humbles himself will be exalted. (Luke 14:8–11)

Again and again, Christ had emphasized this truth: If you want to be great in the kingdom, you must become the servant of all.

It is astonishing how little this truth penetrated the disciples' consciousness, even after three years with Jesus. But on the final night of His earthly ministry, not one of them had the humility to pick up the towel and washbasin and perform the task of a servant (John 13:1–17). So Jesus did it Himself.

John *did* eventually learn the balance between ambition and humility. In fact, humility is one of the great virtues that comes through in his writings.

Throughout John's Gospel, for instance, he never once mentions his own name. (The only "John" who is mentioned by name in the Gospel of John is John the Baptist.) The apostle John refuses to speak of himself in reference to himself. Instead, he speaks of himself in reference to Jesus. He never paints himself in the foreground as a hero, but uses every reference to himself to honor Christ. Rather than write his name, which might focus attention on him, he refers to himself as "the disciple whom Jesus loved" (John 13:23; 20:2; 21:7, 20), giving glory to Jesus for having loved such a man. In fact, he seems utterly in awe of the marvel that Christ loved him. Of course, according to John 13:1–2, Jesus loved *all* His apostles to perfection. But it seems there was a unique way in which John gripped this reality, and he was humbled by it.

In fact, it is John's Gospel alone that records in detail Jesus' act of washing the disciples' feet. It is clear that Jesus' own humility on the night of His betrayal made a lasting impression on John.

John's humility also comes through in the gentle way he appeals to his readers in every one of his epistles. He calls them "little children," "beloved"—and he includes himself as a brother and fellow child of God (cf. 1 John 3:2). There's a tenderness and compassion in those expressions that shows his humility. His last contribution to the canon was the book of Revelation, where he describes himself as "your brother and companion in the tribulation and kingdom and patience of Jesus Christ" (Revelation 1:9). Even though he was the last remaining apostle and the patriarch of the church, we never find him lording it over anyone.

Somewhere along the line, John's ambition found balance in humility. John himself was mellowed—although he remained courageous, confident, bold, and passionate.

HE LEARNED THE BALANCE OF SUFFERING AND GLORY

As noted, in his early years, the apostle John had a thirst for glory and an aversion to suffering. His thirst for glory is seen in his desire for the chief throne. His aversion to suffering is seen in the fact that he and the other apostles forsook Jesus and fled on the night of His arrest (Mark 14:20).

Both desires are perfectly understandable. After all, John had seen Jesus' glory firsthand on the Mount of Transfiguration, and he treasured Jesus' promise that he would share that glory (Matthew 19:28–29). How could he *not* desire such a blessing? On the other hand, no one but a madman enjoys suffering.

There was nothing inherently sinful about John's desire to participate in the glory of Jesus' eternal kingdom. Christ had promised him a throne and an inheritance in glory. Moreover, it is my conviction that when we see Christ's glory fully unveiled we will finally understand why the glory of Christ is the greatest reward of all in heaven. One glimpse of Jesus in the fullness of His glory will be worth all the pain and sorrow and suffering we have endured here on earth (cf. Psalm 17:15; 1 John 3:2). Participation in Christ's glory is therefore a fitting desire for every child of God.

But if we desire to participate in heavenly glory, we

must also be willing to partake of earthly sufferings. This was the apostle Paul's desire: "That I may know Him and the power of His resurrection, and the fellowship of His sufferings, being conformed to His death" (Philippians 3:10). Paul wasn't saying he had a masochistic lust for pain; he was simply recognizing that glory and suffering are inseparable. Those who desire the reward of glory must be willing to endure the suffering.

Suffering is the price of glory. We are "heirs of God and joint heirs with Christ, if indeed we suffer with Him, that we may also be glorified together" (Romans 8:17). Jesus taught this principle again and again. "If anyone desires to come after Me, let him deny himself, and take up his cross, and follow Me. For whoever desires to save his life will lose it, but whoever loses his life for My sake will find it" (Matthew 16:24–25). "Unless a grain of wheat falls into the ground and dies, it remains alone; but if it dies, it produces much grain. He who loves his life will lose it, and he who hates his life in this world will keep it for eternal life" (John 12:24–25).

Suffering is the prelude to glory. Our suffering as believers is the assurance of the glory that is yet to come (1 Peter 1:6–7). And "the sufferings of this present time are not worthy to be compared with the glory which shall be revealed in us" (Romans 8:18). Meanwhile, those who thirst for glory must balance that desire with a willingness to suffer.

All the disciples needed to learn this. Remember, they *all* wanted the chief seats in glory. But Jesus said there is a price for those seats. Not only are those seats reserved for the humble, but those who sit in those seats will first be prepared for the place of honor by enduring the humility of suffering. That is why Jesus told James and John that before they would receive any throne at all, they would be required to "drink the cup that I drink, and be baptized with the baptism that I am baptized with" (Mark 10:38).

How eagerly and how naively James and John assured the Lord that they would be able to drink of the cup He would drink and be baptized with a baptism of suffering! "They said to Him, 'We are able'" (v. 39). At that moment they had no real clue what they were volunteering for. They were like Peter, boasting that they would follow Jesus to the death—but when faced with the opportunity, they all forsook Him and fled.

Thankfully, Christ does not regard such failures as final. All eleven of the disciples fled on the night of Jesus' betrayal and arrest. But every one of them was recovered, and every one of them ultimately learned to suffer willingly for Christ's sake.

In fact, all of them except John suffered and ultimately died for the faith. They were martyred one by one in the prime of life. John was the only disciple who lived to old age. But he suffered, too, in ways the others did not. He was still enduring earthly anguish and persecution long after the others were already in glory.

On the night of Jesus' arrest, John probably began to understand the bitterness of the cup he would have to drink. We know from his account of Jesus' trial that he and Peter followed Jesus to the house of the high priest (John 18:15). There he watched as Jesus was bound and beaten. As far as we know, John was the only disciple who was an actual eyewitness to Jesus' crucifixion. He was standing close enough to the cross for Jesus to see him (John 19:26). He probably watched as the Roman soldiers drove in the nails. He was there when a soldier finally pierced his Lord's side with a spear. And perhaps as he watched he remembered that he had agreed to partake of this same baptism. If so, he surely realized then and there how awful the cup was he had so easily volunteered to drink!

When John's brother James became the church's first martyr, John bore the loss in a more personal way than the others. As each of the other disciples was martyred one by one, John suffered the grief and pain of additional loss. These were his friends and companions. Soon he alone was left. In some ways, that may have been the most painful suffering of all.

Virtually all reliable sources in early church history attest to the fact that John became the pastor of the church the apostle Paul had founded at Ephesus. From there, during a great persecution of the church under the Roman Emperor Domitian (brother and successor of Titus, who destroyed Jerusalem), John was banished to a prison community on Patmos, one of the small Dodecanese Islands in the Aegean Sea off the west coast of modern Turkey. He lived in a cave there. It was while there that he received and recorded the apocalyptic visions described in the book of Revelation (cf. Revelation 1:9). I have been to the cave in which he is thought to have lived and in which he is believed to have written the Apocalypse. It was a harsh environment for an aged man. He was cut off from those whom he loved, treated with cruelty and reproach, and made to sleep on a stone slab with a rock for a pillow as the years passed slowly.

But John learned to bear suffering willingly. There is no complaint about his sufferings anywhere in his epistles or the book of Revelation. It is certain that he wrote Revelation under the most extreme kind of hardship and deprivation. But he makes scant mention of his difficulties, referring to himself as "both your brother and companion in the tribulation and kingdom and patience of Jesus Christ" (Revelation 1:9). Notice that in the same breath he mentioned "tribulation," he speaks of the patience that enabled him to bear his sufferings willingly. He was looking forward calmly to the day when he would partake in the promised glory of the kingdom. That is the right balance and a healthy perspective. He had learned to look beyond his earthly sufferings in anticipation of the heavenly glory.

John got the message. He learned the lessons. He grasped the character of Christ in a powerful way. And he became a choice human model of what righteous, Christlike character ought to be.

Powerful proof of this is seen in a vignette from the cross. Remember, John is the only one of the apostles whom the biblical record places as an eyewitness to the crucifixion. John himself describes the scene as Jesus looked down from the cross and saw His mother, Mary, along with her sister, another Mary (wife of Clopas), Mary Magdalene, and John (John 19:25). John writes, "When Jesus therefore saw His mother, and the disciple whom He loved standing by, He said to His mother, 'Woman, behold your son!' Then He said to the disciple, 'Behold your mother!' And from that hour that disciple took her to his own home" (vv. 26–27).

Obviously, John had learned the lessons he needed to learn. He had learned to be a humble, loving servant—or else Jesus would not have given him the care of His own mother. He told Peter, "Feed My sheep" (John 21:17). He told John, "Care for My mother." Several witnesses in early church history record that John never left Jerusalem and never left the care of Mary until she died.

John reminds me of many seminary graduates whom I have known, including myself as a younger man. I recall when I came out of seminary. I was loaded to the gills with truth but somewhat short on patience. It was a strong temptation to come blasting into the church, dump the truth on everyone, and expect an immediate response. I needed to learn patience, tolerance, mercy, grace, forgiveness, tenderness, compassion—all the characteristics of love. It is wonderful to be bold and thunderous, but love is the necessary balance. John is a superb model for such young men.

It may seem amazing that Jesus loved a man who wanted to burn up the Samaritans. He loved a man who was obsessed with status and position. He loved a man who forsook Him and fled rather than suffer for His sake. But in loving John, Jesus transformed him into a different man—a man who modeled the same kind of love Jesus had shown him.

We noted earlier that John used the word *truth* some forty-five times in his Gospel and epistles. But it is interesting that he also used the word *love* more than eighty times. Clearly, he learned the balance Christ taught Him. He learned to love others as the Lord had loved him. Love became the anchor and centerpiece of the truth he was most concerned with.

In fact, John's theology is best described as a theology of love. He taught that God is a God of love, that God loved His own Son, that God loved the world, that God is loved by Christ, that Christ loved His disciples, that Christ's disciples loved Him, that all men should love Christ, that we should love one another, and that love fulfills the law. Love was a critical part of every element of John's teaching. It was the dominant theme of his theology.

And yet his love never slid into indulgent sentimentality. To the very end of his life John was still a thunderous defender of the truth. He lost none of his intolerance for lies. In his epistles, written near the end of his life, he was still thundering out against errant Christologies, against anti-Christian deceptions, against sin, and against immorality. He was in that sense a Son of Thunder to the end. I think the Lord knew that the most powerful advocate of love needed to be a man who never compromised the truth.

Another favorite word of John's was *witness*. He used it nearly seventy times. He referrs to the witness of John the Baptist, the witness of Scripture, the witness of the Father, the witness of Christ, the witness of the miracles, the witness of the Holy Spirit, and the witness of the apostles. In each case, these were witnesses to the *truth*. So his love for the truth remained undiminished.

In fact, I am convinced John leaned on Jesus' shoulder (John 13:3), not only because he enjoyed the pure love his Lord gave him, but also because he wanted to hear every word of truth that came out of the mouth of Christ.

John died, by most accounts, around A.D. 98, during the reign of Emperor Trajan. Jerome says in his commentary on Galatians that the aged apostle John was so frail in his final days at Ephesus that he had to be carried into the church. One phrase was constantly on his lips: "My little children, love one another." Asked why he always said this, he replied, "It is the Lord's command, and if this alone be done, it is enough."

Thus the fishermen of Galilee—Peter, Andrew, James, and John—became fishers of men on a tremendous scale, gathering souls into the church. In a sense, they are still casting their nets into the sea of the world by their testimony in the Gospels and their epistles. They are still bringing multitudes of people to Christ. Although they were common men, theirs was an uncommon calling.

6

Philip—The Bean Counter

Philip answered Him, "Two hundred denarii worth of bread is not sufficient for them, that every one of them may have a little."

—John 6:7

IN THE FOUR BIBLICAL LISTS of the twelve apostles, the fifth name on every list is Philip. As we noted in chapter 2, this apparently signifies that Philip was the leader of the second group of four. As far as the biblical record is concerned, Philip plays something of a minor role compared to the four men in group one, but he nonetheless is mentioned on several occasions, so he emerges from the larger group of twelve as a distinct character in his own right.

Philip is a Greek name, meaning "lover of horses." He must also have had a Jewish name, because all twelve apostles were Jewish. But his Jewish name is never given. Greek civilization had spread through the Mediterranean after the conquests of Alexander the Great in the fourth century B.C., and many people in the Middle East had adopted the Greek language, Greek culture, and Greek customs. They were known as "Hellenists" (cf. Acts 6:1). Perhaps Philip came from a family of Hellenistic Jews. Custom would have dictated that he have a Hebrew name as well, but for whatever reasons, he seems to have used his Greek name exclusively. So we know him only as Philip.

Don't confuse him with Philip the deacon, the man we meet in Acts 6 who became an evangelist and led the Ethiopian eunuch to Christ. Philip the apostle was a completely different individual.

The apostle Philip "was from Bethsaida, the city of Andrew and Peter" (John 1:44). Since they were all God-fearing Jews, Philip probably grew up attending the same synagogue as Peter and Andrew. Because of the relationship that existed between them and the sons of Zebedee, Philip was possibly acquainted with all four. There is good biblical evidence that Philip, Nathanael, and Thomas were all fishermen from Galilee, because in John 21, after the resurrection, when the apostles returned to Galilee and Peter said, "I am going fishing" (John 21:3), the others who were there all answered, "We are going with you also." According to John 21:2, that group included "Simon Peter, Thomas called the Twin, Nathanael of Cana in Galilee, the sons of Zebedee, and two others of His disciples." The unnamed "two others" were most likely Philip and Andrew, because elsewhere they are always seen in the company of the men who are named in that passage.

If all seven of these men were professional fishermen, they were most likely all friends and close coworkers a long time before they followed Christ. This shows what a close-knit group the apostles were, with at least half of the group—including all the core members—having come from one small region, most likely engaged in the same occupation, and probably having known and befriended each other long before they became disciples.

In a sense that is somewhat surprising. We might have

expected Jesus to take a different approach in choosing the Twelve. After all, He was appointing them to the formidable task of being apostles, proxies for Him after He departed the earth, men with full power of attorney to speak and act on His behalf. You might think He would scour the whole earth to find the most gifted and qualified men. But instead, He singled out a small group of fishermen, a diverse yet common group of men with unexceptional talents and average abilities who already knew each other. And He said, "They will do."

All He really required of them was availability. He would draw them to Himself, train them, gift them, and empower them to serve Him. Because they would preach *Jesus'* message and do miracles by *His* power, these rugged fishermen were better suited to the task than a group of glittering prodigies trying to operate on their own talent might have been. After all, even these men behaved like prima donnas at times. So perhaps one of the reasons Christ selected and called this particular group is that for the most part they already got along well with one another. In any case, after already choosing Peter, Andrew, and John, Jesus located and called Philip, a native of the same little village from which Peter and Andrew originally hailed.

What do we know about Philip? Matthew, Mark, and Luke give no details at all about him. All the vignettes of Philip appear in the Gospel of John. And from John's Gospel, we discover that Philip was a completely different kind of person from either Peter, Andrew, James, or John. In John's narrative, Philip is often paired with Nathanael (also known as Bartholomew), so we can assume the two of them were close comrades. But Philip is singularly different from even his closest companion. He is unique among all the disciples.

Piecing together all that the apostle John records about him, it seems Philip was a classic "process person." He was a facts-and-figures guy—a by-the-book, practical-minded, non-forward-thinking type of individual. He was the kind who tends to be a corporate killjoy, pessimistic, narrowly focused, sometimes missing the big picture, often obsessed with identifying reasons things can't be done rather than finding ways to do them. He was predisposed to be a pragmatist and a cynic—and sometimes a defeatist—rather than a visionary.

HIS CALL

We first meet Philip in John 1, the day after Jesus had first called Andrew, John, and Peter. You will remember that Jesus had called those first three in the wilderness, where they were sitting at the feet of John the Baptist. John pointed them to the Messiah, and they left John to follow Jesus.

John writes, "The following day Jesus wanted to go to Galilee, and He found Philip and said to him, 'Follow Me'" (John 1:43). Apparently, Philip was also in the wilderness with John the Baptist, and before returning to Galilee, Jesus sought him out and invited him to join the other disciples.

Peter, Andrew, and John (and likely James as well) had more or less found Jesus. To be precise, they had been directed to Him by John the Baptist. So this is the first time we read that Jesus Himself actually sought and found one of them.

That is not to say He didn't sovereignly seek and call the rest. In fact, we know that He had chosen them all before the foundation of the world. In John 15:16, Jesus told them, "You did not choose Me, but I chose you and appointed you." But in the descriptions of how they first encountered Christ, this language is unique to the call of Philip. He is the first one whom Jesus physically sought out, and the first one to whom Jesus actually said, "Follow Me."

It is interesting, incidentally, to note that at the *end* of His earthly ministry, Jesus had to say, "Follow Me" to Peter (John 21:19, 22). Peter apparently still needed that encouragement after his failure on the night of Jesus' betrayal. But Philip was the first to hear and obey those words. From the outset, Jesus actively sought Philip. He found him. He invited him to follow. And He found in Philip an eager and willing disciple.

It is obvious that Philip already had a seeking heart. Of course, a seeking heart is always evidence that God is sovereignly drawing the person, for as Jesus said, "No one can come to Me unless the Father who sent Me draws him" (John 6:44); and again, "No one can come to Me unless it has been granted to him by My Father" (v. 65).

Philip's seeking heart is evident in how he responded to Jesus. "Philip found Nathanael and said to him, 'We have found Him of whom Moses in the law, and also the prophets, wrote; Jesus of Nazareth, the son of Joseph'" (John 1:45). Obviously, Philip and Nathanael, like the first four disciples, had been studying the Law and the Prophets and were seeking the Messiah. That is why they had all gone to the wilderness to hear John the Baptist in the first place. So when Jesus came to Philip and said, "Follow Me," his ears, his eyes, and his heart were already open, and he was prepared to follow.

Notice something interesting about the expression Philip used with Nathanael: *"We* have found *Him."* As far as Philip was concerned, he had found the Messiah rather than being found by Him. Here we see the classic tension between sovereign election and human choice. Philip's call is a perfect illustration of how both exist in perfect harmony. The Lord found Philip, but Philip felt he found the Lord. Both things were true from the human perspective. But from a biblical perspective, we know that God's choice is the determinative one. "You did not choose Me, but I chose you and appointed you" (John 15:16).

Still, from a human perspective—from *Philip's* point of view—this was the end of his search. By God's grace, he had been a faithful and true seeker. He was devoted to the Word of God, and he believed the Old Testament promise of a Messiah. Now he had found Him—or rather had been found by Him.

Philip not only had a seeking heart, but he also had the heart of a personal evangelist. His first response upon meeting Jesus was to find his friend Nathanael and tell him about the Messiah.

I am convinced, by the way, that friendships provide the most fertile soil for evangelism. When the reality of Christ is introduced into a relationship of love and trust that has already been established, the effect is powerful. And it seems that invariably, when someone becomes a true follower of Christ, that person's first impulse is to want to find a friend and introduce that friend to Christ. That dynamic is seen in Philip's spontaneous instinct to go find Nathanael and tell him about the Messiah.

The language Philip used betrayed his amazement at discovering who the Messiah was. The One of whom Moses wrote, and the One foretold by the prophets, was none other than "Jesus of Nazareth, the son of Joseph," a lowly carpenter's son.

Nathanael, as we shall see in the chapter that follows, was at first nonplused. "Nathanael said to him, 'Can anything good come out of Nazareth?'" (John 1:46).

Bethsaida was slightly north of Nazareth, but both were in Galilee, not far from each other. Nathanael himself came from Cana (John 21:2), a village just north of Nazareth. Nazareth by all measures would have been a more significant place than Cana, so there may have been some local rivalry reflected in Nathanael's skepticism.

But Philip was undaunted: "Come and see" (1:46). The ease with which Philip believed is remarkable. In human terms, no one had brought Philip to Jesus. He was like Simeon, "waiting for the Consolation of Israel, and the Holy Spirit was upon him" (Luke 2:25). He knew the Old Testament promises. He was ready. He was expectant. His heart was prepared. And he received Jesus gladly, unhesitatingly, as Messiah. No reluctance. No disbelief. It mattered not to him what kind of one-horse town the Messiah had grown up in. He knew instantly that he had come to the end of his search.

That is frankly out of character for Philip, and it reveals to what a great degree the Lord had prepared his heart. His *natural* tendency might have been to hold back, doubt, ask questions, and wait and see. As we are about to discover, he was not usually a very decisive person. But thankfully, in this case, He was already being drawn to Christ by the Father. And as Jesus said, "All that the Father gives Me *will* come to Me" (John 6:37, emphasis added).

THE FEEDING OF THE FIVE THOUSAND

Our next glimpse of Philip occurs in John 6, at the feeding of the five thousand. We referred to this episode in chapter 1. We took a closer look at it in chapter 3 when we studied the character of Andrew. We return now for another look at the feeding of the five thousand, this time through Philip's eyes. And here we discover what Philip as a natural man was like. We already know he was a student of the Old Testament. We know he interpreted it literally and believed in the Messiah. So when the Messiah came to him and said, "Follow Me," he embraced Jesus immediately and followed Him without hesitation. That was Philip's spiritual side. His heart was right. He was a man of faith. But often he was a man of *weak* faith.

Here his personality begins to show through. John describes how a great multitude had sought out Jesus and found Him on a mountainside with His disciples. As we saw in chapter 1, to say this was a crowd of five thousand doesn't do justice to the size of the multitude. John 6:10 says there were five thousand *men* in the crowd. There must have been several more thousand women and children. (Ten or twenty thousand would not be impossible). In any case, it was a huge throng, and according to Matthew 14:15, evening was approaching. The people needed to eat.

John 6:5 says, "Then Jesus lifted up His eyes, and seeing a great multitude coming toward Him, He said to Philip, 'Where shall we buy bread, that these may eat?'"

Why did He single Philip out and ask him? John says, "This He said to test him, for He Himself knew what He would do" (v. 6).

Philip was apparently the apostolic administrator—the bean counter. It is likely that he was charged with arranging meals and logistics. We know that Judas was in charge of keeping the money (John 13:29), so it makes sense that someone was also charged with coordinating the acquisition and distribution of meals and supplies. It was a task that certainly suited Philip's personality. Whether officially or unofficially, he seems to have been the one who was always concerned with organization and protocol. He was the type of person who in every meeting says, "I don't think we can do that"—the master of the impossible. And apparently, as far as he was concerned, almost everything fit into that category.

So Jesus was testing him. He wasn't testing him to find out what he was thinking; Jesus already knew that (cf. John 2:25). He wasn't asking for a plan; John says Jesus also already knew what He Himself was going to do. He was testing Philip so that Philip would reveal to himself what he was like. That is why Jesus turned to Philip, the classic administrative personality, and asked, "How do you propose to feed all these people?"

Of course, Jesus knew exactly what Philip was thinking. I believe Philip had already begun counting heads. When the crowd started moving in, he was already doing estimates. It was late in the day; this was a huge crowd; they were going to be hungry. And eating in those days was no easy thing. There were no fast-food franchises on that mountainside. So by the time Jesus asked the question, Philip already had his calculations prepared: "Philip answered Him, 'Two hundred denarii worth of bread is not sufficient for them, that every one of them may have a little'" (John 6:7). He had apparently been thinking through the difficulties of the food supply from the moment he first saw the crowd. Instead of thinking, *What a glorious occasion! Jesus is going to teach this crowd. What a tremendous opportunity for the Lord!*—all pessimistic Philip could see was the impossibility of the situation.

Philip had been there when the Lord created wine out of water (John 2:2). He had already seen numerous times when Jesus had healed people, including several creative and regenerative miracles. But when he saw that great crowd, he began to feel overwhelmed by the impossible. He lapsed into materialistic thinking. And when Jesus tested his faith, he responded with open unbelief. *It can't be done.*

From a purely human perspective, he was absolutely right. A denarius was one day's wages for a common laborer (cf. Matthew 20:2). In other words, between all the disciples—at least twelve of them and probably many more—they had no more than eight months' worth of a single day-laborer's wages to meet their own needs. That is not a large sum, considering all that had to be done to care for the disciples' own food and lodging. With such a small amount, they couldn't afford even a meager snack for so many people. Philip was probably thinking, *One denarius would buy twelve wheat biscuits. Barley's cheaper. So with one denarius we could buy twenty barley biscuits. If we get the small biscuits and break them in half . . . Nah, it simply can't be done.* He had already figured out that four thousand barley cakes would never be enough to go around. His thoughts were pessimistic, analytical, and pragmatic—completely materialistic and earthbound.

One of the supreme essentials of leadership is a sense of vision—and this is especially true for anyone whose Master is Christ. But Philip was obsessed with mundane matters and therefore overwhelmed by the impossibility of the immediate problem. He knew too much arithmetic to be adventurous. The reality of the raw facts clouded his faith. He was so obsessed with this temporal predicament that he was oblivious to the transcendental possibilities that lay in Jesus' power. He was so enthralled with common-sense calculations that he didn't see the opportunity the situation presented. He *should* have said, "Lord, if You want to feed them, feed them. I'm just going to stand back and watch how You do it. I know You can do it, Lord. You made wine at Cana and fed Your children manna in the wilderness. Do it. We will tell everyone to get in line, and You just make the food." That would have been the right response. But Philip was convinced it simply couldn't be done. The limitless supernatural power of Christ had completely escaped his thinking.

On the other hand, Andrew seemed to have a glimmer of the possible. He found one little boy with two pickled fish and five barley crackers and brought him to Christ. Even Andrew's faith was challenged by the colossal size of the logistical problem. He said to Jesus, "There is a lad here who has five barley loaves and two small fish, but what are they among so many?" (v. 9). Either Andrew had some faint ray of hope that Jesus would do *something* (because he brought the boy to Jesus anyway), or he was influenced by Philip's pessimism, and by this act supported the claim that the situation was impossible.

Either way, Philip lost the opportunity to see the reward of faith; and the action of Andrew (which probably indicated some meager degree of faith) was honored. As Jesus taught them elsewhere, "If you have faith as a mustard seed, you will say to this mountain, 'Move from here to there,' and it will move; and nothing will be impossible for you" (Matthew 17:20).

Philip needed to learn that lesson. *Everything* seemed impossible to him. He needed to set aside his materialistic, pragmatic, common-sense concerns and learn to lay hold of the supernatural potential of faith.

THE VISIT OF THE GREEKS

John 12 gives us another insight into Philip's character. Again, we see his overanalytical temperament. He was concerned too much about methods and protocol. He lacked boldness and vision. It made him too timid and too apprehensive. And when he has another opportunity to step out in faith, he misses it again.

John 12:20–21 says, "Now there were certain Greeks among those who came up to worship at the feast. Then they came to Philip, who was from Bethsaida of Galilee, and asked him, saying, 'Sir, we wish to see Jesus.'" These were either God-fearing Gentiles or full-fledged proselytes to Judaism who were coming to Jerusalem to worship God at the Passover. This was the final Passover of the Old Testament economy, during which Jesus Himself would be slain as the true Lamb of God. He was on His way to Jerusalem to die for the sins of the world.

These Greeks were very interested in Jesus. They sought out Philip in particular. Perhaps because of his Greek name, they thought he was the best contact. Or maybe they had learned that he was more or less the administrator of the group, the one who made all the arrangements on behalf of the disciples. Again we see that whether Philip held that position officially or by default, he seems to have been the one in charge of operations. So these men approached him to arrange a meeting with Jesus.

Philip, being the typical administrative type, probably carried around in his head a full manual of protocols and procedures. (In fact, if he was like many administrators I have known, he might have had an actual written policy manual, which he fastidiously devised and insisted on following to the letter. He strikes me as that kind of by-the-book type of person.) Somehow these Greeks knew he was the policy person, so they asked him to arrange a meeting with Jesus.

It was not a difficult or complex request. And yet Philip

seems to have been unsure what to do with them. If he checked the manual on Gentiles and Jesus, he might have noticed that Jesus said on one occasion when He sent the disciples out, "Do not go into the way of the Gentiles, and do not enter a city of the Samaritans. But go rather to the lost sheep of the house of Israel" (Matthew 10:5–6). On another occasion, Jesus said, "I was not sent except to the lost sheep of the house of Israel" (Matthew 15:24).

Was that principle meant to prohibit Gentiles from ever being introduced to Jesus? Of course not. Jesus was simply identifying the normal priority of His ministry: "to the Jew first and also to the Greek" (Romans 2:10). It was a general principle, not an ironclad law. Greeks and other Gentiles were expressly included among those to whom He ministered. Jesus Himself had originally revealed that He was the Messiah to a Samaritan woman. Although the focus of His ministry was to Israel first and foremost, He was, after all, the Savior of the world, not just Israel. "He came to His own, and His own did not receive Him. But as many as received Him, to them He gave the right to become children of God, to those who believe in His name" (John 1:11–12).

But people like Philip don't appreciate general rules of thumb; they want every rule to be rigid and inviolable. There was no protocol in the manual for introducing Greeks to Jesus. And Philip wasn't prepared to do something so unconventional.

Nonetheless, Philip had a good heart. So he took the Greeks to Andrew. Andrew would bring anyone to Jesus. So "Philip came and told Andrew, and in turn Andrew and Philip told Jesus" (John 12:22). Obviously, Philip was not a decisive man. There was no precedent for introducing Gentiles to Jesus, so he enlisted Andrew's help before doing anything. This way no one could fault Philip for not going by the book. After all, Andrew was *always* bringing people to Jesus. Andrew would get the blame if anyone objected.

We may safely assume that Jesus received the Greeks gladly. He Himself said, "the one who comes to Me I will by no means cast out" (John 6:37). John 12 doesn't record anything about Jesus' meeting with the Greeks except the discourse Jesus gave on that occasion:

> Jesus answered them, saying, "The hour has come that the Son of Man should be glorified. Most assuredly, I say to you, unless a grain of wheat falls into the ground and dies, it remains alone; but if it dies, it produces much grain. He who loves his life will lose it, and he who hates his life in this world will keep it for eternal life. If anyone serves Me, let him follow Me; and where I am, there My servant will be also. If anyone serves Me, him My Father will honor." (12:23–26)

In short, He preached the gospel to them and invited them to become His disciples.

Was it the right thing to bring those Greeks to Jesus? Absolutely. Jesus Himself welcomes all comers to drink freely of the water of life (Revelation 22:17). It would have been wrong to turn those men away. Philip seemed to know that in his heart, even if his head was obsessed with protocol and procedure.

THE UPPER ROOM

Our final glimpse of Philip comes just a short time later, in the Upper Room with the disciples on the occasion of the

Last Supper. It is significant to note that this was the last night of Jesus' earthly ministry—the eve of His crucifixion. The formal training of the Twelve had officially come to an end. And yet their faith was still pathetically weak. This was the same evening when they sat around the table arguing about who was the greatest, rather than taking up the towel and basin and washing Jesus' feet. Many of the most important lessons He had taught them appear to have gone unheeded. As Jesus said, they were "foolish . . . and slow of heart to believe" (Luke 24:25).

This was true of Philip in particular. Of all the foolish, impetuous, heartbreakingly ignorant statements that occasionally escaped the lips of the disciples, none was more disappointing than Philip's remark in the Upper Room.

That night Jesus' heart was heavy. He knew what lay ahead for Him on the following day. He knew His time with the disciples was at an end, and although they still seemed rather ill-prepared from a purely human perspective, He was going to send the Holy Spirit to empower them as His witnesses. His earthly work with them was nearly finished. He was sending them out as sheep in the midst of wolves (cf. Matthew 10:16). So He was eager to comfort them and encourage them about the Holy Spirit, who would come to empower them.

He urged them not to be troubled in their hearts and promised them He was going to prepare a place for them (John 14:1–2). He further promised to return to receive them to Himself so that they could be where He was going (v. 3). Then He added this: "And where I go you know, and the way you know" (v. 4). Obviously, the *where* was heaven, and the *way* there was the way He had outlined in the gospel.

But they were slow to catch his meaning, and Thomas probably spoke for them all when he said, "Lord, we do not know where You are going, and how can we know the way?" (v. 5).

Jesus said to him, "I am the way, the truth, and the life. No one comes to the Father except through Me" (John 14:6). By now His meaning certainly ought to have been clear. He was going to the Father in heaven, and the only way there for them was through faith in Christ. Of course, that is one of the key biblical texts about the exclusivity of Christ. He was expressly teaching that no one can go to heaven who does not trust Him and embrace Him alone as Savior. He is the way—the *only* way—to the Father.

Then Jesus added an explicit claim about His own deity: "If you had known Me, you would have known My Father also; and from now on you know Him and have seen Him" (John 14:7). He was stating in the clearest possible language that He is God. Christ and His Father are of the same essence. To know Christ is to know the Father, because the different Persons of the Trinity are one in their very essence. Jesus *is* God. To see Him is to see God. They had both seen Him and known Him, so in effect, they already knew the Father as well.

It was at this point that Philip spoke up: "Philip said to Him, 'Lord, show us the Father, and it is sufficient for us'" (v. 8).

"Show us the Father"? How could Philip say such a thing, immediately on the heels of what Jesus had just told them? This is profoundly sad. You would think that by the time Philip got to this point, so long a time after he had begun to follow Jesus, he would know better. All that time, he had heard Jesus teach. He had witnessed untold numbers of miracles. He had seen people healed of the worst kinds of diseases and deformities. He had been there when Jesus cast out demons. He had spent time in intimate

fellowship with Christ, day in and day out, twenty-four hours a day, seven days a week, for many months. If he had truly known Christ, he would have known the Father also (v. 7). How could he now say, "Show us the Father"? Where had he been?

"Jesus said to him, 'Have I been with you so long, and yet you have not known Me, Philip? He who has seen Me has seen the Father; so how can you say, "Show us the Father"?' " (v. 9). What did Philip think had been going on for the past two or three years? How could Philip of all people, who had responded with such enthusiastic faith at the beginning, be making a request like this at the end? Where was his faith?

Jesus asked him, "Do you not believe that I am in the Father, and the Father in Me? The words that I speak to you I do not speak on My own authority; but the Father who dwells in Me does the works. Believe Me that I am in the Father and the Father in Me, or else believe Me for the sake of the works themselves" (vv. 10–11). Jesus was saying in essence, "I am to the Father what you are to Me. I am the Father's apostle. I am His *shaliah*. I act with His full power of attorney.

"More than that, I am one with the Father. I am in the Father and the Father is in Me. We share the same divine essence."

Notice the appeal: "Do you not believe? . . . *Believe*"! Philip had already embraced Jesus as Messiah. Christ was urging him to take his faith to its logical conclusion: Philip was already in the presence of the living and eternal God Himself. He did not need to see any greater miracles. He did not need any more dramatic proof. "Show us the Father"? What was he saying? What did he think Jesus had been doing?

For three years Philip had gazed into the very face of God, and it still was not clear to him. His earthbound thinking, his materialism, his skepticism, his obsession with mundane details, his preoccupation with business details, and his small-mindedness had shut him off from a full apprehension of whose presence he had enjoyed.

Philip, like the other disciples, was a man of limited ability. He was a man of weak faith. He was a man of imperfect understanding. He was skeptical, analytical, pessimistic, reluctant, and unsure. He wanted to go by the book all the time. Facts and figures filled his thoughts. So he was unable to grasp the big picture of Christ's divine power, Person, and grace. He was slow to understand, slow to trust, and slow to see beyond the immediate circumstances. He still wanted more proof.

If we were interviewing Philip for the role to which Jesus called him, we might say, "He's out. You can't make him one of the twelve most important people in the history of the world."

But Jesus said, "He's exactly what I'm looking for. My strength is made perfect in weakness. I'll make him into a preacher. He'll be one of the founders of the church. I will make him a ruler in the kingdom and give him an eternal reward in heaven. And I will write his name on one of the twelve gates of the New Jerusalem." Thankfully, the Lord uses people like Philip—lots of them.

Tradition tells us that Philip was greatly used in the spread of the early church and was among the first of the apostles to suffer martyrdom. By most accounts he was put to death by stoning at Heliopolis, in Phrygia (Asia Minor), eight years after the martyrdom of James. Before his death, multitudes came to Christ under his preaching.

Philip obviously overcame the human tendencies that

so often hampered his faith, and he stands with the other apostles as proof that "God has chosen the foolish things of the world to put to shame the wise, and God has chosen the weak things of the world to put to shame the things which are mighty; and the base things of the world and the things which are despised God has chosen, and the things which are not, to bring to nothing the things that are, that no flesh should glory in His presence" (1 Corinthians 1:27–29).

7

NATHANAEL—THE GUILELESS ONE

Nathanael answered and said to Him, "Rabbi, You are the Son of God! You are the King of Israel!"

—JOHN 1:49

PHILIP'S CLOSEST COMPANION, NATHANAEL, is listed as Bartholomew in all four lists of the Twelve. In the Gospel of John he is always called Nathanael. *Bartholomew* is a Hebrew surname meaning "son of Tolmai." *Nathanael* means "God has given." So he is Nathanael, son of Tolmai, or Nathanael Bar-Tolmai.

The synoptic Gospels and the book of Acts contain no details about Nathanael's background, character, or personality. In fact, they each mention him only once—when they list all twelve disciples. John's Gospel features Nathanael in just two passages: in John 1, where his call is recorded, and in John 21:2, where he is named as one of those who returned to Galilee and went fishing with Peter after Jesus' resurrection and before the ascension.

According to John 21:2, Nathanael came from the small town of Cana in Galilee, the place where Jesus did

His first miracle, changing water into wine (John 2:11). Cana was very close to Jesus' own hometown, Nazareth.

As we saw in the previous chapter, Nathanael was brought to Jesus by Philip immediately after Philip was sought and called by Christ. Philip and Nathanael were apparently close friends, because in each of the synoptic Gospels' lists of the twelve apostles, the names of Philip and Bartholomew are linked. In the earliest church histories and many of the early legends about the apostles, their names are often linked as well. Apparently, they were friends throughout the years of their journey with Christ. Not unlike Peter and Andrew (who were so often named together as brothers) and James and John (who likewise were brothers), we find these two always side by side, not as brothers, but as close companions.

Virtually everything we know about Nathanael Bar-Tolmai comes from John's account of his call to discipleship. Remember, that event took place in the wilderness, shortly after Jesus' baptism, when John the Baptist pointed to Christ as the Lamb of God who takes away the sin of the world (John 1:29). Andrew, John, and Peter (and possibly James as well) were the first to be called (vv. 35–42). The next day, having purposed to go to Galilee, Jesus sought out Philip and called him, too (v. 43).

According to verse 45, "Philip found Nathanael." They were obviously friends. Whether this was a business relationship, a family relationship, or just a social relation-ship, Scripture does not say. But Philip obviously was close to Nathanael, and he knew Nathanael would be interested in the news that the long-awaited Messiah had finally been identified. In fact, he couldn't wait to share the news with him. So he immediately pursued him and brought him to Jesus.

Apparently Nathanael was found by Philip in or near the same place where Philip was found by the Lord Himself. The brief description of how Nathanael came to Jesus is full of insight into his character. From it, we learn quite a lot about what kind of person Nathanael was.

HIS LOVE OF SCRIPTURE

One striking fact about Nathanael is obvious from how Philip announced to him that he had found the Messiah: "Philip found Nathanael and said to him, 'We have found Him of whom Moses in the law, and also the prophets, wrote'" (John 1:45). Obviously, the truth of Scripture was something that mattered to Nathanael. Philip knew Nathanael, so he knew Nathanael would be intrigued by the news that Jesus was the One prophesied by Moses and the prophets in Scripture. Therefore, when Philip told Nathanael about the Messiah whom he had found, he did so from the standpoint of Old Testament prophecy. The fact that Philip introduced Jesus this way suggests that Nathanael *knew* the Old Testament prophecies.

This probably indicates that Nathanael and Philip were students of the Old Testament together. In all likelihood, they had come to the wilderness to hear John the Baptist together. They had a shared interest in the fulfillment of Old Testament prophecy. Philip obviously knew the news of Jesus would excite Nathanael.

Notice that he didn't say to him, "I found a man who has a wonderful plan for your life." He didn't say, "I found a man who will fix your marriage and your personal problems and give your life meaning." He didn't appeal to Nathanael on the basis of how Jesus might make

Nathanael's life better. Philip spoke of Jesus as the fulfillment of Old Testament prophecies, because he knew that would pique Nathanael's interest. Nathanael, as an eager student of the Old Testament, was already a seeker after divine truth.

Incidentally, it appears that all the apostles, with the exception of Judas Iscariot, were to some degree already true seekers after divine truth before they met Jesus. They were already being drawn by the Spirit of God. Their hearts were open to the truth and hungry to know it. They were sincere in their love for God and their desire to know the truth and receive the Messiah. In that sense they were very different from the religious establishment, which was dominated by hypocrisy and false piety. The disciples were the real thing.

Most likely, Philip and Andrew had pored long hours over the Scripture together, searching the Law and the Prophets to discern the truth about the coming of the Messiah. And the fact that they were so well trained in Scripture no doubt explains why they were so quick to respond to Jesus. In Nathanael's case, this would become especially evident. He was able to recognize Jesus clearly and instantly because he had a clear understanding of what the Scripture said about Him. Nathanael knew what the promises said, so he recognized the fulfillment when he saw it. He knew Him of whom Moses and the prophets had written, and he recognized Jesus as that One after the briefest of conversations with Him. Nathanael sized Him up quickly and received Him on the spot. The reason that was possible was because Nathanael had been such a diligent student of Scripture.

Philip told him, "[It is] Jesus of Nazareth, the son of Joseph." "Jesus" was a common name—*Y'shua* in its Aramaic form. It is the same name rendered "Joshua" in the Old Testament. It meant, significantly, "Yahweh is salvation" ("for He will save His people from their sins"—Matthew 1:21). Philip was using the expression "son of Joseph" as a kind of surname—"Jesus Bar-Joseph," just as his friend was "Nathanael Bar-Tolmai." That is how people were commonly identified. (It was the Hebrew equivalent of modern surnames like Josephson or Johnson. People throughout history have been identified this way—with surnames derived from their fathers.)

There must have been a certain amount of surprise in the voice of Philip. It was as if he were saying, "You'll never believe this, but Jesus, son of Joseph, the carpenter's son from Nazareth is the Messiah!"

HIS PREJUDICE

Verse 46 then gives us a further insight into Nathanael's character. Although he was as a student of Scripture and a searcher for the true knowledge of God; although he had strong spiritual interests and had been faithful, diligent, and honest in his devotion to the Word of God; he was human. He had certain prejudices. Here is his response: "Can anything good come out of Nazareth?"

He *might* have said, "As I read the Old Testament, Micah the prophet says Messiah comes out of Bethlehem [Micah 5:2], not Nazareth." He could have said, "But Philip, Messiah is identified with Jerusalem, because He's going to reign in Jerusalem." But the depth of his prejudice comes through in the words he chose: "Can anything good come out of Nazareth?"

That was not a rational or biblical objection; it was

based on sheer emotion and bigotry. It reveals what contempt Nathanael had for the whole town of Nazareth. Frankly, Cana wasn't such a prestigious town, either. To this day it is utterly unexceptional. Unless you are looking for the shrine built on the supposed location where Jesus turned water to wine, you probably won't want to go there. Cana was off the beaten track, while Nazareth was at least at a crossroads. To travel from the Mediterranean to Galilee, people traveled through Nazareth. One of the main routes going north and south between Jerusalem and Lebanon passed through Nazareth. No one ever "passed through" Cana; Cana was a side trip from everything. So the lack of anything attractive in Nazareth doesn't fully explain Nathanael's prejudice. His remark probably reflects some kind of civic rivalry between Nazareth and Cana.

Nazareth was a rough town. Its culture was largely unrefined and uneducated. (It is still much the same today.) It isn't a particularly picturesque place. Although it has a nice setting on the slopes of the hills in Galilee, it is not a very memorable town, and it was even less so in Jesus' time. The Judaeans looked down on all Galileans, but even the Galileans looked down on the Nazarenes. Nathanael, though he came from an even more lowly village, was simply echoing the Galileans' general contempt for Nazareth. This was the same kind of regional pride that might cause someone from, say, Cleveland, to speak with disdain about Buffalo.

Here again we see that God takes pleasure in using the common, weak, and lowly things of this world to confound the wise and powerful (cf. 1 Corinthians 1:27). He even calls people from the most despised locations. He can also take a flawed person who is blinded by prejudice, and He can change that person into someone used to transform the world. In the end the only explanation is the power of God, so all the glory goes to Him.

It was inconceivable to Nathanael that the Messiah would come out of a tacky place like Nazareth. It was an uncultured place, full of evil, corrupt, and populated with sinful people. Nathanael simply did not anticipate that anything good could come from there. And he was oblivious to the rather obvious fact that he himself had come from an equally contemptible community.

Prejudice is ugly. Generalizations based on feelings of superiority, not on fact, can be spiritually debilitating. Prejudice cuts a lot of people off from the truth. As a matter of fact, much of the nation of Israel rejected their Messiah because of prejudice. They did not believe their Messiah should come out of Nazareth, either. It was inconceivable to them that the Messiah and all His apostles would come from Galilee. They mocked the apostles as uneducated Galileans. The Pharisees taunted Nicodemus by saying, "Are you also from Galilee? Search and look, for no prophet has arisen out of Galilee" (John 7:52). They did not like the fact that Jesus spoke against the religious establishment from Jerusalem. And from the religious leaders down to the people sitting in the synagogues, it was to some degree their prejudice that caused them to reject Him. This happened even in Jesus' own hometown. They derided Jesus as Joseph's son (Luke 4:22). He was without honor even in His own country, because he was nothing but a carpenter's son (v. 24). And the entire synagogue in Nazareth—His own synagogue, where He had grown up—were so filled with prejudice against Him that after He preached a single message to them, they tried to take Him to a cliff on the edge of town and throw Him off to kill Him (vv. 28–29).

Prejudice skewed their view of the Messiah. The people of Israel were prejudiced against Him as a Galilean and a Nazarene. They were prejudiced against Him as an uneducated person outside the religious establishment. They were particularly prejudiced against His message. And their prejudice against Him shut them off from the gospel. They refused to hear Him because they were cultural and religious bigots.

John Bunyan understood the danger of prejudice. In his famous allegory *The Holy War,* he pictures the forces of Immanuel coming to bring the gospel to the town of Mansoul. They directed their assault on Mansoul at the Ear-gate, because faith comes by hearing. But Diabolus, the enemy of Immanuel and His forces, wanted to hold Mansoul captive to hell. So Diabolus decided to meet the attack by stationing a special guard at Ear-gate. The guard he chose was "one old Mr. Prejudice, an angry and ill-conditioned fellow." According to Bunyan, they made Mr. Prejudice "captain of the ward at that gate, and put under his power sixty men, called deaf men; men advantageous for that service, forasmuch as they mattered no words of the captains, nor of the soldiers." That is a very vivid description of precisely how many people are rendered impervious to the truth of the gospel. Their own prejudice renders them deaf to the truth.

Men's ears are closed to the gospel by many kinds of prejudice—racial prejudice, social prejudice, religious prejudice, and intellectual prejudice. Prejudice effectively caused the majority of the Jewish nation to remain deaf to the Messiah. Satan had stationed at the Ear-gate of Israel Mr. Prejudice and his band of deaf men. That is why when Jesus "came to His own, . . . His own did not receive Him" (John 1:11).

John Bunyan used the imagery of deafness. The apostle Paul used the metaphor of blindness: "If our gospel is veiled, it is veiled to those who are perishing, whose minds the god of this age has blinded, who do not believe, lest the light of the gospel of the glory of Christ, who is the image of God, should shine on them" (2 Corinthians 4:3–4). Rendered deaf and blind by prejudice against the truth, they missed the message. It's still that way today.

Nathanael lived in a society that was prejudicial by temperament. In reality, all sinful people are. We make prejudicial statements. We draw prejudiced conclusions about individuals, classes of people, and whole societies. Nathanael, like the rest of us, had that sinful tendency. And his prejudice caused him at first to be skeptical when Philip told him the Messiah was a Nazarene.

Fortunately, his prejudice wasn't strong enough to keep him from Christ. "Philip said to him, 'Come and see'" (v. 46). That is the right way to deal with prejudice: Confront it with the facts. Prejudice is feeling-based. It is subjective. It does not necessarily reflect the reality of the matter. So the remedy for prejudice is an honest look at objective reality—"come and see."

And Nathanael went. Fortunately, his prejudiced mind was not as powerful as his seeking heart.

HIS SINCERITY OF HEART

The most important aspect of Nathanael's character is expressed from the lips of Jesus. Jesus knew Nathanael already. He "had no need that anyone should testify of man, for He knew what was in man" (John 2:25). So His first words upon seeing Nathanael were a powerful commendation of Nathanael's character. Jesus saw Nathanael coming toward Him and said of him, "Behold, an Israelite indeed, in whom is no deceit!" (John 1:47).

Can you imagine a more wonderful thing than to have words of approval like that come out of the mouth of Jesus? It would be one thing to hear that at the end of your life, along with, "Well done, good and faithful servant; you have been faithful over a few things, I will make you ruler over many things. Enter into the joy of your lord" (cf. Matthew 25:21, 23). We often hear eulogies at funerals that extol the virtues of the deceased. But how would you like Jesus to say that about you from the very start?

This speaks volumes about Nathanael's character. He was pure-hearted from the beginning. Certainly, he was human. He had sinful faults. His mind was tainted by a degree of prejudice. But His heart was not poisoned by deceit. He was no hypocrite. His love for God, and His desire to see the Messiah, were genuine. His heart was sincere and without guile.

Jesus refers to him as "an Israelite indeed." The word in the Greek text is *alethos,* meaning "truly, genuinely." He was an authentic Israelite.

This is not a reference to his physical descent from Abraham. Jesus was not talking about genetics. He was linking Nathanael's status as a true Israelite to the fact that he was without deceit. His guilelessness is what defined him as a true Israelite. For the most part, the Israelites of Jesus' day were not real, because they were hypocrites. They were phonies. They lived life with a veneer of spirituality, but it was not real, and therefore they were not genuine spiritual children of Abraham. Nathanael, however, was real.

In Romans 9:6–7, the apostle Paul says, "For they are not all Israel who are of Israel, nor are they all children because they are the seed of Abraham." In Romans 2:28–29, he writes, "He is not a Jew who is one outwardly, nor is circumcision that which is outward in the flesh; but he is a Jew who is one inwardly; and circumcision is that of the heart, in the Spirit, not in the letter; whose praise is not from men but from God."

Here was an authentic Jew, one of the true spiritual offspring of Abraham. Here was one who worshiped the true and living God without deceit and without hypocrisy. Nathanael was the authentic item. Jesus would later say, in John 8:31, "If you abide in My word, you are My disciples indeed." The Greek word is the same—*alethos*.

Nathanael was a true disciple from the start. There was no hypocrisy in him. This is very unusual, and it was particularly rare in first-century Israel. Remember, Jesus indicted the entire religious establishment of His day as hypocrites. Matthew 23:13–33 records an amazing diatribe against the scribes and Pharisees in which Jesus calls them hypocrites from every possible angle. The synagogues were full of hypocrites, too. From the highest leaders to the people on the street, hypocrisy was a plague on that culture. But here was a true, nonhypocritical Jew. Here was a man whose heart was circumcised, cleansed of defilement. His faith was authentic. His devotion to God was real. He was without guile, not like the scribes and Pharisees. He was a truly righteous man—flawed by sin as we all are—but justified before God through a true and living faith.

HIS EAGER FAITH

Because his heart was sincere and his faith was real, Nathanael overcame his prejudice. His response to Jesus and the narrative that follows reveal his true character. At first, he was simply amazed that Jesus seemed to know anything about him. "Nathanael said to Him, 'How do You know me?'" (John 1:48).

We have to assume that Nathanael was still questioning whether this Man could truly be the Messiah. It was not that he questioned Philip's judgment; Philip was his friend, so he surely knew enough about Philip to know that Philip—the indecisive process-person—wouldn't have made any hasty judgment. It was certainly not that he questioned Scripture or that he was prone to skepticism. It was just that this man from Nazareth did not seem to fit the picture of the Messiah in Nathanael's mind. Jesus was the son of a carpenter, a no-name, non-descript man from a town that had no connection to any prophecy. (Nazareth did not even exist in the Old Testament.) And now Jesus had spoken to him as if he knew all about him and could even see inside his heart. Nathanael was just trying to come to grips with it all.

"How do You know me?" He might have meant, "Are You just flattering me? Are You trying to make me one of Your followers by paying me compliments? How could You possibly know what is in my heart?"

"Jesus answered and said to him, 'Before Philip called you, when you were under the fig tree, I saw you.'" (v. 48). This put a whole different spin on things. This was not flattery; it was omniscience! Jesus wasn't physically present to see Nathanael under the fig tree; Nathanael knew that. Suddenly he realized he was standing in the presence of Someone who could see into his very heart with an omniscient eye.

What was the significance of the fig tree? It was most likely the place where Nathanael went to study and meditate on Scripture. Houses in that culture were mostly small, one-room affairs. Most of the cooking was done inside, so a fire was kept burning even in the summer. The house could get full of smoke and stuffy. Trees were planted around houses to keep them cool and shaded. One of the best trees to plant near a house was a fig tree, because it bore wonderful fruit and gave good shade. Fig trees grow to a height of only about fifteen feet. They have a fairly short, gnarled trunk, and their branches are low and spread as far as twenty-five or thirty feet. A fig tree near a house provided a large, shady, protected place outdoors. If you wanted to escape the noise and stifling atmosphere of the house, you could go outside and rest under its shade. It was a kind of private outdoor place, perfect for meditation, reflection, and solitude. No doubt that is where Nathanael went to study Scripture and pray.

In effect, Jesus was saying, "I know the state of your heart because I saw you under the fig tree. I knew what you were doing. That was your private chamber. That is where you would go to study and pray. That's where you would go to meditate. And I saw you in that secret place. I knew what you were doing." It was not only that Jesus saw his *location*, but that He saw his *heart* as well. He knew the sincerity of Nathanael's character because He saw right into him when he was under the fig tree.

That was enough for Nathanael. He "answered and said to Him, 'Rabbi, You are the Son of God! You are the King of Israel!' " (v. 49).

John's whole Gospel was written to prove that Jesus is the Son of God (John 20:31). John's first words are a powerful declaration of Jesus' deity ("In the beginning was the Word, and the Word was with God, and the Word was God.") Every point in his Gospel is designed to prove that

Jesus is the Son of God—sharing the same essence as God—by highlighting His miracles, His sinless character, the divine wisdom of His teaching, and His attributes, which are the very attri-butes of God. John is writing to show the many ways in which Jesus manifested Himself as God. And here in the first chapter he gives the testimony of Nathanael that this Jesus is the omniscient Son of God. He is of the very same essence as God.

Remember, this is the very same truth Nathanael's friend Philip still hadn't quite grasped two years later, because he said to Jesus in the Upper Room, "Show us the Father" (John 14:8–9). What Philip didn't get until the end, his friend Nathanael understood at the very start.

Nathanael knew the Old Testament. He was familiar with what the prophets had said. He knew whom to look for. And now, regardless of the fact that Jesus came from Nazareth, His omniscience, His spiritual insight, His ability to read the heart of Nathanael was enough to convince Nathanael that He was indeed the true Messiah.

Nathanael's familiarity with the Old Testament messianic prophecies is clearly seen in his reply to Jesus ("You are the Son of God! You are the King of Israel!"). Psalm 2 clearly indicated that the Messiah would be the Son of God. Many Old Testament prophecies spoke of Him as "King of Israel," including Zephaniah 3:15 ("The LORD has taken away your judgments, He has cast out your enemy. The King of Israel, the LORD, is in your midst; You shall see disaster no more") and Zechariah 9:9 ("Rejoice greatly, O daughter of Zion! Shout, O daughter of Jerusalem! Behold, your King is coming to you; He is just and having salvation, lowly and riding on a donkey, a colt, the foal of a donkey"). Micah 5:2, the same verse that predicted His birth in Bethlehem, referred to him as "The

One to be Ruler in Israel, whose goings forth are from of old, from everlasting"—identifying Him not only as King but also as the Eternal One. So when Nathanael saw proof of Jesus' omniscience, he instantly recognized Him as the promised Messiah, the Son of God and King of Israel.

Nathanael was like Simeon, who lifted up the infant Jesus and said, "Lord, now You are letting Your servant depart in peace, according to Your word; for my eyes have seen Your salvation which You have prepared before the face of all peoples, a light to bring revelation to the Gentiles, and the glory of Your people Israel" (Luke 2:29–32). He recognized Jesus instantly as the One he had been waiting for. Nathanael, a careful student of Scripture, was a true Jew who waited for the Messiah and knew that when He came He would be Son of God and King. He was never one of the half-committed. He came to full understanding and total commitment on day one.

"Jesus answered and said to him, 'Because I said to you, "I saw you under the fig tree," do you believe? You will see greater things than these.' And He said to him, 'Most assuredly, I say to you, hereafter you shall see heaven open, and the angels of God ascending and descending upon the Son of Man'" (John 1:51). He affirmed Nathanael's faith and promised that he would see even greater things than a simple show of Jesus' omniscience. If one simple statement about the fig tree was enough to convince Nathanael that this was the Son of God and the King of Israel, he had not seen anything yet. From here on out, everything he would see would enrich and enlarge his faith.

Most of the disciples struggled just to come to the place where Nathanael stood after his first meeting with Christ. But for Nathanael, the ministry of Christ only affirmed what he already knew to be true. How wonderful to see someone so trustworthy and trusting from the very beginning, so that for him the whole three years with Jesus was just an unfolding panorama of supernatural reality!

In the Old Testament, Jacob had a dream in which "a ladder was set up on the earth, and its top reached to heaven; and there the angels of God were ascending and descending on it" (Genesis 28:12). Jesus' words to Nathanael were a reference to that Old Testament account. *He* was the ladder. And Nathanael would see the angels of God ascending and descending upon Him. In other words, Jesus *is* the ladder that connects heaven and earth.

That's all we know about Nathanael from Scripture. Early church records suggest that he ministered in Persia and India and took the gospel as far as Armenia. There is no reliable record of how he died. One tradition says he was tied up in a sack and cast into the sea. Another tradition says he was crucified. By all accounts, he was martyred like all the apostles except John.

What we *do* know is that Nathanael was faithful to the end because he was faithful from the start. Everything he experienced with Christ and whatever he experienced after the birth of the New Testament church ultimately only made his faith stronger. And Nathanael, like the other apostles, stands as proof that God can take the most common people, from the most insignificant places, and use them to His glory.

8

MATTHEW—THE TAX COLLECTOR; AND THOMAS—THE TWIN

> *As Jesus passed on from there, He saw a man named Matthew sitting at the tax office. And He said to him, "Follow Me." So he arose and followed Him.*
>
> —MATTHEW 9:9

> *Then Thomas, who is called the Twin, said to his fellow disciples, "Let us also go, that we may die with Him."*
>
> —JOHN 11:16

A S WE HAVE SEEN ALL ALONG, one of the facts that stands out in the lives of all twelve apostles is how ordinary and unrefined they were when Jesus met them. All twelve, with the exception of Judas Iscariot, were from Galilee. That whole region was predominantly rural, consisting of small towns and villages. Its people were not elite. They were not known for their education. They were the commonest of the common. They were fishermen and farmers.

Such were the disciples as well. Christ deliberately

passed over those who were aristocratic and influential and chose men mostly from the dregs of society.

That is how it has always been in God's economy. He exalts the humble and lays low those who are proud. "Out of the mouth of babes and nursing infants [He has] ordained strength" (Psalm 8:2). "For He brings down those who dwell on high, the lofty city; He lays it low, He lays it low to the ground, He brings it down to the dust. The foot shall tread it down; the feet of the poor and the steps of the needy" (Isaiah 26:5–6). God told Israel, "I will leave in your midst a meek and humble people, and they shall trust in the name of the LORD" (Zephaniah 3:12). "Thus says the Lord GOD: 'Remove the turban, and take off the crown; nothing shall remain the same. Exalt the humble, and humble the exalted'" (Ezekiel 21:26).

It should be no surprise, then, that Christ disdained religious elitism. The religious leaders of Jesus' day (like the vast majority of religious celebrities even today) were blind leaders of the blind. Most members of the Jewish establishment in Jesus' day were so spiritually blind that when the Messiah came and did miracles before their eyes, they still did not see Him as the Messiah. They saw Him rather as an interloper and an intruder. They regarded Him as an enemy. And from the very outset, from the first time He preached in public, they sought a way to have Him murdered (Luke 4:28–29).

In the end, it was the chief priests and ruling council of Israel who led the crowd in a cry for Jesus' blood. The religious establishment hated Him. So it is no wonder that when the time came for Jesus to choose and appoint apostles, He looked away from the religious elite and chose instead simple men of faith who were, by every earthly standard, commonplace.

It wasn't that the self-righteous religious leaders did not believe in Jesus' miracles. Nowhere on the pages of the Gospel record did anyone ever deny the *reality* of Jesus' miracles. Who could deny them? There were too many, and they had been done too publicly to be dismissed by even the most skeptical gainsayers. Of course, some desperately tried to attribute Jesus' miracles to the power of Satan (Matthew 12:24). No one, however, ever denied that the miracles were *real*. Anyone could see that He had the power to cast out demons and do miracles at will. No one could honestly question whether He truly had power over the supernatural world.

But what irritated the religious leaders was not the miracles. They could have lived with the fact that He could walk on water or that He could make food to feed thousands of people. What they could *not* tolerate was being called sinners. They would not acknowledge themselves as poor, prisoners, blind, and oppressed (Luke 4:18). They were too smugly self-righteous. So when Jesus came (as John the Baptist had come before Him) preaching repentance and saying they were sinners, wretched, poor, blind, lost people under the bondage of their own iniquity, needing forgiveness and cleansing—they could not and would not tolerate that. Therefore it was ultimately because of His *message* that they hated Him, vilified Him, and finally executed Him.

That is precisely why when it came time for Him to appoint apostles, He chose lowly, ordinary men. These were men who were not reluctant to acknowledge their own sinfulness.

MATTHEW, THE PUBLICAN

In all likelihood, none of the Twelve was more notorious as a sinner than Matthew. He is called by his Jewish name, "Levi the son of Alphaeus," in Mark 2:14. Luke refers to him as "Levi" in Luke 5:27–29, and as "Matthew" when he lists the Twelve in Luke 6:15 and Acts 1:13.

Matthew, of course, is the author of the Gospel that bears his name. For that reason, we might expect to have a lot of detail about this man and his character. But the fact of the matter is that we know very little about Matthew. The only thing we know for sure is he was a humble, self-effacing man who kept himself almost completely in the background throughout his lengthy account of Jesus' life and ministry. In his entire Gospel he mentions his own name only two times. (Once is where he records his call, and the other is when he lists all twelve apostles.)

Matthew was a tax collector—a publican—when Jesus called him. That is the *last* credential we might expect to see from a man who would become an apostle of Christ, a top leader in the church, and a preacher of the gospel. After all, tax collectors were the most despised people in Israel. They were hated and vilified by all of Jewish society. They were deemed lower than Herodians (Jews loyal to the Idumean dynasty of Herods) and more worthy of scorn than the occupying Roman soldiers. Publicans were men who had bought tax franchises from the Roman emperor and then extorted money from the people of Israel to feed the Roman coffers and to pad their own pockets. They often strong-armed money out of people with the use of thugs. Most were despicable, vile, unprincipled scoundrels.

Matthew 9:9 records the call of this man. It comes out of nowhere, completely catching the reader by surprise: "As

Jesus passed on from [Capernaum], He saw a man named Matthew sitting at the tax office. And He said to him, 'Follow Me.' So he arose and followed Him." That is the only glimpse of Matthew we have from his own Gospel.

Matthew goes on in the next few verses to say, "Now it happened, as Jesus sat at the table in the house, that behold, many tax collectors and sinners came and sat down with Him and His disciples" (v. 10). Luke reveals that this was actually an enormous banquet that Matthew himself held at his own house in Jesus' honor. It seems he invited a large number of his fellow tax collectors and various other kinds of scoundrels and social outcasts to meet Jesus. As we saw in the case of Philip and Andrew, Matthew's first impulse after following Jesus was to bring his closest friends and introduce them to the Savior. He was so thrilled to have found the Messiah that he wanted to introduce Jesus to everyone he knew. So he held a large banquet in Jesus' honor and invited them all.

Luke records what happened on that occasion: "Then Levi gave Him a great feast in his own house. And there were a great number of tax collectors and others who sat down with them. And their scribes and the Pharisees complained against His disciples, saying, 'Why do You eat and drink with tax collectors and sinners?' Jesus answered and said to them, 'Those who are well have no need of a physician, but those who are sick. I have not come to call the righteous, but sinners, to repentance'" (Luke 5:29–32).

Why did Matthew invite tax gatherers and other lowlifes? Because they were the only kind of people he knew. They were the only ones who would associate with a man like Matthew. He didn't know any of the social elite well enough to invite them to his house. He was a tax collector, and tax collectors were on the same level socially as harlots (Matthew 21:32). For a *Jewish* man like Matthew to be a tax collector was even worse. His occupation made him a traitor to the nation, a social pariah, the rankest of the rank. He would also have been a religious outcast, forbidden to enter any synagogue.

Therefore Matthew's only friends were the riffraff of society—petty criminals, hoodlums, prostitutes, and their ilk. They were the ones he invited to his house to meet Jesus. Jesus and the apostles, according to Matthew's own account, gladly came and ate with such people.

Of course, the people of the religious establishment were outraged and scandalized. They wasted no time voicing their criticism to the disciples. But Jesus replied by saying sick people are the very ones who need a physician. He had not come to call the self-righteous, but sinners, to repentance. In other words, there was nothing He could do for the religious elite as long as they insisted on keeping up their pious, hypocritical veneer. But people like Matthew who were prepared to confess their sin could be forgiven and redeemed.

It is interesting to note that three tax collectors are specifically mentioned in the Gospels, and each one of them found forgiveness. There was Zaccheus, in Luke 19:2–10; the publican mentioned in the parable of Luke 18:10–14; and Matthew. Furthermore, Luke 15:1 says that "all the tax collectors and the sinners drew near to Him to hear Him." Luke 7:29 says after Jesus commended John the Baptist's ministry, that "when all the people heard Him, even the tax collectors justified God, having been baptized with the baptism of John." Jesus admonished the religious leaders with these words: "Assuredly, I say to you that tax collectors and harlots enter the kingdom of God before you. For John came to you in the way of righteousness, and you did not believe him; but tax collectors and harlots believed him; and when you saw it, you did not afterward relent and believe him" (Matthew 21:31–32).

The parable of the publican and the sinner in Luke 18:10–14 might well have been based on an actual incident. Jesus said,

> Two men went up to the temple to pray, one a Pharisee and the other a tax collector. The Pharisee stood and prayed thus with himself, "God, I thank You that I am not like other men; extortioners, unjust, adulterers, or even as this tax collector. I fast twice a week; I give tithes of all that I possess." And the tax collector, standing afar off, would not so much as raise his eyes to heaven, but beat his breast, saying, "God, be merciful to me a sinner!" I tell you, this man went down to his house justified rather than the other; for everyone who exalts himself will be humbled, and he who humbles himself will be exalted.

Notice that the tax collector stood "afar off." He had to. He would not have been permitted past the court of the Gentiles in the temple. In fact, tax collectors had to keep their distance from any group, because they were so hated. The Jewish Talmud taught that it was righteous to lie and deceive a tax collector, because that was what a professional extortioner deserved.

Obviously, tax collectors had a certain amount that was legitimate to collect for the government (cf. Matthew 22:21; Romans 13:7). But there was an unspoken agreement with the Roman emperor that they could assess whatever other fees and additional taxes they could collect, and they were allowed to keep a percentage for themselves.

There were two kinds of tax collectors, the *Gabbai* and the *Mokhes*. The Gabbai were general tax collectors. They collected property tax, income tax, and the poll tax. These taxes were set by official assessments, so there was not as much graft at this level. The Mokhes, however, collected a duty on imports and exports, goods for domestic trade, and virtually anything that was moved by road. They set tolls on roads and bridges, they taxed beasts of burden and axles on transport wagons, and they charged a tariff on parcels, letters, and whatever else they could find to tax. Their assessments were often arbitrary and capricious.

There were two kinds of Mokhes—the Great Mokhes and the Little Mokhes. A Great Mokhes stayed behind the scenes and hired others to collect taxes for him. (Zaccheus was apparently a Great Mokhes—a "chief tax collector"—Luke 19:2). Matthew was evidently a Little Mokhes, because he manned a tax office where he dealt with people face to face (Matthew 9:9). He was the one the people saw and resented most. He was the worst of the worst. No self-respecting Jew in his right mind would ever choose to be a tax collector. He had effectively cut himself off not only from his own people, but also from his God. After all, since he was banned from the synagogue and forbidden to sacrifice and worship in the temple, he was in essence worse off religiously than a Gentile.

Therefore it must have been a stunning reality to Matthew when Jesus chose him. It came out of the blue. By Matthew's own account, Jesus saw him sitting in the tax office and simply said, "Follow Me" (Matthew 9:9).

Matthew instantly and without hesitation "arose and followed Him." He abandoned the tax office. He left his toll booth and walked away from his cursed profession forever.

The decision was irreversible as soon as he made it. There was no shortage of money-grubbing piranha who coveted a tax franchise like Matthew's, and as soon as he stepped away, you can be sure that someone else stepped in and took over. Once Matthew walked away, he could never go back. Nor did he ever regret his decision.

What was it in a man like Matthew that caused him to drop everything at once like that? We might assume that he was a materialist. And at one time he must have been, or he never would have gotten into a position like that in the first place. So why would he walk away from everything and follow Jesus, not knowing what the future held?

The best answer we can deduce is that whatever Matthew's tortured soul may have experienced because of the profession he had chosen to be in, down deep inside he was a Jew who knew and loved the Old Testament. He was spiritually hungry. At some point in his life, most likely *after* he had chosen his despicable career, he was smitten with a gnawing spiritual hunger and became a true seeker. Of course, God was seeking and drawing *him,* and the draw was irresistible.

We know that Matthew knew the Old Testament very well, because his Gospel quotes the Old Testament ninety-nine times. That is more times than Mark, Luke, and John combined. Matthew obviously had extensive familiarity with the Old Testament. In fact, he quotes out of the Law, out of the Psalms, and out of the Prophets—every section of the Old Testament. So he had a good working knowledge of all the Scriptures that were available to him. He must have pursued his study of the Old Testament on his own, because he couldn't hear the Word of God explained in any synagogue. Apparently, in a quest to fill the spiritual void in his life, he had turned to the Scriptures.

He believed in the true God. And because he knew the record of God's revelation, he understood the promises of the Messiah. He must have also known about Jesus, because sitting on the crossroads in a tax booth, he would have heard information all the time about this miracle worker who was banishing disease from Palestine, casting demons out of people, and doing miracles. So when Jesus showed up and called him to follow Him, he had enough faith to drop everything and follow. His faith is clearly indicated not only in the immediacy of his response, but also in the fact that after following Jesus, he held this evangelistic banquet in his home.

This is virtually all we know of Matthew: He knew the Old Testament, he believed in God, he looked for the Messiah, he dropped everything immediately when he met Jesus, and in the joy of his new-found relationship, he embraced the outcasts of his world and introduced them to Jesus. He became a man of quiet humility who loved the outcasts and gave no place to religious hypocrisy—a man of great faith and complete surrender to the lordship of Christ. He stands as a vivid reminder that the Lord often chooses the most despicable people of this world, redeems them, gives them new hearts, and uses them in remarkable ways.

Forgiveness is the thread that runs through Matthew 9 after the account of Matthew's conversion. Of course, even as a tax collector, Matthew knew his sin, his greed, his betrayal of his own people. He knew he was guilty of graft, extortion, oppression, and abuse. But when Jesus said to him, "Follow Me," Matthew knew there was inherent in that command a promise of the forgiveness of his sin. His heart had long hungered for such forgiveness. And that is why he arose without hesitation and devoted the rest of his life to following Christ.

We know that Matthew wrote his Gospel with a Jewish audience in mind. Tradition says he ministered to the Jews both in Israel and abroad for many years before being martyred for his faith. There is no reliable record of how he was put to death, but the earliest traditions indicate he was burned at the stake. Thus this man who walked away from a lucrative career without ever giving it a second thought remained willing to give his all for Christ to the very end.

THOMAS, THE PESSIMIST

The final apostle in the second group of four is also a familiar name: Thomas. He is usually nicknamed "Doubting Thomas," but that may not be the most fitting label for him. He was a better man than the popular lore would indicate.

It probably is fair, however, to say that Thomas was a somewhat negative person. He was a worrywart. He was a brooder. He tended to be anxious and angst-ridden. He was like Eeyore in Winnie the Pooh. He anticipated the worst all the time. Pessimism, rather than doubt, seems to have been his besetting sin.

Thomas, according to John 11:16 (KJV), was also called "Didymus," which means "the twin." Apparently he had a twin brother or a twin sister, but his twin is never identified in Scriptures.

Like Nathanael, Thomas is mentioned only once each in the three synoptic Gospels. In each case, he is simply named with the other eleven apostles in a list. No details about him are given by Matthew, Mark, or Luke. We learn everything we know about his character from John's Gospel.

It becomes obvious from John's record that Thomas had a tendency to look only into the darkest corners of life. He seemed always to anticipate the worst of everything. Yet despite his pessimism, some wonderfully redeeming elements of his character come through in John's account of him.

John's first mention of Thomas is found in John 11:16.

It is a single verse, but it speaks volumes about Thomas's real character.

In this context, John is describing the prelude to the raising of Lazarus. Jesus had left Jerusalem because His life was in jeopardy there, and "He went away again beyond the Jordan to the place where John was baptizing at first, and there He stayed" (John 10:40). Great crowds of people came out to hear Jesus preach. John says, "And many believed in Him there" (v. 42). This may have been the most fruitful time of ministry the disciples had witnessed in all the time since they had begun to follow Christ. People were responsive. Souls were being converted. And Jesus was able to minister freely without the opposition of the religious rulers of Jerusalem.

But something happened to interrupt their time in the wilderness. John writes, "Now a certain man was sick, Lazarus of Bethany, the town of Mary and her sister Martha. It was that Mary who anointed the Lord with fragrant oil and wiped His feet with her hair, whose brother Lazarus was sick" (John 11:1–2). Bethany was on the outskirts of Jerusalem. And Jesus had formed a close and loving relationship with this little family who lived there. He loved them with a special affection. He had stayed with them, and they had provided for His needs.

Now His dear friend Lazarus was sick, and Mary and Martha sent word to Jesus saying, "Lord, behold, he whom You love is sick" (v. 3). They knew if Jesus came to see Lazarus, He would be able to heal him.

This presented a quandary. If Jesus went that close to Jerusalem, he was walking into the very teeth of the worst kind of hostility. John 10:39 says the Jewish leaders were seeking to seize Him. They were already determined to kill Him. He had eluded their grasp once already, but if He returned to Bethany, they were certain to find out, and they would try again to seize Him.

The disciples must have breathed a sigh of relief when Jesus answered, "This sickness is not unto death, but for the glory of God, that the Son of God may be glorified through it" (John 11:4). What He *meant,* of course, was that Lazarus's death would not be the *ultimate* result of his sickness. The Son of God would glorify Himself by raising Lazarus from the dead. Jesus knew, of course, that Lazarus would die. In fact, He knew the very hour of his death.

John writes, "Now Jesus loved Martha and her sister and Lazarus. So, when He heard that he was sick, He stayed two more days in the place where He was" (vv. 5–6). At first glance, that seems a strange juxtaposition of statements: Jesus loved Lazarus and his family, so He stayed put while Lazarus was dying. He deliberately tarried to give Lazarus time to die. But this *was* an act of love, because ultimately, the blessing they received when Lazarus was raised from the dead was a greater blessing than if he had merely been healed of his sickness. It glorified Jesus in a greater way. It strengthened their faith in Him immeasurably more. Therefore Jesus waited a couple of extra days so that Lazarus was already dead four days by the time He arrived (v. 39).

Of course, Jesus, with His supernatural knowledge, knew exactly when Lazarus died. That is *why* He waited. "Then after this He said to the disciples, 'Let us go to Judea again'" (v. 7).

The disciples thought this was crazy. They said, "Rabbi, lately the Jews sought to stone You, and are You going there again?" (v. 8). They frankly did not want to go back to Jerusalem. The ministry in the wilderness was phenomenal. In Jerusalem they all risked being stoned. Now was not a good time for a visit to Bethany, which was virtually within sight of the temple, where Jesus' bitterest enemies had their headquarters.

Jesus' answer is interesting. He gives them an illustration. "Are there not twelve hours in the day? If anyone walks in the day, he does not stumble, because he sees the light of this world. But if one walks in the night, he stumbles, because the light is not in him" (vv. 9–10). In other words, there was no need for Him to skulk around like a common criminal. He was determined to do His work in the bright light of day, because that's what you do in order *not* to stumble. Those who were walking in darkness are the ones in danger of stumbling—particularly the religious leaders who were secretly looking for a way to kill Him.

He said that to the disciples to calm them down. They obviously did not want to go back and die. But Jesus reassured them they had nothing to fear. And of course, He knew His time to die was in God's timing, not His enemies'. Our Lord made His purpose clear when He said, "Our friend Lazarus sleeps, but I go that I may wake him up" (v. 11).

The disciples missed His meaning. They said, "Lord, if he sleeps he will get well" (v. 12). If he's only asleep, why not let him rest? After all, Jesus had already said his sickness was not unto death. The disciples couldn't see the urgency of the situation. It sounded to them like Lazarus was already on the road to recovery.

"However, Jesus spoke of his death, but they thought that He was speaking about taking rest in sleep. Then Jesus said to them plainly, 'Lazarus is dead. And I am glad for your sakes that I was not there, that you may believe. Nevertheless let us go to him'" (vv. 13–15).

Now they understood. Jesus *had* to go back. He was determined to do so. There would be no talking Him out of it. To them, it must have seemed like the worst possible disaster. They were floundering in fear. They were convinced that if Jesus returned to Bethany, He would be killed. But He had made up His mind.

It was at this point that Thomas spoke up. Here is where we meet him for the first time in all the Gospel records. "Then Thomas, who is called the Twin, said to his fellow disciples, 'Let us also go, that we may die with Him'" (v. 16).

Now that is pessimistic, and that's typical for Thomas. But it is a heroic pessimism. He could see nothing but disaster ahead. He was convinced Jesus was heading straight for a stoning. But if that is what the Lord was determined to do, Thomas was grimly determined to go and die with Him. You have to admire his courage.

It is not easy to be a pessimist. It is a miserable way to live. An optimist might have said, "Let's go; everything will work out. The Lord knows what He is doing. He says we won't stumble. We will be fine." But the pessimist says, "He's going to die, and we're going to die with Him." Thomas at least had the courage to be loyal, even in the face of his pessimism. It is much easier for an optimist to be loyal. He always expects the best. It is hard for a pessimist to be loyal, because he is convinced the worst is going to happen. This is heroic pessimism. This is real courage.

Thomas was devoted to Christ. He may have been the equal to John in this regard. When we think about someone who loved Jesus and was intimate with Him, we usually think of John, because he was always near Jesus. But it is clear from this account that Thomas did not want to live without Jesus. If Jesus was going to die, Thomas was prepared to die with Him. In essence he says, "Guys, suck it up; let's go and die. Better to die and be with Christ than to be left behind."

Thomas was an example of strength to the rest of the apostles. It appears they collectively followed his lead at this point and said, "OK, let's go and die"—because they *did* go with Him to Bethany.

Thomas obviously had a deep devotion to Christ that could not be dampened even by his own pessimism. He had no illusion that following Jesus would be easy. All he could see were the jaws of death opening to swallow him. But he followed Jesus with an undaunted courage. He was resolved to die if necessary with his Lord rather than forsake Him. He would rather die than be left behind and separated from Christ.

Thomas's profound love for the Lord shows up again in John 14. You'll recall from our study of Philip that Jesus was telling them of His imminent departure. "I go to prepare a place for you" (John 14:2). "And where I go you know, and the way you know" (v. 4).

In verse 5 Thomas speaks: "Thomas said to Him, 'Lord, we do not know where You are going, and how can we know the way?'" Again we see his pessimism. In essence, he was saying, "You're leaving. We'll never get where you are going. We don't even know *how* to get there. How are we supposed to get there? It was a better plan for us to die with You, because then there's no separation. If we died together, we would all be together. But if You just go, how are we ever going to find You? We don't even know how to get there."

Here is a man with deep love. He is a man whose relationship with Christ was so strong that he never wanted to be severed from Him. His heart was broken as he heard Jesus speak of leaving them. He was shattered. The thought of losing Christ paralyzed him. He had become so attached to Jesus in those years that he would have been glad to die with Christ, but he could not think of living without Him. You have to admire his devotion to Christ.

This was overwhelming for Thomas. And his worst fears came to pass. Jesus died and he didn't.

We pick up the next picture of Thomas in John 20. After Jesus' death, all the disciples were in deep sorrow. But they all got together to comfort one another. Except for Thomas. John 20:24 says, "Thomas, called the Twin, one of the twelve, was not with them."

It is too bad he wasn't there, because Jesus came and appeared to them. They had locked themselves in a room somewhere (most likely the Upper Room in Jerusalem). John writes, "The doors were shut where the disciples were assembled, for fear of the Jews" (v. 19). Suddenly, although the doors and windows were sealed shut, "Jesus came and stood in the midst, and said to them, 'Peace be with you.' When He had said this, He showed them His hands and His side. Then the disciples were glad when they saw the Lord" (vv. 19–20).

Thomas missed the whole thing. Why wasn't he there? It is possible that he was so negative, so pessimistic, such a melancholy person, that he was absolutely destroyed, and he was probably off somewhere wallowing in his own misery. He could see only the worst of everything. Now his worst fear had been realized. Jesus was gone, and Thomas was sure he would never see Him again. He may have still been thinking he would never find the way to get where Jesus was. He was no doubt regretting the fact that he did not die with Jesus, as he had been so determined to do in the first place.

Thomas may well have felt alone, betrayed, rejected, forsaken. It was over. The One he loved so deeply was gone, and it tore his heart out. He was not in a mood to socialize. He was brokenhearted, shattered, devastated, crushed. He just wanted to be alone. He simply couldn't take the banter. He wasn't in a mood to be in a crowd, even with his friends.

"The other disciples therefore said to him, 'We have seen the Lord'" (v. 25). They were exuberant. They were ecstatic. They were eager to share the good news with Thomas.

But someone in the kind of mood Thomas was in was not going to be cheered up so easily. He was still being a hopeless pessimist. All he could see was the bad side of things, and this was just too good to be true. "So he said to them, 'Unless I see in His hands the print of the nails, and put my finger into the print of the nails, and put my hand into His side, I will not believe'" (v. 25).

It is because of that statement that he has been nick-named "Doubting Thomas." But don't be too hard on Thomas. Remember, the other disciples did not believe in the resurrection until they saw Jesus, either. Mark 16:10–11 says after Mary Magdalene saw Him, "She went and told those who had been with Him, as they mourned and wept. And when they heard that He was alive and had been seen by her, they did not believe." The two disciples on the road to Emmaus walked with Him a long distance before they even realized who He was. And then "they went and told it to the rest, but they did not believe them either" (v. 13). When Jesus showed up in the room where the disciples are gathered, "He showed them His hands and side" (John 20:20). *Then* they believed. So they were *all* slow to believe. What set Thomas apart from the other ten was not that his doubt was greater, but that his sorrow was greater.

John 20:26 says that eight days passed after Jesus appeared to the disciples again. Finally Thomas's ragged grief had eased a bit, apparently. Because when the apostles were returned to the room where Jesus appeared to them, this time Thomas was with them. Once again, "Jesus came, the doors being shut, and stood in the midst, and said, 'Peace to you!' " (v. 26).

No one needed to tell Jesus what Thomas had said, of course. He looked right at Thomas and said, "Reach your finger here, and look at My hands; and reach your hand here, and put it into My side. Do not be unbelieving, but believing" (v. 27). The Lord was amazingly gentle with him. Thomas had erred because he was more or less wired to be a pessimist. But it was the error of a profound love. It was provoked by grief, brokenheartedness, uncertainty, and the pain of loneliness. No one could feel the way Thomas felt unless he loved Jesus the way Thomas loved Him. So Jesus was tender with him. He understands our weaknesses (Hebrews 4:15). So He understands our doubt. He sympathizes with our uncertainty. He is patient with our pessimism. And while recognizing these as weaknesses, we must also acknowledge Thomas's heroic devotion to Christ, which made him understand that it would be better to die than to be separated from his Lord. The proof of his love was the profoundness of his despair.

Then Thomas made what was probably the greatest statement ever to come from the lips of the apostles: "My Lord and my God!" (v. 28). Let those who question the deity of Christ meet Thomas.

Suddenly, Thomas's melancholy, comfortless, negative, moody tendencies were forever banished by the appearance of Jesus Christ. And in that moment he was transformed into a great evangelist. A short time later, at Pentecost, along with the other apostles, he was filled with the Holy Spirit and empowered for ministry. He, like his comrades, took the gospel to the ends of the earth.

There is a considerable amount of ancient testimony

that suggests Thomas carried the gospel as far as India. There is to this day a small hill near the airport in Chennai (Madras), India, where Thomas is said to have been buried. There are churches in south India whose roots are traceable to the beginning of the church age, and tradition says they were founded under the ministry of Thomas. The strongest traditions say he was martyred for his faith by being run through with a spear—a fitting form of martyrdom for one whose faith came of age when he saw the spear mark in his Master's side and for one who longed to be reunited with his Lord.

TWO TRANSFORMED

It's interesting that God used a publican like Matthew and a pessimist like Thomas. Matthew was once the vilest of sinners—a wretched, despicable outcast. Thomas was a tender-hearted, moody, melancholy individual. But both of them were transformed by Christ in the same way He transformed the others. Are you beginning to get the idea of what kind of people God uses? He can use *anyone*. Personality, status, and family background are all immaterial. The one thing all these men except Judas had in common was a willingness to acknowledge their own sinfulness and look to Christ for grace. He met them with grace, mercy, and forgiveness and transformed their lives into lives that would glorify Him. He does that for all who truly trust Him.

9

JAMES—THE LESS;
SIMON—THE ZEALOT;
AND JUDAS (NOT ISCARIOT)—
THE APOSTLE WITH
THREE NAMES

*James the son of Alphaeus, and Simon called
the Zealot; Judas the son of James . . .*

—LUKE 6:15–16

THE FINAL GROUP OF FOUR APOSTLES is the least known to us, except for Judas Iscariot, who made himself notorious by selling Christ to be crucified. This group seems to have been less intimate with Christ than the other eight disciples. They are virtually silent in the Gospel narratives. Little is known about any of them, except the fact that they were appointed to be apostles. We'll deal with three of them in this chapter, and save Judas Iscariot, the traitor, for the final chapter.

It must be borne in mind that the apostles were men who gave up everything to follow Christ. Peter spoke for them all when he said, "See, we have left all and followed You" (Luke 18:28). They had left houses, jobs, lands, family, and friends to follow Christ. Their sacrifice was heroic.

With the exception of Judas Iscariot, they all became valiant and intrepid witnesses.

We don't actually see much of their heroism in the Gospel records, because the Gospel writers—two of them apostles (Matthew and John) and the other two (Mark and Luke) close friends of apostles—honestly portrayed their weaknesses as well as their strengths. The apostles are not presented to us as mythic figures, but as real people. They are not depicted as prominent celebrities, but as ordinary men. That is why, as far as the Gospel accounts are concerned, the apostles give color and life to the descriptions of Jesus' life, but they are rarely in the foreground. They are never major role players.

When they do come to the foreground, it is often to manifest doubt, disbelief, or confusion. Sometimes we see them thinking more highly of themselves than they ought to think. Sometimes they speak when they ought to remain silent and seem clueless about things they ought to have understood. Sometimes they exhibit more confidence in their own abilities and their own strengths than they should. So their shortcomings and weaknesses show up more often than their strengths. In that sense, the raw honesty of the Gospel accounts is amazing.

Meanwhile, there are very few manifestations of any great acts by the apostles. We are told that they were empowered to heal, raise the dead, and cast out demons, but even that is narrated in such a way as to highlight the apostles' imperfections (cf. Mark 9:14–29). The one place in all the Gospels where a specific apostle does something truly extraordinary is when Peter began to walk on water—but he immediately found himself sinking.

The Gospel records simply do not portray these men as heroes. Their heroism played out after Jesus went back to heaven, sent the Holy Spirit, and empowered them. Suddenly we begin to see them acting differently. They are strong and courageous. They perform great miracles. They preach with a newfound boldness. But even then, the biblical record is sparse. Primarily, all we see are Peter, John, and later the apostle Paul (who was added to their number as "one born out of due time"—1 Corinthians 15:8). The rest of them went on into obscurity.

The legacy of their true greatness is the church, a living, breathing organism which they helped found and of which they became the very foundation stones ("Jesus Christ Himself being the chief cornerstone"—Ephesians 2:20). The church, now some two thousand years old, exists today because these men launched the expansion of the gospel of Jesus Christ to the ends of the earth. And their heroism will be rewarded and commemorated throughout eternity in the New Jerusalem, where their names will be permanently etched into the foundation of that city.

The Gospels are the record of how Jesus trained them. Scripture deliberately records more about Jesus and His teaching than it does about the lives of these men. It all serves to remind us that the Lord loves to use weak and common people. If the faults and character flaws of the apostles seem like a mirror of your own weaknesses, take heart. These are the kinds of people the Lord delights to use.

The one thing that set these men apart from others in the Gospel accounts was the durability of their faith. Nowhere does this come through more clearly than in John 6, shortly after the feeding of the five thousand, when crowds of people began to flock around Jesus, hoping for more free food. At that very point, Jesus began to preach a message that many found shocking and offensive. He described Himself as the true manna from heaven (v. 32).

That was shocking enough, because by describing Himself as having come down from heaven (v. 41), He was claiming to be God. The Jewish leaders and the people understood this correctly as a claim of deity (v. 42). Jesus responded by saying again that He was the true bread of life (v. 48). He then added that He would give His flesh for the life of the world, and said, "Whoever eats My flesh and drinks My blood has eternal life, and I will raise him up at the last day. For My flesh is food indeed, and My blood is drink indeed. He who eats My flesh and drinks My blood abides in Me, and I in him" (vv. 54–56). Obviously, He was not talking about literal cannibalism; He was using vivid imagery to speak of the absolute commitment He required of His followers.

John writes, "Therefore many of His disciples, when they heard this, said, 'This is a hard saying; who can understand it?'" (v. 60). The word "disciples" in that verse refers to the larger group of followers who followed Jesus, not the Twelve in particular. John goes on to say, "From that time many of His disciples went back and walked with Him no more" (John 6:66). On that very day, many of the dozens of disciples who had sat under Jesus' teaching and witnessed His miracles stopped following Him. His sayings were too hard and His demands too rigorous for them. But not the Twelve. They remained resolutely with Jesus.

And as the crowd dissipated in shock, Jesus looked around at the Twelve and said, "Do you also want to go away?" (v. 67). Now was the time to leave, if they were inclined to do so.

Peter spoke for the group when he answered, "Lord, to whom shall we go? You have the words of eternal life" (v. 68). They were staying with Him no matter what. Except for Judas Iscariot, they were men of true faith.

Jesus knew all along that some of His disciples were not

true believers, and He knew that Judas would betray Him. He told them, " 'But there are some of you who do not believe.' For Jesus knew from the beginning who they were who did not believe, and who would betray Him" (v. 64). In verse 70, He answers Peter, "Did I not choose you, the twelve, and one of you is a devil?" He knew their hearts. Except for Judas, they had made the break with their past permanently. They had given up everything to follow Jesus.

That is the single most heroic fact about them revealed in the Gospels. And Judas's failure to make that commitment, while pretending that he had, was what made him so despicable.

As we examine this last group of apostles, we discover that although Scripture says very little about them, they nonetheless have their own distinctions.

JAMES, SON OF ALPHAEUS

The ninth name in Luke's list of the apostles (Luke 6:14–16) is "James the son of Alphaeus" (v. 15). The *only* thing Scripture tells us about this man is his name. If he ever wrote anything, it is lost to history. If he ever asked Jesus any questions or did anything to stand out from the group, Scripture does not record it. He never attained any degree of fame or notoriety. He was not the kind of person who stands out. He was utterly obscure. He even had a common name.

There are several men with the name *James* in the New Testament. We have already met James the son of Zebedee. There was another James, who was the son of Mary and Joseph and therefore a half brother of Christ (Galatians 1:19). The James who was Jesus' half brother apparently became a leader in the Jerusalem church. He was the spokesman who delivered the ruling at the Jerusalem Council in Acts 15:13–21. He is also thought to be the same James who penned the New Testament epistle that bears his name. He is not the same James named as one of the apostles in the third band of four.

Practically all we know about the James with whom we are concerned is that he was the son of Alphaeus (Matthew 10:3; Mark 3:18; Luke 6:15; Acts 1:13). In Mark 15:40, we learn that James's mother was named Mary. That verse, together with Matthew 27:56 and Mark 15:47 mention another of this woman's sons, Joses. Joses must have been well-known as a follower of the Lord (though not an apostle), because his name is mentioned repeatedly. Their mother, Mary, was obviously a devoted follower of Christ as well. She was an eyewitness to the crucifixion. She is also one of the women who came to prepare Jesus' body for burial (Mark 16:1).

Aside from those scant details that can be gleaned about his family, this James is utterly obscure. His lack of prominence is even reflected in his nickname. In Mark 15:40 he is referred to as "James the Less."

The Greek word for "Less" is *mikros.* It literally means "little." Its primary meaning is "small in stature," so it could refer to his physical features. Perhaps he was a short or small-framed man.

The word can also speak of someone who is young in age. He might have been younger than James the son of Zebedee, so that this title would distinguish him as the younger of the two. In fact, even if this is not what his nickname mainly referred to, it is probably true that he was younger than the other James; otherwise he would more likely have been known as "James the Elder."

But the name most likely refers to his influence. As we have already seen, James the son of Zebedee was a man of prominence. His family was known to the high priest (John 18:15–16). He was part of the Lord's most intimate inner circle. He was the better-known of the two Jameses. Therefore, James the son of Alphaeus was known as "James the Less." *Mikros.* "Little James."

It may well be that all these things were true of James, so that he was a small, young, quiet person who stayed mostly in the background. That would all be consistent with the low profile he had among the Twelve. We might say his distinguishing mark was his obscurity.

That in itself is a significant fact. Apparently he sought no recognition. He displayed no great leadership. He asked no critical questions. He demonstrated no unusual insight. Only his name remains, while his life and his labors are immersed in obscurity.

But he was one of the Twelve. The Lord selected him for a reason, trained and empowered him like the others, and sent him out as a witness. He reminds me of those unnamed people mentioned in Hebrews 11:33–38:

> . . . who through faith subdued kingdoms, worked right-eousness, obtained promises, stopped the mouths of lions, quenched the violence of fire, escaped the edge of the sword, out of weakness were made strong, became valiant in battle, turned to flight the armies of the aliens. Women received their dead raised to life again. And others were tortured, not accepting deliverance, that they might obtain a better resurrection. Still others had trial of mockings and scourgings, yes, and of chains and imprisonment. They were stoned, they were sawn in two, were tempted, were slain with the sword. They wandered about in sheepskins

and goatskins, being destitute, afflicted, tormented; of whom the world was not worthy. They wandered in deserts and mountains, in dens and caves of the earth.

Eternity will reveal the names and the testimonies of these, like James the Less, whom this world barely remembers and knows nothing about.

Early church history is also mostly silent about this man named James. Some of the earliest legends about him confuse him with James the brother of the Lord. There is some evidence that James the Less took the gospel to Syria and Persia. Accounts of his death differ. Some say he was stoned; others say he was beaten to death; still others say he was crucified like his Lord.

In any case, we can be certain that he became a powerful preacher like the others. He surely performed "the signs of an apostle . . . in signs and wonders and mighty deeds" (2 Corinthians 12:12). And His name will be inscribed on one of the gates of the heavenly city.

Here's an interesting thought about James, son of Alphaeus: You may recall that according to Mark 2:14, Levi (Matthew) was the son of a man named Alphaeus as well. It could be that this James was the brother of Matthew. After all, Peter and Andrew were brothers and James and John were brothers. Why not these two? There is no effort on the part of Scripture to distinguish between the two Alphaeuses. On the other hand, Matthew and James are nowhere identified as brothers. We simply don't know whether they were or not.

Another interesting question about James's lineage comes to light when we compare Mark 15:40 with John 19:25. Both verses mention two other Marys who were standing by the cross of Jesus with Mary the Lord's mother.

Mark 15:40 mentions "Mary Magdalene, and Mary the mother of James the less and of Joses." John 19:25 names "[Jesus'] mother's sister, Mary the wife of Clopas, and Mary Magdalene." It is possible, perhaps even likely, that Jesus' mother's sister ("Mary the wife of Clopas") and "Mary the mother of James the less" are the same person. ("Clopas" may have been another name for Alphaeus, or James's mother might have remarried after his father died). That would have made James the Less Jesus' cousin.

Was James the cousin of our Lord? Was he the brother of Matthew? We don't know. Scripture doesn't expressly tell us. The disciples' importance did not stem from their pedigree. Had that been important, Scripture would have recorded it for us. What made these men important was the Lord whom they served and the message they proclaimed. If we lack details about the men themselves, that is OK. Heaven will reveal the full truth of who they were and what they were like. In the meantime, it is enough to know that they were chosen by the Lord, empowered by the Spirit, and used by God to carry the gospel to the world of their day.

All the men themselves more or less disappear from the biblical narrative within a few years after Pentecost. In no case does Scripture give us a full biography. That is because Scripture always keeps the focus on the power of Christ and the power of the Word, not the men who were merely instruments of that power. These men were filled with the Spirit and they preached the Word. That is all we really need to know. The vessel is not the issue; the Master is.

No one epitomizes that truth better than James the Less, son of Alphaeus. He may have been able to claim that he was Matthew's brother or Jesus' cousin, but he went quietly unnoticed through the entire Gospel narrative. This world remembers next to nothing about him. But in eternity, he will receive a full reward (Mark 10:29–31).

SIMON THE ZEALOT

The next name given in Luke 6:15 is "Simon called the Zealot." In Matthew 10:4 and Mark 3:18, he is called "Simon the Cananite." That is not a reference to the land of Canaan or the village of Cana. It comes from the Hebrew root *qanna,* which means "to be zealous."

Simon was apparently at one time a member of the political party known as the Zealots. The fact that he bore the title all his life may also suggest that he had a fiery, zealous temperament. But that term in Jesus' day signified a well-known and widely feared outlaw political sect, and Simon had apparently been a member of that sect.

The historian Josephus described four basic parties among the Jews of that time. The *Pharisees* were fastidious about the Law; they were the religious fundamentalists of their time. The *Sadducees* were religious liberals; they denied the supernatural. They were also rich, aristocratic, and powerful. They were in charge of the temple. The *Essenes* are not mentioned in Scripture at all, but both Josephus and Philo describe them as ascetics and celibates who lived in the desert and devoted their lives to the study of the Law. The fourth group, the *Zealots,* were more politically minded than any group besides the Herodians. The Zealots hated the Romans, and their goal was to overthrow the Roman occupation. They advanced their agenda primarily through terrorism and surreptitious acts of violence.

The Zealots were extremists in every sense. Like the Pharisees, they interpreted the law literally. Unlike the

Pharisees (who were willing to compromise for political reasons), the Zealots were militant, violent outlaws. They believed only God Himself had the right to rule over the Jews. And therefore they believed they were doing God's work by assassinating Roman soldiers, political leaders, and anyone else who opposed them.

The Zealots were hoping for a Messiah who would lead them in overthrowing the Romans and restore the kingdom to Israel with its Solomonic glory. They were red-hot patriots, ready to die in an instant for what they believed in. Josephus wrote of them:

> Of the fourth sect of Jewish philosophy, Judas the Galilean was the author. These men agree in all other things with the Pharisaic notions; but they have an inviolable attachment to liberty, and say that God is to be their only Ruler and Lord. They also do not value dying any kinds of death, nor indeed do they heed the deaths of their relations and friends, nor can any such fear make them call any man lord. And since this immovable resolution of theirs is well known to a great many, I shall speak no further about that matter; nor am I afraid that any thing I have said of them should be disbelieved, but rather fear, that what I have said is beneath the resolution they show when they undergo pain. And it was in Gessius Florus's time that the nation began to grow mad with this distemper, who was our procurator, and who occasioned the Jews to go wild with it by the abuse of his authority, and to make them revolt from the Romans.[1]

The revolt Josephus describes "in Gessius Florus's time" occurred in A.D. 6, when a group of Zealots waged a violent rebellion against a Roman census tax. The Zealots' leader and founder, also mentioned by Josephus, was Judas the Galilean, who is named in Acts 5:37.

The Zealots were convinced that paying tribute to a pagan king was an act of treason against God. That view found widespread acceptance among people who were already overburdened by Roman taxation. Judas the Galilean seized the opportunity, organized forces, and went on a rampage of murder, plunder, and destruction. From their headquarters in the Galilee region, Judas and his followers carried out guerilla-style warfare and terrorist acts against the Romans. Soon, however, the Romans crushed the rebellion, killed Judas of Galilee, and crucified his sons.

The Zealot party merely went underground. Their acts of terror became more selective and more secretive. As noted in chapter 2, they formed a party of secret assassins called *sicarii*—"dagger-men"—because of the deadly, curved daggers they carried in the folds of their robes. They would sneak up behind Roman soldiers and politicians and stab them in the back, between the ribs, expertly piercing the heart.

They liked to burn Roman targets in Judea, then retreat to the remote areas of Galilee to hide. As Josephus described them in the quotation cited above, their willingness to suffer any kind of death or endure any amount of pain—including the torture of their own kindred—was well known. The Romans might torture them and kill them, but they could not quench their passion.

Many historians believe that when the Romans sacked Jerusalem under Titus Vespasian in A.D. 70, that terrible holocaust was largely precipitated by the Zealots. During the siege of Rome, after the Roman army had already surrounded the city and cut off supplies, the Zealots actually began killing fellow Jews who wanted to negotiate with Rome to end the siege. They allowed no one to surrender who wanted to save his or her own life. When Titus saw how hopeless the situation was, he destroyed the city, massacring thousands of its inhabitants, and carried off the treasures of the temple. So the Zealots' blind hatred of Rome and everything Roman ultimately provoked the destruction of their own city. The spirit of their movement was an insane, and ultimately self-destructive, fanaticism.

Josephus suggests that the name *Zealots* was a misnomer, "as if they were zealous in good undertakings, and were not rather zealous in the worst actions, and extravagant in them beyond the example of others."[2]

Simon was one of them. It is interesting that when Matthew and Mark list the Twelve, they list Simon just before Judas Iscariot. When Jesus sent the disciples out two by two in Mark 6:7, it is likely that Simon and Judas Iscariot were a team. They probably both originally followed Christ for similar political reasons. But somewhere along the line, Simon became a genuine believer and was transformed. Judas Iscariot never really believed.

When Jesus did not overthrow Rome, but instead talked of dying, some might have expected Simon to be the betrayer—a man of such deep passion, zeal, and political conviction that he would align himself with terrorists. But that was before He met Jesus.

Of course, as one of the Twelve, Simon also had to associate with Matthew, who was at the opposite end of the political spectrum, collecting taxes for the Roman government. At one point in his life, Simon would probably have gladly killed Matthew. In the end, they became spiritual brethren, working side by side for the same cause—the spread of the gospel—and worshiping the same Lord.

It is amazing that Jesus would select a man like Simon

to be an apostle. But he was a man of fierce loyalties, amazing passion, courage, and zeal. Simon had believed the truth and embraced Christ as his Lord. The fiery enthusiasm he once had for Israel was now expressed in his devotion to Christ.

Several early sources say that after the destruction of Jerusalem, Simon took the gospel north and preached in the British Isles. Like so many of the others, Simon simply disappears from the biblical record. There is no reliable record of what happened to him, but all accounts say he was killed for preaching the gospel. This man who was once willing to kill and be killed for a political agenda within the confines of Judea found a more fruitful cause for which to give his life—in the proclamation of salvation for sinners out of every nation, tongue, and tribe.

JUDAS, SON OF JAMES

The last name on the list of faithful disciples is "Judas, the son of James." The name *Judas* in and of itself is a fine name. It means "Jehovah leads." But because of the treachery of Judas Iscariot, the name *Judas* will forever bear a negative connotation. When the apostle John mentions him, he calls him "Judas (not Iscariot)" (John 14:22).

Judas the son of James actually had three names. (Jerome referred to him as "Trinomious"—the man with three names.) In Matthew 10:3, he is called "Lebbaeus, whose surname was Thaddaeus." *Judas* was probably the name given him at birth. *Lebbaeus* and *Thaddaeus* were essentially nicknames. *Thaddaeus* means "breast child"— evoking the idea of a nursing baby. It almost has a derisive sound, like "mamma's boy." Perhaps he was the youngest in his family, and therefore the baby among several siblings—specially cherished by his mother. His other name, *Lebbaeus,* is similar. It is from a Hebrew root that refers to the heart—literally, "heart child."

Both names suggest he had a tender, childlike heart. It is interesting to think of such a gentle soul hanging around in the same group of four apostles as Simon the Zealot. But the Lord can use both kinds. Zealots make great preachers. But so do tender-hearted, compassionate, gentle, sweet-spirited souls like Lebbaeus Thaddaeus. Together, they contribute to a very complex and intriguing group of twelve apostles. There's at least one of every imaginable personality.

Like the other three faithful members of the third apostolic group, Lebbaeus Thaddaeus is more or less shrouded in obscurity. But that obscurity should not cloud our respect for them. They all became mighty preachers.

The New Testament records one incident involving this Judas Lebbaeus Thaddaeus. To see it, we return to the apostle John's description of Jesus' Upper-Room Discourse. In John 14:21, Jesus says, "He who has My commandments and keeps them, it is he who loves Me. And he who loves Me will be loved by My Father, and I will love him and manifest Myself to him."

Then John adds, "Judas (not Iscariot) said to Him, 'Lord, how is it that You will manifest Yourself to us, and not to the world?'" (v. 22). Here we see the tender-hearted humility of this man. He doesn't say anything brash or bold or overconfident. He doesn't rebuke the Lord like Peter once did. His question is full of gentleness and meekness and devoid of any sort of pride. He couldn't believe that Jesus would manifest Himself to this rag-tag group of eleven, and not to the whole world.

After all, Jesus was the Savior of the world. He was the

rightful heir of the earth—King of kings and Lord of lords. They had always assumed that He came to set up His kingdom and subdue all things to Himself. The good news of forgiveness and salvation was certainly good news for all the world. And the disciples knew it well, but the rest of the world was still, by and large, clueless. So Lebbaeus Thaddaeus wanted to know, "Why are you going to disclose Yourself to us and not to the whole world?"

This was a pious, believing disciple. This was a man who loved his Lord and who felt the power of salvation in his own life. He was full of hope for the world, and in his own tender-hearted, childlike way he wanted to know why Jesus wasn't going to make Himself known to everyone. He was obviously still hoping to see the kingdom come to earth. We certainly can't fault him for that; that is how Jesus taught His disciples to pray (Luke 11:2).

Jesus gave him a marvelous answer, and the answer was as tender as the question. "Jesus answered and said to him, 'If anyone loves Me, he will keep My word; and My Father will love him, and We will come to him and make Our home with him'" (John 14:23). Christ would manifest Himself to anyone who loves Him.

Judas Lebbaeus Thaddaeus was still thinking in the political and material realm. "How come You haven't taken over the world yet? Why don't You just manifest Yourself to the world?"

Jesus' answer meant, "I'm not going to take over the world externally; I'm going to take over hearts, one at a time. If anyone loves Me, he will keep My Word. And if he keeps My Word, My Father and I will come to him and together we'll set up the kingdom in his heart."

Most of the early tradition regarding Lebbaeus Thaddaeus suggests that a few years after Pentecost, he took the gospel north, to Edessa, a royal city in Mesopotamia, in the region of Turkey today. There are numerous ancient accounts of how he healed the king of Edessa, a man named Abgar. In the fourth century, Eusebius the historian said the archives at Edessa (now destroyed) contained full records of Thaddaeus's visit and the healing of Abgar.[3]

The traditional apostolic symbol of Judas Lebbaeus Thaddaeus is a club, because tradition says he was clubbed to death for his faith.

Thus this tender-hearted soul followed his Lord faithfully to the end. His testimony was as powerful and as far-reaching as that of the better-known and more outspoken disciples. He, like them, is proof of how God uses perfectly ordinary people in remarkable ways.

10

JUDAS—THE TRAITOR

*Then Judas, who was betraying Him, answered
and said, "Rabbi, is it I?"*

—MATTHEW 26:25

THE MOST NOTORIOUS AND UNIVERSALLY SCORNED of all the disciples is Judas Iscariot, the betrayer. His name appears last in every biblical list of apostles, except for the list in Acts 1, where it doesn't appear at all. Every time Judas is mentioned in Scripture, we also find a notation about his being a traitor. He is the most colossal failure in all of human history. He committed the most horrible, heinous act of any individual, ever. He betrayed the perfect, sinless, holy Son of God for a handful of money. His dark story is a poignant example of the depths to which the human heart is capable of sinking. He spent three years with Jesus Christ, but for all that time his heart was only growing hard and hateful.

The other eleven apostles are all great encouragements to us because they exemplify how common people with typical failings can be used by God in *un*common, remarkable ways. Judas, on the other hand, stands as a warning about the evil potential of spiritual carelessness, squandered opportunity, sinful lusts, and hardness of the heart. Here was a man who drew as close to the Savior as it is humanly possible to be. He enjoyed every privilege Christ affords. He was intimately familiar with everything Jesus taught. Yet he remained in unbelief and went into a hopeless eternity.

Judas was as common as the rest, without earthly credentials and without any characteristics that made him stand out from the group. He began exactly like the others had begun. But he never laid hold of the truth by faith, so he was never transformed like the rest. While they were increasing in faith as sons of God, he was becoming more and more a child of hell.

The New Testament tells us plenty about Judas—enough to accomplish two things: First, the life of Judas reminds us that it is possible to be near Christ and associate with Him closely (but superficially) and yet become utterly hardened in sin. Second, Judas reminds us that no matter how sinful a person may be, no matter what treachery he or she may attempt against God, the purpose of God cannot be thwarted. Even the worst act of treachery works toward the fulfillment of the divine plan. God's sovereign plan cannot be overthrown even by the most cunning schemes of those who hate Him.

HIS NAME

Judas's name is a form of *Judah*. The name means "Jehovah leads," which indicates that when he was born his parents must have had great hopes for him to be led by God. The irony of the name is that no individual was ever more clearly led by Satan than Judas was.

His surname, *Iscariot,* signifies the region he came from. It is derived from the Hebrew term *ish* ("man") and the name of a town, Kerioth—"man of Kerioth." Judas probably came from Kerioth-hezron (cf. Joshua 15:25), a humble town in the south of Judea. He was apparently the only one of the apostles who did not come from Galilee. As we know, many of the others were brothers, friends, and working companions even before meeting Christ. Judas was a solitary figure who entered their midst from afar. Although there is no evidence that he was ever excluded or looked down upon by the rest of the group, he may have thought of himself as an outsider, which would have helped him justify his own treachery.

The Galilean disciples' unfamiliarity with Judas would have aided and abetted him in his deception. The others knew little about his family, his background, or his life before he became a disciple. So it was easy for him to play the hypocrite. He was able to work his way into a place of trust, which we know he did, because he ultimately became the treasurer of the group and used that position to pilfer funds (John 12:6).

Judas's father was named Simon (John 6:71). This Simon is otherwise unknown to us. It was a common name, obviously, because two of the disciples (Peter and the Zealot) were also named Simon. Beyond that, we know nothing of Judas's family or social background.

Judas was ordinary in every way, just like the others. It is significant that when Jesus predicted one of them would betray Him, no one pointed the finger of suspicion at Judas (Matthew 26:22–23). He was so expert in his hypocrisy that no one seemed to distrust him. But Jesus knew his heart from the beginning (John 6:64).

HIS CALL

The call of Judas is not recorded in Scripture. It is obvious, however, that he followed Jesus willingly. He lived in a time of heightened messianic hope, and like most in Israel, he was eager for the Messiah to come. When he heard about Jesus, he must have become convinced that this must be the true Messiah. Like the other eleven, he left whatever other enterprise he may have been engaged in and began to follow Jesus full-time. Judas even stayed with Jesus when less-devoted disciples began to leave the group (John 6:66–71). He had given his life to following Jesus. But he never gave Jesus his heart.

Judas was probably a young, zealous, patriotic Jew who did not want the Romans to rule and who hoped Christ would overthrow the foreign oppressors and restore the kingdom to Israel. He obviously could see that Jesus had powers like no other man. There was plenty of reason for a man like Judas to be attracted to that.

It is equally obvious, however, that Judas was not attracted to Christ on a spiritual level. He followed Jesus out of a desire for selfish gain, worldly ambition, avarice, and greed. He sensed Jesus' power, and he wanted power like that for himself. He was not interested in the kingdom for salvation's sake or for Christ's sake. He was interested only in what he could get out of it. Wealth, power, and prestige were what fueled his ambitions.

It is clear, on the one hand, that he *chose* to follow. He continued following even when following became difficult. He persisted in following even though it required him to be a more clever hypocrite in order to cover up the reality of what he really was.

On the other hand, Jesus also chose him. The tension

between divine sovereignty and human choice is manifest in Judas's calling, just as it is manifest in the calling of the other apostles. They had all chosen Jesus, but He chose them first (John 15:16). Judas had likewise chosen to follow Jesus. And yet he had also been chosen *by* Jesus, but not for redemption. His role of betrayal was ordained before the foundation of the world and even prophesied in the Old Testament.

Psalm 41:9, a messianic prophecy, says, "Even my own familiar friend in whom I trusted, who ate my bread, has lifted up his heel against me." Jesus cited that verse in John 13:18 and said its fulfillment would come in His own betrayal. Psalm 55:12–14 says, "For it is not an enemy who reproaches me; then I could bear it. Nor is it one who hates me who has exalted himself against me; then I could hide from him. But it was you, a man my equal, my companion and my acquaintance. We took sweet counsel together, and walked to the house of God in the throng." That passage also foretold the treachery of Judas. Zechariah 11:12–13 says, "They weighed out for my wages thirty pieces of silver. And the LORD said to me, 'Throw it to the potter'; that princely price they set on me. So I took the thirty pieces of silver and threw them into the house of the LORD for the potter." Matthew 27:9–10 identifies that as another prophecy about Judas. So Judas's role was foreordained.

Scripture even says that when Jesus chose Judas, He *knew* Judas would be the one to fulfill the prophecies of betrayal. He knowingly chose him to fulfill the plan.

And yet Judas was in no sense coerced into doing what he did. No invisible hand forced him to betray Christ. He acted freely and without external compulsion. He was responsible for his own actions. Jesus said he would bear the guilt of his deed throughout eternity. His own greed, his own ambition, and his own wicked desires were the only forces that constrained him to betray Christ.

How do we reconcile the fact that Judas's treachery was prophesied and predetermined with the fact that he acted of his own volition? There is no need to reconcile those two facts. They are not in contradiction. God's plan and Judas's evil deed concurred perfectly. Judas did what he did because his heart was evil. God, who works all things according to the counsel of His own will (Ephesians 1:11), had foreordained that Jesus would be betrayed and that He would die for the sins of the world. Jesus Himself affirmed both truths in Luke 22:22: "Truly the Son of Man goes as it has been determined, but woe to that man by whom He is betrayed!"

Spurgeon said this about the tension between divine sovereignty and human choice:

> If . . . I find taught in one part of the Bible that everything is fore-ordained, that is true; and if I find, in another Scripture, that man is responsible for all his actions, that is true; and it is only my folly that leads me to imagine that these two truths can ever contradict each other. I do not believe they can ever be welded into one upon any earthly anvil, but they certainly shall be one in eternity. They are two lines that are so nearly parallel, that the human mind which pursues them farthest will never discover that they converge, but they do converge, and they will meet some-where in eternity, close to the throne of God, whence all truth doth spring.1

God ordained the events by which Christ would die, and yet Judas carried out his evil deed by his own choice, unfettered and uncoerced by any external force. Both things are true. The perfect will of God and the wicked purposes of Judas concurred to bring about Christ's death. Judas did it for evil, but God meant it for good (cf. Genesis 50:20). There is no contradiction.

From a human perspective, Judas had the same potential as the others. The difference is that he was never really drawn to the Person of Christ. He saw Him only as a means to an end. Judas's secret goal was personal prosperity—gain for himself. He never embraced Jesus' teaching by faith. He never had an ounce of true love for Christ. His heart had never been changed, and therefore the light of truth only hardened him.

Judas had every opportunity to turn from his sin—as much opportunity as was ever afforded anyone. He heard numerous appeals from Christ urging him *not* to do the deed he was planning to do. He heard every lesson Jesus taught during His ministry. Many of those lessons applied directly to him: the parable of the unjust steward (Luke 16:1–13); the message of the wedding garment (Matthew 22:11–14); and Jesus' preaching against the love of money (Matthew 6:19–34), against greed (Luke 13:13–21), and against pride (Matthew 23:1–12). Jesus had even candidly told the Twelve, "One of you is a devil" (John 6:70). He cautioned them about the woe that would come to the person who betrayed him (Matthew 26:24). Judas listened to all of that unmoved. He never applied the lessons. He just kept up his deceit.

HIS DISILLUSIONMENT

Meanwhile, Judas was becoming progressively more disillusioned with Christ. No doubt at the start, *all* the apostles thought of the Jewish Messiah as an oriental monarch who would defeat the enemies of Judea, rid Israel of pagan occupation, and reestablish the Davidic kingdom in unprecedented glory. They knew Jesus was a miracle worker. He obviously had power over the kingdom of darkness. He also had authority to command the physical world. No one ever taught the way He taught, spoke the way He spoke, or lived the way He lived. As far as the disciples were concerned, He was the obvious fulfillment of the Old Testament messianic promises.

But Jesus did not always fulfill their personal expectations and ambitions. To be perfectly honest, their expectations were not all spiritually motivated. We see evidence of this from time to time, such as when James and John asked for the chief seats in the kingdom. Most of them had hoped to see an earthly, materialistic, political, military, and economic kingdom. Although they had left all to follow Jesus, they did so with an expectation that they would be rewarded (Matthew 19:27). The Lord assured them they *would* be rewarded, but their full and final reward would be in the age to come (Luke 18:29–30). If they were counting on immediate, material rewards, they were going to be disappointed.

The rest of the apostles had begun to catch on slowly that the true Messiah was not what they at first expected. They embraced the su-perior understanding of the biblical promises Jesus unfolded to them. Their love for Christ overcame their worldly ambitions. They received His teaching about the spiritual dimension of the kingdom, and they gladly became partakers.

Judas, meanwhile, simply became disillusioned. For the most part, he hid his disappointment under his blanket of hypocrisy, probably because he was looking for a way to get some money out of the years he had invested with Jesus. The worldliness in his heart was never conquered. He never embraced the spiritual kingdom of Christ. He remained an outsider, albeit secretly.

The few glimpses of Judas that are shown to us from time to time in the Gospels suggest that he had long been growing progressively more disillusioned and embittered but kept it hidden from everyone. As early as John 6, during Jesus' Galilean ministry, Jesus referred to Judas as "a devil." Jesus knew what no one else knew: Judas was becoming disgruntled already. He was still unbelieving, unrepentant, and unregenerate; and he was growing more and more hardhearted all the time.

By the time Jesus and the apostles went to Jerusalem for the Passover in the last year of Jesus' earthly ministry, Judas's spiritual disenfranchisement was complete. At some point in those final few days, his disillusionment turned to hate, and hate mixed with greed finally turned to treachery. Judas probably convinced himself that Jesus had stolen his life—robbed him of two years of money-making potential. That sort of thinking ate away at him until finally he became the monster who betrayed Christ.

HIS AVARICE

Shortly after the raising of Lazarus, and just before Jesus' Triumphal Entry into Jerusalem, Jesus and the disciples returned to Bethany, on the outskirts of the city. This was the place where Lazarus had been raised and where he lived with his sisters, Mary and Martha. Jesus was invited to a meal at the home of one "Simon the Leper" (Matthew 26:6). His dear friend Lazarus was present with Mary and

Martha, who were helping serve the meal. John 12:2–3 records what happened: "There they made Him a supper; and Martha served, but Lazarus was one of those who sat at the table with Him. Then Mary took a pound of very costly oil of spikenard, anointed the feet of Jesus, and wiped His feet with her hair. And the house was filled with the fragrance of the oil."

This act was shocking in its extravagance. Not only was it an overt act of worship, but it also had the appearance of wastefulness. Obviously perfume—especially such an expensive fragrance—is designed to be used in small amounts. Once poured out, it cannot be reused. To pour out a pound of expensive oil and use it to anoint someone's feet gave the appearance of gross excess.

"Then one of His disciples, Judas Iscariot, Simon's son, who would betray Him, said, 'Why was this fragrant oil not sold for three hundred denarii and given to the poor?'" (vv. 4–5). Three hundred denarii was a lot of money for perfume by any measure. Remember, a denarius was basically a working man's daily wage (Matthew 20:2). Three hundred denarii is a full year's wages (allowing for Sabbaths and holidays off). I have purchased costly perfume for my wife, but I would never think of spending a year's wages on one dose of perfume! This was an amazingly lavish act on the part of a family who must have had some means.

Judas's response was a clever ploy. He feigned concern for the poor. Apparently, his protest seemed reasonable to the other apostles, too, because Matthew 26:8 says they all echoed Judas's indignation. What an expert Judas had become in his hypocrisy! The apostle John, reflecting on this incident years later, wrote, "This he said, not that he cared for the poor, but because he was a thief, and had the money box; and he used to take what was put in it" (John

12:6). Of course, neither John nor any of the other apostles saw through Judas's deceit at the time, but in retrospect, and writing his book under the Holy Spirit's inspiration, John told us plainly what Judas's motive was: sheer greed.

Jesus responded to Judas in verse 7: "Let her alone; she has kept this for the day of My burial. For the poor you have with you always, but Me you do not have always." Given the circumstances, and since Jesus knew perfectly well what was in Judas's heart, this seems a rather mild rebuke. He could have blasted Judas with a fierce condemnation and exposed his real motives, but He did not.

Nonetheless, the gentle reprimand seems to have made Judas resent Jesus even more. He did not repent. He did not even examine his own heart. In fact, this incident seems to have been the turning point in his thinking. Three hundred denarii would have been a lot to add to the treasury, offering a prime opportunity for Judas to skim money for his own pocket. Because of Jesus' willingness to receive such lavish worship, Judas missed a prime opportunity to embezzle funds.

It appears to have been the last straw as far as Judas was concerned, because immediately after telling the story of Jesus' anointing, Matthew says, "Then one of the twelve, called Judas Iscariot, went to the chief priests and said, 'What are you willing to give me if I deliver Him to you?' And they counted out to him thirty pieces of silver. So from that time he sought opportunity to betray Him" (Matthew 26:14–16). He crept away, left Bethany, walked about a mile and a half to Jerusalem, met with the chief priests, and sold Jesus to His enemies for a pocketful of coins. Thirty pieces of silver. That is all he could get. According to Exodus 21:32, it was the price of a slave. It was not much money. But it was all he could negotiate.

The contrast is staggering: Our Lord is anointed with overwhelming love by Mary and betrayed with overwhelming hate by Judas at the same time.

Notice that this is the first time Judas had ever exposed himself in any way. Up to that point, He had blended in perfectly with the rest of the group. This is the first time on record that he spoke out as an individual, and it is the first time he merited any kind of direct rebuke from Christ. Apparently, that is all that was needed to provoke his betrayal. He had kept his bitterness and disillusionment bottled up as long as he could. Now it spilled forth in secret treachery.

HIS HYPOCRISY

John 13:1 begins the apostle John's lengthy account of what happened in the Upper Room on the night of Jesus' arrest. Having already taken money to betray Christ, Judas came back, blended into the group, and pretended nothing unusual had happened. John says it was the devil who put it in the heart of Judas to betray Jesus (v. 2). That is no surprise. Again, Judas did what he did willingly, without any coercion. Satan could not *force* him to betray Jesus. But Satan through some means suggested the plot, tempted Judas to do this thing, and planted the very seed of treachery in his heart. Judas's heart was so hostile to the truth and so filled with evil that Judas became a willing instrument of Satan himself.

It was at this very point that Jesus gave the apostles a lesson in humility by washing their feet. He washed the feet of all twelve, which means He even washed the feet of Judas. Judas sat there and let Jesus wash his feet and remained utterly unmoved. The world's worst sinner was also the world's best hypocrite.

Peter, on the other hand, was deeply moved by Jesus' act of humility. At first he was ashamed and refused to let Jesus wash his feet. But when Jesus said, "If I do not wash you, you have no part with Me," (v. 8), Peter replied, "Lord, not my feet only, but also my hands and my head!" (v. 9).

Jesus replied, "He who is bathed needs only to wash his feet, but is completely clean; and you are clean, *but not all of you*" (v. 10, emphasis added). A buzz must have gone around the room when He said that. There were only twelve of them, and Jesus was saying that someone in the group was not clean. Matthew adds, "For He knew who would betray Him; therefore He said, 'You are not all clean'" (v. 11).

In verses 18–19, Jesus spoke even more directly: "I do not speak concerning all of you. I know whom I have chosen; but that the Scripture may be fulfilled, 'He who eats bread with Me has lifted up his heel against Me.' Now I tell you before it comes, that when it does come to pass, you may believe that I am He." Of course, He was saying Judas's act was the fulfillment of Psalm 41:9.

All of that seems to have gone over the heads of most of the apostles. So in verse 21, Jesus makes an even more explicit prediction about the impending act of betrayal: "When Jesus had said these things, He was troubled in spirit, and testified and said, 'Most assuredly, I say to you, one of you will betray Me.'" All the disciples except Judas were perplexed and deeply troubled by this. They apparently began to examine their own hearts, because Matthew 26:22 says, "They were exceedingly sorrowful, and each of them began to say to Him, 'Lord, is it I?'" Even Judas, ever careful to keep up the appearance of being like everyone else, asked, "Rabbi, is it I?" (v. 25). But in his case there had been no sincere self-examination. He asked the question only because he was worried about how the others perceived him; he already knew that he was the one of whom Jesus spoke.

The apostle John concludes his account of this incident:

> Now there was leaning on Jesus' bosom one of His disciples, whom Jesus loved. Simon Peter therefore motioned to him to ask who it was of whom He spoke. Then, leaning back on Jesus' breast, he said to Him, "Lord, who is it?" Jesus answered, "It is he to whom I shall give a piece of bread when I have dipped it." And having dipped the bread, He gave it to Judas Iscariot, the son of Simon. Now after the piece of bread, Satan entered him. Then Jesus said to him, "What you do, do quickly." But no one at the table knew for what reason He said this to him. For some thought, because Judas had the money box, that Jesus had said to him, "Buy those things we need for the feast," or that he should give something to the poor. Having received the piece of bread, he then went out immediately. And it was night. (John 12:23–30)

The day of salvation closed for Judas. Divine mercy gave way to divine judgement. Judas was in essence handed over to Satan. Sin had triumphed in his heart. Satan moved in.

Notice, however, that even though Jesus had just spoken of the betrayer and had given Judas the morsel to identify him, it *still* did not compute in the minds of the apostles. No one seemed to anticipate that Judas would be the traitor. So expert was he in his hypocrisy that he fooled everyone but Jesus, right up to the very end.

Jesus sent him away. That is easy to understand. Jesus is

pure, sinless, spotless, and holy. Here was this wretched, evil presence into whom Satan had literally entered. Jesus was not about to have the first communion service with the devil and Judas present in the room. *Get out.*

Only after Judas had left did our Lord institute the Lord's Supper. To this day, when we come to the Lord's Table, we are instructed to examine ourselves lest we come hypocritically to the table and bring judgment upon ourselves (1 Corinthians 11:27–32).

The apostle John says that throughout this entire episode, until Judas left the company of apostles, Jesus was deeply "troubled in spirit" (John 13:21). Of course He was troubled! This wicked, wretched, Satan-possessed presence was polluting the fellowship of the apostles. Judas's ingratitude, His rejection of Jesus' kindness, the hate Judas secretly harbored for Jesus, the repulsiveness of the presence of Satan, the heinousness of sin, the horrors of knowing that the gaping jaws of hell were awaiting one of His closest companions—all of that troubled and agitated Jesus. No wonder he sent Judas away.

HIS BETRAYAL

Judas apparently went straight from the Upper Room to the Sanhedrin. He reported to them that the final breach had been made, and he now knew where they could apprehend Jesus under cover of darkness. Judas had been secretly seeking a convenient opportunity to betray Jesus ever since making his bargain with the Sanhedrin (Mark 14:11). Now the time had come.

Remember, Judas did not act in a moment of insanity. This was not a sudden impulse. It was not an act borne only out of passion. This dark deed was deliberately planned and premeditated. He had been planning this for days, if not weeks or even months. He had already taken the money for it (Matthew 26:15). He had just been waiting for an opportune hour. Along the way, he had continued his campaign of embezzlement, kept up the hypocritical facade, and carried on with the rest of the apostles as if he were truly one of them. But now Jesus had spoken openly to the other disciples about Judas's plot to betray Him. Judas had nearly been unmasked in front of the others. It was time for him to act.

What had he been waiting for anyway? According to Luke 22:6, Judas had been seeking an opportunity "to betray [Jesus] to them *in the absence of the multitude*" (emphasis added). He was a coward. He knew the popularity of Jesus. He was afraid of the crowd. Like every hypocrite, he was obsessed with concerns about what people thought of him, so he was hoping to betray Jesus as quietly as possible. He was looking for the doorway to hell that was most convenient. And when he found it, he plunged right in.

So at the very moment when Jesus was instituting the Lord's Supper in the Upper Room, Judas was making arrangements for His capture. He knew Jesus regularly went to Gethsemane to pray with His disciples. Luke 22:39 says it was Jesus' custom to go there. John 18:2 says Judas "knew the place; for Jesus often met there with His disciples." So Judas knew exactly where to bring the authorities to capture Jesus.

The next time we see Judas is in John 18, when his conspiracy of betrayal reaches its culmination. The evening was at its end. Jesus had gone from the Upper Room to His customary place of prayer in the little olive grove known as

Gethsemane. There He poured out his heart to the Father in such agony that His sweat became as great drops of blood. He had left eight of the disciples some distance away and gone deep into the garden with Peter, James, and John (Mark 14:32–33).

"Then Judas, having received a detachment of troops, and officers from the chief priests and Pharisees, came there with lanterns, torches, and weapons" (John 18:3). The "detachment of troops" was most likely a Roman cohort from the Antonio Fortress, adjacent to the temple. A full cohort numbered about six hundred men. No exact figure is given, but all the Gospel writers say it was a great multitude (Matthew 26:47; Mark 14:43; Luke 22:47)—probably hundreds of soldiers. They obviously expected the worst. They came armed to the teeth.

"Jesus therefore, knowing all things that would come upon Him, went forward and said to them, 'Whom are you seeking?'" (John 18:4). He did not wait for Judas to single him out; He did not try to hide; He "went forward," presenting Himself to them, and said, "I am He" (v. 5).

Judas had a prearranged signal to identify Jesus: "Whomever I kiss, He is the One; seize Him" (Matthew 26:48). What a diabolical way to point out Jesus! But his wretchedness was so profound and his hypocrisy so malicious that he seemingly had no conscience. Furthermore, since Jesus stepped forward and identified Himself, the signal would have been unnecessary, but Judas—cynic and scoundrel that he had become—kissed Him anyway (Mark 14:45).

"Jesus said to him, 'Judas, are you betraying the Son of Man with a kiss?'" (Luke 22:48). Kissing is a mark of homage, love, affection, tenderness, respect, and intimacy. Judas's feigned feelings for Christ only made his deed that much darker. It was a devious hypocrisy, trying to keep up the veneer of respect even to the bitter end.

Jesus, ever gracious, even addressed him as "Friend" (Matthew 26:50). Jesus had never been anything but friendly to Judas, but Judas was no true friend of Jesus (cf. John 15:14). He was a betrayer and a deceiver. His kisses were the kisses of the worst kind of treachery.

Judas profaned the Passover that night. He profaned the Lamb of God. He profaned the Son of God. He profaned the place of prayer. He betrayed his Lord with a kiss.

HIS DEATH

Judas sold Jesus for a pittance. But as soon as the deal was complete, Judas's conscience immediately came alive. He found himself in a hell of his own making, hammered by his own mind for what he had done. The money, which had been so important to him before, now did not matter. Matthew 27:3–4 says, "Then Judas, His betrayer, seeing that He had been condemned, was remorseful and brought back the thirty pieces of silver to the chief priests and elders, saying, 'I have sinned by betraying innocent blood.'"

His remorse was not the same as repentance, as subsequent events clearly show. He was sorry, not because he had sinned against Christ, but because his sin did not satisfy him the way he had hoped.

The chief priests and elders were unsympathetic. "They said, 'What is that to us? You see to it!'" (v. 4). They had what they wanted. Judas could do what he liked with the money. Nothing would undo his treachery now.

Matthew says, "Then he threw down the pieces of silver in the temple and departed, and went and hanged himself" (v. 5). Judas was already in a hell of his own making. His conscience would not be silenced, and that is the very essence of hell. Sin brings guilt, and Judas's sin brought him unbearable misery. Again, his remorse was not genuine repentance. If that were the case, he would not have killed himself. He was merely sorry because he did not like what he felt.

Sadly, he did not seek the forgiveness of God. He did not cry out for mercy. He did not seek deliverance from Satan. Instead, he tried to silence his conscience by killing himself. This was the grief of a madman who had lost control.

Matthew concludes his account of Judas: "But the chief priests took the silver pieces and said, 'It is not lawful to put them into the treasury, because they are the price of blood.' And they consulted together and bought with them the potter's field, to bury strangers in. Therefore that field has been called the Field of Blood to this day" (Matthew 27:6–8).

Acts 1:18–19 adds a final note to the tragedy of Judas, with more detail about his death and the acquisition of the Field of Blood: "This man purchased a field with the wages of iniquity; and falling headlong, he burst open in the middle and all his entrails gushed out. And it became known to all those dwelling in Jerusalem; so that field is called in their own language, Akel Dama, that is, Field of Blood."

Some have imagined a contradiction between Matthew and Acts, but all apparent discrepancies are easily reconciled. Matthew indicates that the priests purchased the field with Judas's blood money. Thus it is true that Judas acquired the field "with the wages of iniquity." It was purchased *for* him by the chief priests, but the purchase was made with his money. The field became his possession. His heirs—if he had any—would inherit the field. So it is correct to say that "purchased a field with the wages of iniquity," even though the field was purchased *for* him, by proxy.

Why this particular field? Because it was the very place where Judas hanged himself. Apparently he chose a tree on an overhang above some jagged rocks. (There is a place that precisely fits that description in the field in Jerusalem where tradition says Judas hanged himself.) Either the rope or the tree branch broke, and Judas fell headlong onto the rocks. The biblical description is graphic and ugly: "He burst open in the middle and all his entrails gushed out" (Acts 18:1). Judas was such a tragic figure that he couldn't even kill himself the way he wanted to. Nonetheless, he died.

This is virtually the last word in Scripture about Judas: "His entrails gushed out." His life and his death were grotesque tragedies. He was a child of hell and a son of perdition, and he went to his own place where he belonged. Jesus said these chilling words: "It would have been good for that man if he had never been born" (Mark 14:21).

THE MORAL OF HIS LIFE

We can draw some important lessons from the life of Judas. *First,* Judas is a tragic example of lost opportunity. He heard Jesus teach day in and day out for some two years. He could have asked Jesus any question he liked. He could have sought and received from the Lord any help he needed. He could have exchanged the oppressive burden of his sin for an easy yoke. Christ had given an open invitation for anyone to do so (Matthew 11:28–30). Yet in the end Judas was damned because of his own failure to heed what he heard.

Second, Judas is the epitome of wasted privilege. He was

given the highest place of privilege among all the Lord's followers, but he squandered that privilege—cashed it in for a fistful of coins he decided he did not really want after all. What a stupid bargain!

Third, Judas is the classic illustration of how the love of money is a root of all kinds of evil (1 Timothy 6:10).

Fourth, Judas exemplifies the ugliness and danger of spiritual betrayal. Would that Judas were the only hypocrite who ever betrayed the Lord, but that is not so. There are Judases in every age—people who seem to be true disciples and close followers of Christ but who turn against Him for sinister and selfish reasons. Judas's life is a reminder to each of us about our need for self-examination (cf. 2 Corinthians 13:5).

Fifth, Judas is proof of the patient, forebearing goodness and loving-kindness of Christ. "The LORD is good to all, and His tender mercies are over all His works" (Psalm 145:9). He even shows His loving-kindness to a reprobate like Judas. Remember, Jesus was still calling him "Friend," even in the midst of Judas's betrayal. Jesus never showed Judas anything but kindness and charity, even though the Lord knew all along what Judas was planning to do. In no sense was Judas driven to do what he did by Christ.

Sixth, Judas demonstrates how the sovereign will of God cannot be thwarted by any means. His betrayal of Christ seemed at first glance like Satan's greatest triumph ever. But in reality, it signalled utter defeat for the devil and all his works (Hebrews 2:14; 1 John 3:8).

Seventh, Judas is a vivid demonstration of the deceitfulness and fruitlessness of hypocrisy. He is the branch spoken of in John 15:6 that does not abide in the True Vine. That branch bears no fruit, is cut off, and is thrown into the fire to be destroyed. Judas was so expert at his hypocrisy that none of the other eleven ever suspected him. But he could never fool Jesus. Nor can any hypocrite. And Christ is the righteous Judge who will render to every person his due (John 5:26–27). Hypocrites like Judas will have no one but themselves to blame for the destruction of their souls.

When Judas bartered away the life of Christ, he was in effect selling his own soul to the devil. The tragedy of his life was a tragedy of his own making. He ignored the light he had been exposed to for all those years, and thus he relegated himself to eternal darkness.

After Jesus' resurrection, Judas's office was filled by Matthias (Acts 1:16–26). The apostle Peter said, "For it is written in the Book of Psalms: 'Let his dwelling place be desolate, and let no one live in it'; and, 'Let another take his office'" (v. 20). Matthias was selected because he had been with Jesus and the other apostles "from the baptism of John to that day when He was taken up from us" (v. 22).

Nothing is known of Matthias other than that. His name appears only twice in Scripture, both times in Acts 1, the account of how he was chosen. Thus in the end, another perfectly ordinary man was chosen to fill the place of that extraordinary villain. And so along with the other eleven, Matthias became a powerful witness of Jesus' resurrection (v. 22)—one more ordinary man whom the Lord elevated to an extraordinary calling.

NOTES

INTRODUCTION

1. Alexander Balman Bruce, *The Training of the Twelve* (New York: Doubleday, 1928), 29–30.

CHAPTER 2

1. John C. Maxwell, *The 21 Irrefutable Laws of Leadership* (Nashville: Thomas Nelson, 1998), 71.

2. The King James and New King James Versions seem to suggest that this event occurred after the meal—"supper being ended . . ." Other versions say it occurred "during supper . . ." (NASB) or while "the evening meal was being served" (NIV). The Greek word translated "ended" in the KJV is *ginomai,* a verb with a broad range of meanings, including "to be assembled, to be brought to pass, to be finished." The context makes it clear that it was the preparation of the meal, and not the eating of it, that was "finished" when Jesus arose to wash feet. Obviously, it was after this that Jesus dipped the sop and handed it to Judas (v. 26). So the foot-washing obviously occurred (as protocol demanded) before the meal, not afterward.

3. Eusebius, *Ecclesiastical History,* 3:1, 30.

CHAPTER 3

1. John C. Pollock, *Moody: A Biographical Portrait of the Pacesetter in Modern Evangelism* (New York: Macmillan, 1963), 13.

2. Richard Ellsworth Day, *Bush Aglow: The Life Story of Dwight Lyman Moody* (Philadelphia: Judson, 1936), 65.

CHAPTER 4

1. Eusebius, *Ecclesiastical Church History* 2.9.2–3.

CHAPTER 9

1. Josephus, *Antiquities* 18.6.
2. Josephus, *Wars of the Jews* 4.3.9.
3. Eusebius, *Ecclesiastical History* 1.13.5.

CHAPTER 10

1. Charles H. Spurgeon, "A Defense of Calvinism" in Susannah Spurgeon and Joseph Harrald, eds., *The Autobiography of Charles H. Spurgeon,* 4 vols. (Philadelphia: American Baptist Publication Society, 1895), 1:177.

ABOUT THE AUTHOR

J OHN MACARTHUR, THE AUTHOR OF NUMEROUS BEST-SELLING books that have touched millions of lives, is pastor-teacher of Grace Community Church in Sun Valley, California, and president of The Master's College and Seminary. He is also president of Grace to You, the ministry that produces the internationally syndicated radio program *Grace to You* and a host of print, audio, and Internet resources. He also authored the notes in the Gold Medallion Award-winning *The MacArthur Study Bible*. John and his wife, Patricia, have four children (all married), who have given them thirteen grandchildren. For more information, contact Grace to You at 1-800-55-GRACE.

JOHN MACARTHUR

FIGHTING FOR CERTAINTY *in an* AGE *of* DECEPTION

THE TRUTH WAR

COMING SOON!

An Excerpt
from
THE TRUTH WAR

1

CAN TRUTH SURVIVE IN A POSTMODERN SOCIETY?

Jesus answered, "You say rightly that I am a king. For this cause I was born, and for this cause I have come into the world, that I should bear witness to the truth. Everyone who is of the truth hears My voice." Pilate said to Him, "What is truth?"

—JOHN 18:37–38

Considering who stood before him and the gravity of the issues he was being asked to decide, Pilate's attitude was astonishingly dismissive. But he did raise a vital question: *What is "truth"?*

Where, after all, does this concept come from, and why is it so basic to all human thought? Every idea we have, every relationship we cultivate, every belief we cherish, every fact we know, every argument we make, every conversation we engage in, and every thought we think presupposes that there is such a thing as "truth." The idea is an essential concept, without which the human mind could not function.

Even if you are one of those trendy thinkers who claims to be skeptical about whether "truth" is really a useful category anymore, to express that opinion you must presume that truth *is* meaningful on some fundamental level. One of the most basic, universal, and undeniable axioms of all human thought is the absolute necessity of truth. (And we might add that the necessity of absolute truth is its close corollary.)

A BIBLICAL DEFINITION

So what is truth?

Here is a simple definition drawn from what the Bible teaches: *Truth is that which is consistent with the mind, will, character, glory, and being of God.* Even more to the point: *truth is the self-expression of God.* That is the biblical meaning of *truth*, and it is the definition I employ throughout this book. Because the definition of truth flows from God, truth is *theological*.

Truth is also *ontological*—which is a fancy way of saying it is the way things really are. Reality is what it is because God declared it so and made it so. Therefore God is the author, source, determiner, governor, arbiter, ultimate standard, and final judge of all truth.

The Old Testament refers to the Almighty as the "God of truth" (Deuteronomy 32:4; Psalm 31:5; Isaiah 65:16). When Jesus said of Himself, "I *am* . . . the truth (John 14:6, emphasis added), He was thereby making a profound claim about His own deity. He was also making it clear that *all* "truth" must ultimately be defined in terms of God and His eternal glory. After all, Jesus is "the brightness of [God's] glory and the express image of His person" (Hebrews 1:3).

He is truth incarnate—the perfect expression of God and therefore the absolute embodiment of all that is true.

Jesus also said that the written Word of God is truth. It does not merely contain nuggets of truth; it *is* pure, unchangeable, and inviolable truth which (according to Jesus) "cannot be broken" (John 10:35). Praying to His heavenly Father on behalf of His disciples, He said this: "Sanctify them by Your truth. Your word is truth" (John 17:17). Moreover, the Word of God is eternal truth "which lives and abides forever" (1 Peter 1:23).

Of course there cannot be any discord or difference of opinion between the *written* Word of God (Scripture) and the *incarnate* Word of God (Jesus). In the first place, truth by definition cannot contradict itself. Second, Scripture is called "the word of Christ" (Colossians 3:16). It is *His* message; *His* self-expression. In other words, the truth of Christ and the truth of the Bible are of the very same character. They are in perfect agreement in every respect. Both are equally true. God has revealed Himself to humanity through Scripture and through His Son. Both perfectly embody the essence of what truth is.

Remember, Scripture also says God reveals basic truth about Himself in nature. The heavens declare His glory (Psalm 19:1). His other invisible attributes (such as His wisdom, power, and beauty) are on constant display in what He has created (Romans 1:20). Knowledge of Him is inborn in the human heart (Romans 1:19), and a sense of the moral character and loftiness of His law is implicit in every human conscience (Romans 2:15). Those things are universally self-evident truths. According to Romans 1:20, denial of the spiritual truths we know innately always involves a deliberate and culpable unbelief. And for those who wonder whether basic truths about God and His moral standards really are stamped on the human heart, ample proof can be found in the long history of human law and religion. To suppress this truth is to dishonor God, displace His glory, and incur His wrath (vv. 19–20).

Still, the only infallible interpreter of what we see in nature or know innately in our own consciences is the explicit revelation of Scripture. Since Scripture is also the one place where we are given the way of salvation, entrance into the kingdom of God, and an infallible account of Christ, the Bible is the touchstone to which all truth claims should be brought and by which all other truth must finally be measured.

THE INADEQUACY OF ALL OTHER DEFINITIONS

An obvious corollary of what I am saying is that truth means nothing apart from God. Truth cannot be adequately explained, recognized, understood, or defined without God as the source. Since He alone is eternal and self-existent and He alone is the Creator of all else, He is the fountain of all truth.

If you don't believe that, try defining *truth* without reference to God, and see how quickly all such definitions fail. The moment you begin to ponder the essence of truth, you are brought face-to-face with the requirement of a universal absolute—the eternal reality of God. Conversely, the whole concept of truth instantly becomes nonsense (and every imagination of the human heart therefore turns to sheer foolishness) as soon as people attempt to remove the thought of God from their minds.

That, of course, is precisely how the apostle Paul traced

the relentless decline of human ideas in Romans 1:21–22: "Although they knew God, they did not glorify Him as God, nor were thankful, but became futile in their thoughts, and their foolish hearts were darkened. Professing to be wise, they became fools."

There are serious *moral* implications, too, whenever someone tries to dissociate "truth" from the knowledge of God. Paul went on to write, "Even as they did not like to retain God in their knowledge, God gave them over to a debased mind, to do those things which are not fitting" (Roman 1:28). Abandon a biblical definition of truth, and unrighteousness is the inescapable result. We see it happening before our eyes in every corner of contemporary society. In fact, the widespread acceptance of homosexuality, rebellion, and all forms of iniquity that we see in our society today is a verbatim fulfillment of what Romans 1 says always happens when a society denies and suppresses the essential connection between God and truth.

If you reflect on the subject with any degree of sobriety, you will soon see that even the most fundamental moral distinctions—good and evil, right and wrong, beauty and ugliness, or honor and dishonor—cannot possibly have any true or constant meaning apart from God. That is because truth and knowledge themselves simply have no coherent significance apart from a fixed source, namely, God. How could they? God embodies the very definition of truth. Every truth claim apart from Him is preposterous.

That reality has led to an ominous shift in the world of secular thought in recent years. Human philosophers have sought for thousands of years to explain truth apart from God—and all who have tried have been ultimately unsuccessful. Elaborate systems of thought have been proposed and methodically debunked one after another—like a long chain in which every previous link is broken. For thousands of years, the very best of human philosophies have all utterly failed to account for truth without God.

In fact, the one most valuable lesson humanity ought to have learned from philosophy is that it is impossible to make sense of truth without acknowledging God as the necessary starting point.

THE GREAT "PARADIGM SHIFT"

Lately, many unbelieving intellectuals have admitted the chain is broken and have decided the culprit is the absurdity of any quest for "truth." In effect, they have given up that pursuit as something wholly futile. The world of human ideas is therefore currently in a serious state of flux. On almost every level of society, we are witnessing a profoundly radical "paradigm shift"—a wholesale overhaul in the way people think about truth itself.

Unfortunately, instead of acknowledging what truth demands and yielding to the necessity of belief in the God of truth, contemporary Western thought has devised ways to rid human philosophy of any coherent notion of truth altogether. The concept of truth is therefore under heavy attack in the philosophical community, the academic world, and the realm of worldly religion. The way people think about truth is being totally revamped and the vocabulary of human knowledge completely redefined. The goal, clearly, is to usher every notion of truth off into oblivion.

The goal of human philosophy used to be truth without God. Today's philosophies are open to the notion of God without truth—or to be more accurate, personal "spirituality" in which everyone is free to create his or her own god. Personal gods pose no threat to sinful self-will, because they suit each sinner's personal preferences anyway, and they make no demands on anyone else.

That fact underscores the true reason for every denial of truth: "Men loved darkness rather than light, because their deeds were evil" (John 3:19). Here the Lord Jesus says people reject truth (light) for reasons that are fundamentally moral, not intellectual. Truth is clear—too clear. It reveals and condemns sin. Therefore, "everyone practicing evil hates the light and does not come to the light, lest his deeds should be exposed" (v. 20). Sinners love their sin, so they flee from the light, denying that it even exists.

The war against truth is nothing new, of course. It began in the garden when the serpent said to the woman, "Has God indeed said . . . ?" (Genesis 3:1). A relentless battle has raged ever since—between truth and falsehood, good and evil, light and darkness, assurance and doubt, belief and skepticism, righteousness and sin. It is a savage spiritual conflict that literally spans all of human history. But the ferocity and irrationality of this present onslaught seems quite unprecedented.

The far-reaching ramifications of the recent paradigm shift are obvious already. Over the past generation—and especially the past two decades—we have seen convulsive changes in society's moral values, philosophy, religion, and the arts. The upheaval has been so profound that our grandparents' generation (and practically every prior generation of human history) scarcely would have thought the landscape could possibly change so quickly. Almost no aspect of human discourse has been left unaffected. The traditional, nominal devotion to ideals and moral standards derived from Scripture is dying with the senior generation.

Many believe the paradigm shift has already brought us beyond the age of "modernity" to the next great epoch in the development of human thought: the *postmodern* era.

MODERNITY

Modernity, in simple terms, was characterized by the belief that truth exists and that the scientific method is the only reliable way to determine that truth. In the so-called "modern" era, most academic disciplines (philosophy, science, literature, and education) were driven primarily by rationalistic presuppositions. In other words, modern thought treated human reason as the final arbiter of what is true. The modern mind discounted the idea of the supernatural and looked for scientific and rationalistic explanations for everything. But modern thinkers retained their belief that knowledge of the truth is possible. They were still seeking universal and absolute truths that applied to everyone. Scientific methodologies became the chief means by which modern people sought to gain that knowledge.

Those presuppositions gave birth to Darwinism, which in turn spawned a string of humanistic ideas and worldviews. Most prominent among them were several atheistic, rationalistic, utopian philosophies—including Marxism, fascism, socialism, communism, and theological liberalism.

Modernism's devastating repercussions were soon felt worldwide. Various struggles between those ideologies (and others like them) dominated the twentieth century. All failed. After two world wars, nonstop social revolutions, civil unrest, and a long ideological cold war, modernity was declared dead by most in the academic world. The symbolic death of the modern era was marked by the fall of the

Berlin Wall, one of the more apt and imposing monuments to modern ideology. Because the wall was the ultimate expression modernity's ultimate worldview (communism), its sudden demolition was also a perfect symbol for the collapse of modernity.

Most, if not all, of the major dogmas and worldviews from the modern era are now deemed completely outmoded and hopelessly discredited in virtually every corner of the intellectual and academic world. Even modernist religion's fascination with higher criticism has given way to abstract spirituality.

The overconfident rationalism and human conceit that characterized the modern era has finally—and fittingly—had most of the wind taken out of its sails.

POSTMODERNISM

Accordingly, the new ways of thinking have been collectively nicknamed *postmodern*.

If you have been paying attention to the world around us, you have probably heard that expression a lot recently. The term *postmodernism* has been used increasingly since the 1980s to describe several popular trends in architecture, art, literature, history, culture, and religion. It is not an easy term to explain, because it describes a way of thinking that defies (and even rejects) any clear definition.

Postmodernism in general is marked by *a tendency to dismiss the possibility of any sure and settled knowledge of the truth*. Postmodernism suggests that if objective truth exists, it cannot be known objectively or with any degree of certainty. That is because (according to postmodernists), the subjectivity of the human mind makes knowledge of objective truth impossible. So it is useless to think of truth in objective terms. Objectivity is an illusion. Nothing is certain, and the thoughtful person will never speak with too much conviction about anything. Strong convictions about any point of truth are judged supremely arrogant and hopelessly naive. Everyone is entitled to his own truth.

Postmodernism therefore has no positive agenda to assert anything as true or good. Perhaps you have noticed that only the most heinous crimes are still seen as evil. (Actually, there are many today who are prepared to dispute whether *anything* is "evil," so such language is fast disappearing from public discourse.) That is because the notion of evil itself does not fit in the postmodern scheme of things. If we can't really know anything for certain, how can we judge anything "evil"?

Therefore postmodernism's one goal and singular activity is the systematic deconstruction of every other truth claim. The chief tools being employed to accomplish this are relativism, subjectivism, the denial of every dogma, the dissection and annihilation of every clear definition, the relentless questioning of every axiom, the undue exaltation of mystery and paradox, the deliberate exaggeration of every ambiguity, and above all the cultivation of uncertainty about *everything*.

If you were to challenge me to boil down postmodern thought into its pure essence and identify the gist of it in one single, simple, central characteristic, I would say it is *the rejection of every expression of certainty*. In the postmodern perspective, certainty is regarded as inherently arrogant, elitist, intolerant, oppressive—and therefore always wrong.

The demise of modernity and the resulting blow to rationalistic human arrogance is certainly something to celebrate. From a spiritual perspective, however, the rise of postmodernism has been anything but a positive development.

Postmodernism has resulted in a widespread rejection of truth and the enshrinement of skepticism. Postmodernists despise truth claims. They also spurn every attempt to construct a coherent worldview, labeling all comprehensive ideologies and belief systems "metanarratives," or grand stories. Such "stories," they say, can't possibly do justice to everyone's individual perspective, and therefore they are always inadequate.

Postmodernism's preference for subjectivity over objectivity makes it inherently relativistic. Naturally, the postmodernist recoils from absolutes and does not want to concede any truths that might seem axiomatic or self-evident. Instead, "truth," if acknowledged at all, becomes something infinitely pliable and ultimately unknowable in any objective sense.

Postmodernism therefore signals a major triumph for relativism—the view that "truth" is not fixed and objective, but something individually determined by each person's unique, subjective perception. All this is ultimately a vain attempt to try to eliminate morality and guilt from human life.

GETTING PROPOSITIONS OFF THE PREMISES

One other extremely important point has to be mentioned with regard to postmodern notions of truth: *postmodernists are generally suspicious of rational and logical forms. They especially do not like to discuss truth in plain propositional terms.*

As we are seeing, postmodernism is largely a reaction against the unbridled rationalism of modernity. But many postmodernists' response to rationalism is a serious *over*reaction. Lots of postmodernists seem to entertain the notion that *ir*rationality is superior to rationalism.

Actually, both ways of thinking are dead wrong and equally hostile to authentic truth and biblical Christianity. One extreme is as deadly as the other. *Rationalism* needs to be rejected without abandoning *rationality*.

Rationality (the right use of sanctified reason through sound logic) is never condemned in Scripture. Faith is not irrational. Authentic biblical truth demands that we employ logic and clear, sensible thinking. Truth can always be analyzed and examined and compared under the bright light of other truth, and it does not melt into absurdity. Truth by definition is never self-contradictory or nonsensical. And contrary to popular thinking, it is not "rationalism" to insist that coherence is a necessary quality of all truth. Christ is truth incarnate, and He cannot deny himself (2 Timothy 2:13). Self-denying truth is an absolute contradiction in terms. "No lie is of the truth" (1 John 2:21).

Nor is logic a uniquely "Greek" category that is somehow hostile to the Hebrew context of Scripture. (That is a common myth and a gross oversimplification that is often set forth in support of postmodernism's flirtation with irrationality.) Scripture frequently employs logical devices, such as antithesis, if-then arguments, syllogisms, and propositions. These are all standard logical forms, and Scripture is full of them. (See, e.g., Paul's long string of deductive arguments about the importance of the resurrection in 1 Corinthians 15:12–19.)

Yet we often encounter people enthralled with postmodern ideas who argue vehemently that truth cannot be expressed in bare propositions like mathematical formulae. Even some professing Christians nowadays argue along these lines: "If truth is personal, it cannot be propositional.

If truth is embodied in the person of Christ, then the form of a proposition can't possibly express authentic truth. That is why most of Scripture is told to us in narrative form—as a *story*—not as a set of propositions."

The reason behind postmodernism's contempt for propositional truth is not difficult to understand. A "proposition" is *an idea framed as a logical statement that affirms or denies something, and it is expressed in such a way that it must be either true or false.* There is no third option between true and false. (This is the "excluded middle" in logic.) The whole point of a proposition is to boil a truth-statement down to such pristine clarity that it must be either affirmed or denied. In other words, propositions are the simplest expressions of truth value used to express the substance of what we believe. Postmodernism frankly cannot endure that kind of stark clarity.

In reality, however, postmodernism's rejection of the propositional form turns out to be totally untenable. It is impossible to discuss truth at all—or even tell a story—without resorting to the use of propositions. Until fairly recently, the validity and necessity of expressing truth in propositional form was considered self-evident by virtually everyone who ever studied logic, semantics, philosophy, or theology. Ironically, to make any cogent argument *against* the use of propositions, a person would have to employ propositional statements! So every argument against propositions is instantly self-defeating.

Let's be clear: truth certainly does entail more than bare propositions. There is without question a *personal* element to the truth. Jesus Himself made that point when He declared Himself truth incarnate. Scripture also teaches that faith means receiving Christ for all that He is—knowing Him in a real and personal sense and being indwelt by

Him—not merely assenting to a short list of disembodied truths *about* Him (Matthew 7:21–23).

So it is quite true that faith cannot be reduced to mere assent to a finite set of propositions (James 2:19). I have made that point repeatedly in previous books. Saving faith is more than a merely intellectual nod of approval to the bare facts of a minimalist gospel outline. Authentic faith in Christ involves love for His person and willing surrender to His authority. The human heart, will, and intellect all consent in the act of faith. In that sense, it is certainly correct, even *necessary*, to acknowledge that mere propositions can't do full justice to all the dimensions of truth.

On the other hand, truth simply cannot survive if stripped of propositional content. While it is quite true that believing the truth entails more than the assent of the human intellect to certain propositions, it is equally true that authentic faith never involves anything less. To reject the propositional content of the gospel is to forfeit saving faith, period.

Postmodernists are uncomfortable with propositions for an obvious reason: they don't like the clarity and inflexibility required to deal with truth in propositional form. A proposition is the simplest form of any truth claim, and postmodernism's fundamental starting point is its contempt for all truth claims. The "fuzzy logic" of ideas told in "story" form sounds so much more elastic—even though it really is not. Propositions are necessary building blocks for every means of conveying truth—including stories.

But the attack on propositional expressions of truth is the natural and necessary outworking of postmodernism's general distrust of logic, distaste for certainty, and dislike for clarity. To maintain the ambiguity and pliability of "truth" necessary for the postmodern perspective, clear and definitive propositions must be discounted as a means of expressing truth. Propositions force us to face facts and either affirm or deny them, and that kind of clarity simply does not play well in a postmodern culture.

UNCERTAINTY IS THE NEW TRUTH

Of course, postmodernism is considerably more complex than those few descriptive paragraphs can possibly relate, but that is a sufficient thumbnail sketch of what the expression signifies. We will delve into some of the major characteristics of the postmodern "paradigm shift" here and there throughout the book. But to get us started, let's consider this notion that certainty about *anything* is inherently arrogant.

That view is wildly popular today. The belief that no one can really know anything for certain is emerging as virtually the one dogma postmodernists will tolerate. Uncertainty is the new "truth." Doubt and skepticism have been canonized as a form of "humility." Right and wrong have been redefined in terms of subjective feelings and personal perspectives.

Those views are infiltrating the church too. In some circles within the visible church, cynicism is now virtually regarded as the most splendid of all virtues. I began this book with a prime example of that cynicism, as seen in the so-called Emerging Church movement. A relentless tone of postmodern angst about *too much certainty* pervades that whole movement. No wonder: the Emerging Church began as a self-conscious effort to make Christianity more suitable to a postmodern culture. Emerging Christians are determined to adapt the Christian faith, the structure of the church, the language of faith, and even the gospel message itself to the ideas and rhetoric of postmodernism.

Postmodernity is a major theme in the literature of the Emerging Church movement. Several leading voices in the movement have suggested that postmodernism is something the church should embrace and adopt. Others might be more tentative about endorsing postmodernism entirely, but they insist that Christians at least need to start speaking the postmodern dialect if we want to reach a postmodern generation. That, they say, will require a retooling of the message we bring to the world, not to mention a revamping of the means by which we deliver it. Some in the movement have openly questioned whether there is even any legitimate role for preaching in a postmodern culture. "Dialogue" is the preferred method of communication. Accordingly, some Emerging-style congregations have done away with pastors altogether and replaced them with "narrators." Others have replaced the sermon with a free-ranging dialogue in which no one takes any leading role. For obvious reasons, an authoritative "thus saith the Lord" is not welcome in such a setting.

Of course, the first casualty of that way of thinking is every kind of *certainty*. The central propositions and bedrock convictions of biblical Christianity—such as firm belief in the inspiration and authority of Scripture, a sound understanding of the true gospel, full assurance of salvation, settled confidence in the lordship of Christ, and the narrow exclusivity of Christ as the only way of salvation—do not reconcile well with postmodernism's contempt for clear, authoritative truth claims. The *medium* of postmodern "dialogue" thereby instantly and automatically changes the *message*. And the rhetoric of the Emerging Church movement itself reflects that.

Listen, for example, to how Brian McLaren sums up his views on orthodoxy, certainty, and the question of whether the truths of Christianity are sound and reliable in the first place:

How ironic that I am writing about orthodoxy, which implies to many a final capturing of the truth about God, which is the glory of God. Sit down here next to me in this little restaurant and ask me if Christianity (my version of it, yours, the Pope's, whoever's) is *orthodox*, meaning true, and here's my honest answer: *a little, but not yet.* Assuming by *Christianity* you mean the Christian understanding of the world and God, Christian opinions on soul, text, and culture . . . I'd have to say that we probably have a couple of things right, but a lot of things wrong.[1]

McLaren suggests that clarity itself is of dubious value. He clearly prefers ambiguity and equivocation, and his books are therefore full of deliberate doublespeak. In his introduction to *A Generous Orthodoxy*, he admits, "I have gone out of my way to be provocative, mischievous, and unclear, reflecting my belief that clarity is sometimes overrated, and that shock, obscurity, playfulness, and intrigue (carefully articulated) often stimulate more thought than clarity."[2] A common theme that runs throughout most of McLaren's writings is the idea that "there is great danger in the quest to be right."[3]

Postmodern influences have come into the evangelical movement through other avenues as well. *Beyond Foundationalism: Shaping Theology in a Postmodern Context*, by Stanley Grenz and John Franke, was published in 2001 and has made a significant impact in the evangelical academic community, garnering lots of positive reviews and stimulating numerous papers and lectures from evangelical leaders who evidently find much to agree with in the book.

But as the subtitle suggests, the book pleads for a whole new approach to theology, with the goal of "contextualizing" Christianity for a postmodern culture. "The categories and paradigms of the modern world" are in collapse, the authors note in the book's opening sentence.[4] They go on to assert that Christian theology therefore needs to be rethought, revised, and adapted in order to keep in step and remain relevant in these changing times.

Grenz and Franke argue that the Spirit of God speaks through Scripture, tradition, and culture, and theologians must seek to hear the voice of the Spirit in each one. Moreover, since culture is constantly in flux, they say, it is right and fitting for Christian theology to be in a perpetual state of transition and ferment too. No issue should ever be regarded as finally settled.

The obvious casualty of all this is any sure and certain knowledge of biblical truth. That is okay with Grenz and Franke. They are convinced that every desire to gain a fixed and positive knowledge of any truth actually belongs to the collapsing categories of enlightenment rationalism. That is precisely what they mean by the reference to "foundationalism" in the book's title. They define "Classical foundationalism" as a "quest for complete epistemological certitude."[5]

"Certitude" naturally comes under repeated attack in the book. This culminates in the incredible claim that certainty is ultimately incompatible with hope.[6] Of course, there are some things we don't yet see clearly and still hope for (Romans 8:24–25). But it seems rather far-fetched to conclude that there is nothing we can know with a true and settled certainty.

Some readers have nevertheless found the Grenz-Franke argument persuasive, including John Armstrong. Armstrong is a writer, conference speaker, and former pastor who at one time was a defender of Reformation theology and a student of revival. The name of his ministry, Reformation and Revival, reflected that.

But after reading *Beyond Foundationalism*, Armstrong wrote a series of articles in his ministry newsletter declaring that he has changed his mind about several vital points of doctrine—including faith and understanding, the sacraments, the doctrine of revelation, and Christology—among other things. Crediting Grenz and Franke for helping him see the light, Armstrong wrote, "I have been forced, upon deeper reflection about theological method, to give up what I call epistemological certitude."[7] He goes on to explain: "Reformed dogmaticians and teachers on the conservative side seek a steady, unshakable and certain knowledge. . . . John Franke suggests that the agenda employed by such theologians 'glorifies reason and deifies science.' I have changed my mind about the way to do theology, and I confess I now agree with Franke's conclusion."[8]

Armstrong reveals how far he has moved from his starting point with this statement: "If there is a foundation in Christian theology, and I believe that there must be, then it is not found in the Church, Scripture, tradition or culture."[9] Scripture is not the foundation for Christian doctrine? Then what is? Armstrong's answer echoes the central thesis of *Beyond Foundationalism:* "If we must speak of 'foundations' for Christian faith and its theological enterprise, then we must speak only of the triune God as disclosed in polyphonic fashion through Scripture, the church, and even the world."

Armstrong tries awkwardly to give lip service to the

authority of Scripture by suggesting (in language Karl Barth might have applauded) that our doctrine must "always [be] in accordance with the normative witness to divine self-disclosure contained in Scripture."[10] But even that morsel is instantly snatched away with the other hand and quickly replaced with a wholly subjective, irrational, postmodern hermeneutic: "Theology must be a humble human attempt to 'hear him'—never about rational approaches to texts."[11]

Armstrong identifies the illusion of many under the sway of this error by boasting that his radical turnaround is the epitome of "humility" and "the very essence of servant-leadership."[12] (In accordance with his shifting views, Armstrong has changed the name of his ministry from Reformation and Revival to Act 3—stressing his goal of being "missional" in the third millennium.)

Meanwhile, Armstrong employs caricature and exaggeration to attack the views he himself once held. He claims he has "routinely" heard "prominent Christians say: 'I have never changed my mind—never.'"[13] He cites Wayne Grudem's *Systematic Theology* as an example of the " 'concordance' view of theology. You gather all the verses on a given subject, sort them all out, put them in their proper place in your system, and then develop (or write) a theology, formal or otherwise. This theology is then transferred as if the system itself contains, or is, the truth of God."[14]

Armstrong, Grenz, Franke, and the Emerging postmodernists have blurred the line between certainty and omniscience. They seem to presume that if we cannot know *everything* perfectly, we really cannot know *anything* with any degree of certainty. That is an appealing argument to the postmodern mind, but it is entirely at odds with what Scripture teaches: "We have the mind of Christ" (1 Corinthians 2:16).

That is not to suggest, of course, that we have *exhaustive* knowledge. But we do have *infallible* knowledge of what Scripture reveals, as the Spirit of God teaches us through the Word of God: "We have received, not the spirit of the world, but the Spirit who is from God, that we might know the things that have been freely given to us by God" (1 Corinthians 2:12). The fact that our knowledge grows fuller and deeper—and we all therefore change our minds about *some* things as we gain more and more light—doesn't mean that everything we know is uncertain, out-dated, or in need of an overhaul every few years. The words of 1 John 2:20–21 apply in their true sense to every believer: "You have an anointing from the Holy One, and you know all things. I have not written to you because you do not know the truth, but because you know it, and that no lie is of the truth."

The message coming from postmodernized evangelicals is exactly the opposite: Certainty is overrated. Assurance is arrogant. Better to keep changing your mind and keep your theology in a constant state of flux.

By such means, the ages-old war against truth has moved right into the Christian community, and the church itself has already become a battleground—and ominously, precious few in the church today are prepared for the fight.

We have come to this down a discernible path.

WAR IN THE CHURCH

This is by no means the first time the Truth War has intruded into the church. It has happened in every major era of church history. Battles over the truth were raging inside the Christian community even in apostolic times, when the church was just beginning. In fact, the record of Scripture indicates that false teachers in the church immediately became a significant and widespread problem wherever the gospel went. Virtually all the major epistles in the New Testament address the problem in one way or another. The apostle Paul was constantly engaged in battle against the lies of "false apostles [and] deceitful workers [who transformed] themselves into apostles of Christ" (2 Corinthians 11:13). Paul said that was to be expected. It is, after all, one of the favorite strategies of the evil one: "No wonder! For Satan himself transforms himself into an angel of light. Therefore it is no great thing if his ministers also transform themselves into ministers of righteousness" (vv. 14–15).

It takes a willful naïveté to deny that such a thing could happen in our time. As a matter of fact, it *is* happening on a massive scale. Now is not a good time for Christians to flirt with the spirit of the age. We cannot afford to be apathetic about the truth God has put in our trust. It is our duty to guard, proclaim, and pass that truth on to the next generation (1 Timothy 6:20–21). We who love Christ and believe the truth embodied in His teaching must awaken to the reality of the battle that is raging all around us. We must do our part in the ages-old Truth War. We are under a sacred obligation to join the battle and contend for the faith.

In one narrow respect, the driving idea behind the Emerging Church movement is correct: The current climate of postmodernism *does* represent a wonderful window of opportunity for the church of Jesus Christ. The arrogant rationalism that dominated the modern era is already in its death throes. Most of the world is caught up in disillusionment and confusion. People are unsure about virtually everything and do not know where to turn for truth.

However, the absolute *worst* strategy for ministering the gospel in a climate like this is for Christians to imitate the uncertainty or echo the cynicism of the postmodern perspective—and in effect drag the Bible and the gospel into it. Instead, we need to affirm *against* the spirit of the age that God has spoken with the utmost clarity, authority, and finality through His Son (Hebrews 1:1–2). And we have the infallible record of that message in Scripture (2 Peter 1:19–21).

Postmodernism is simply the latest expression of worldly unbelief. Its core value—a dubious ambivalence toward truth—is merely skepticism distilled to its pure essence. There is nothing virtuous or genuinely humble about it. It is proud rebellion against divine revelation.

In fact, postmodernism's hesitancy about truth is exactly antithetical to the bold confidence Scripture says is the birthright of every believer (Ephesians 3:12). Such assurance is wrought by the Spirit of God Himself in those who believe (1 Thessalonians 1:5). We need to make the most of that assurance and not fear to confront the world with it.

The gospel message in all its component facts is a clear, definitive, confident, authoritative proclamation that Jesus is Lord, and that He gives eternal and abundant life to all who *believe*. We who truly know Christ and have received that gift of eternal life have also received from Him a clear, definitive commission to deliver the gospel message boldly as His ambassadors. If we are likewise not clear and distinct in our proclamation of the message, we are not being good ambassadors.

But we are not merely ambassadors. We are simultaneously soldiers, commissioned to wage war for the defense and dissemination of the truth in the face of countless onslaughts against it. We are *ambassadors*—with a message of good news for people who walk in a land of darkness and dwell in the land of the shadow of death (Isaiah 9:2). And we are *soldiers*—charged with pulling down ideological strongholds and casting down the lies and deception spawned by the forces of evil (2 Corinthians 10:3–5; 2 Timothy 2:3–4).

Notice carefully: our task as ambassadors is to bring good news to *people*. Our mission as soldiers is to overthrow false *ideas*. We must keep those objectives straight; we are not entitled to wage warfare against people or to enter into diplomatic relations with anti-Christian ideas. Our warfare is not against flesh and blood (Ephesians 6:12); and our ambassadorial objective precludes any compromise whatsoever with human philosophies, religious deceit, or any other kind of falsehood (Colossians 2:8).

If those sound like difficult assignments to keep in balance and maintain in proper perspective, they are indeed.

Jude certainly understood this. The Holy Spirit inspired him to write his short epistle to people who were struggling with some of these very same issues. He nevertheless urged them to contend earnestly for the faith against all falsehood, while doing everything possible to deliver souls from destruction: "pulling them out of the fire, hating even the garment defiled by the flesh" (Jude 23).

So we are ambassador-soldiers, reaching out to sinners with the truth even as we make every effort to destroy the lies and other forms of evil that hold them in deadly bondage. That is a perfect summary of every Christian's duty in the Truth War.

Martin Luther, that noble gospel soldier, threw down the gauntlet at the feet of every Christian in every generation after him, when he said:

If I profess with the loudest voice and clearest exposition every portion of the truth of God except precisely that little point which the world and the devil are at that moment attacking, I am not *confessing* Christ, however boldly I may be *professing* Christ. Where the battle rages, there the loyalty of the soldier is proved; and to be steady on all the battlefield besides, is mere flight and disgrace if he flinches at that point.[15]

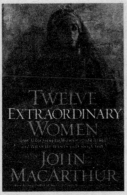

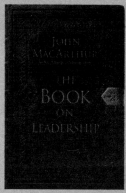

The MacArthur Study Bible

John MacArthur, General Editor

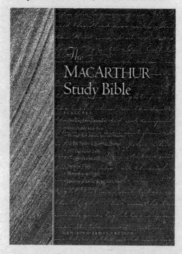

For thirty years, thirty hours a week, John MacArthur poured over every page of Scripture. Explored every verse. Dug into every difficult passage. As he studied, he combined the exegetical skills of a world-class scholar with wisdom and warmth of an experienced pastor. The result is more than just another Study Bible. It is the work of a lifetime. A true classic that will set standards for decades to come.

No other Study Bible does such a thorough job of explaining the historical context, unfolding the meaning of the text, and placing it within a theological framework.

Featuring the word-for-word accuracy of the New King James Version, the *MacArthur Study Bible* is perfect fot serious study. The *MacArthur Study Bible* also contains helpful charts, maps, outlines and articles, along with thousands of study notes personally written by Dr. MacArthur and informed by the research of scholars at the Master's Seminary.

Available in a variety of Hardcover and Leather Editions

**NELSON
BIBLES**

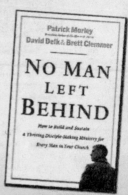